The Practical Guide

for

Independent Consultants

Created to help those who are interested in consulting as a possible new career; those who are getting started; and those already practising who wish to raise their performance.

It assesses the circumstances that lead to the choice of self-employed consulting as an alternative career, and provides experience-based advice and guidance on the many issues integral to the achievement of success

by

Ray Kavanagh & Jon Sebastian

AJ Publishing Ltd

The Publisher and Authors are grateful to Messrs Worsdell & Vintner, Solicitors, of 2 Ivy House Road, Ickenham, Uxbridge, Middlesex UB10 8NE for their guidance and advice concerning Appendices A, B & C of this work.

First published in 1999 in Great Britain by
A J Publishing Limited
11 Great Benty
West Drayton
Middlesex UB7 7UW

Printed and bound in the Republic of Ireland by
ColourBooks Limited
Unit 105 Baldoyle Industrial Estate
Baldoyle
Dublin 13
Ireland

ISBN 1 903118 00 X

Publisher's Reference: ZGCO1A

Companies, institutions and other organisations wishing to make bulk purchases of this title and any other publications by A J Publishing Ltd should contact:

http://www:ajpublishing.co.uk

Table of contents

Chapter 1

Why a need for this guide?

This guide is intended as a workable and realistic source of help and advice to people who are thinking about a change in their career, or who are committed to make a change, or for whom the change so far has not been as successful as had been hoped.

The authors believe that this book can help different types of people:

- Those who are bored and frustrated in a corporate career.
- Those who want to make a career change but are not sure where to start.
- Those who believe that their talents, which are lost in a corporate organisation, can be put to more fulfilling use by working alone.
- Those who yearn for the freedom that self-employment seems to offer but need to know more before gambling on a change.
- Those who are already self-employed consultants.
- Those who have been made redundant but cannot afford to stop working.
- Those who can afford to retire but want to stay active in the business scene.
- Those who work part-time but wish for more work to fill their days.
- Those who run a business and would like to know more what an outside advisor can do for them.

- Those whose formal careers have fallen foul of ageist or sexist policies.

- Those who are casualties of company strategic review, de-manning, down-sizing, take-over, merger, consolidation, centralisation, de-centralisation, policy re-alignment, re-organisation, re-location, re-deployment, re-focussing, re-assessment, re-profiling, re-engineering, re-fashioning.

There are many reasons why self-employment is now seriously considered as a career option by numerous people who previously would never have thought such a notion to be either possible or necessary. Often they have little choice in the matter. Often they make expensive errors through pressures of time and money, lack of planning, inexperience and the shortage of sources of reliable and objective career advice. Often, in this process they choose to pursue independent consulting.

The dual purposes of this book are to help make that a better informed choice, and then to help make that a successful choice.

--- o O o ---

Among the various changes that the business world has witnessed over the last twenty years, one of the most profound has been the emergence of a growing army of accomplished and experienced technicians and advisors who actively sell their expertise to commercial organisations in need of assistance. It is now well accepted that it is uneconomic for a complex organisation to retain among its personnel all the skills and disciplines needed to sustain operations on an efficient and competitive level.

In the simpler and more predictable conditions that once prevailed, it would have been quite realistic for a medium sized company to retain the services of just a modestly sized legal firm, or perhaps even in some cases a single lawyer, to satisfy all the organisation's demands for expert legal advice. Today, complexities of the modern world ordain that ready access to advice is needed for a multiplicity of different requirements. Hence, a company may need help in such diverse areas as the law of contract, copyright, labour, property, and to be able to seek help in conflict of international law, or to understand and satisfy evolving European legislation.

On a more mundane level, the technology that is essential to commercial competence is innately complex but brings with it also its own demands for technical advice and support. The idea of retaining an outside consultant to help decide which machine to acquire, and then to advise on how machine A will inter-act effectively with machine B is accepted as wise practise and economically sensible. Equally, we do not doubt the need to retain access to support facilities and their expert personnel to maintain those machines, and to guard against their failure doing lasting damage to the enterprise.

In both cases, the purchaser of the expert service is aware of the shortcomings in his knowledge, and fears the consequences of failure to make good that deficiency. In that sense, the company manager would no more gamble on his ability correctly to interpret the implications of a complex European court ruling in preference to calling his lawyer, than he would ask his secretary to fix a broken photocopier herself rather than to call a mechanic.

This willingness to refer problems perceived or real to the acknowledged expert is quite usual in circumstances where there is a sense of familiarity with the risk involved – a familiarity because the issue under debate has a tangible quality that is readily felt. The decision to acquire the help is a natural response to a shared concern. While this may be an expensive and overly vigilant choice, there is nonetheless a sense of comfort that this is preferable to the gamble of instigating no precautionary measures at all.

Consulting often faces rather more complex challenges because recognition of the need is sometimes far from obvious. If the manager knows that a new European law will affect his company but he cannot follow the tangled and abstruse language in which it is couched, he will have no choice but to turn to someone who can interpret it for him. If the photocopier no longer copies, the manager's secretary may push all the buttons, reload the paper magazine, give the machine a kick and then be left in no doubt that a mechanic must be called. In both cases, there is clarity about the urgency of the need and little inclination to quibble about the price of the solution, so long as it is immediate and effective.

The consultant often faces a far harder task to convince that his services are necessary. He may be starting out with an unclear mandate and facing doubt in the mind of the recipient over what his services comprise, and whether or not they are really needed. With the difficult question of law or the faulty photocopier, the need is readily apparent. No further identification is necessary because it is the user who takes the problem to the expert for attention.

In consulting, the problem may only be manifest in several disparate effects and the first task is to identify and link the causes, before setting out on a solution. Because the client frequently confuses cause and effect, the consultant may face a complex challenge of detection while also having to prove his own technical credentials, validate his operating techniques and justify possibly iconoclastic corrective action. These features are particularly relevant to the situation faced daily by the general business consultant.

--- o O o ---

Prior to the preparation of this book, the authors debated at length what should be its title. However, as the work proceeded, the title emerged as the natural summation of what we are trying to achieve.

The adjective ***Practical*** accurately reflects the fact that what we have to say is drawn from personal experience and knowledge, and above all from mistakes that we have made in the course of consulting. That experience is diverse and many of the principles we set out have stood the test of time. In our analysis of interview techniques and practises, we have drawn from actual events and circumstances going back to 1973.

The need for a ***Guide*** stems from recognition of an unfortunate outcome of the demographics of modern business. The change process yields a growing number of middle aged managers equipped with valuable skills and experience who cannot find the means adequately to put those advantages to remunerative use. In earlier life, the pattern of training and career selection is well defined through the educational system and by corporate manpower development programs. Later on there is no such supportive system at work and while it may be reasonable that more mature people should be expected to stand on their own two feet, this does not dispel the need for advice and for guidance.

Independent follows in this theme. By middle age, many relish the notion of an independent lifestyle, free from the demands and traumas of the corporatism that governs work, and often too many aspects of social behaviour. Longing for this freedom may be engendered by romantic ideas but the reality can prove a stern test of character for someone who has grown and matured within the womb of the corporate system. The challenge may be the greater because the assumption of independence is often dreamt-of but nonetheless unplanned, the practical issues of which are addressed after the event.

Having become independent, ***Consultant*** regularly forms the answer to the question of what to do next. However, the circumstances surrounding this decision can make it a knee-jerk reaction, and a priority choice driven by an absence of feasible alternatives. The selection of consulting is thus more a corollary to a situation than the logical outcome of a structured program of focussed training and career development. The absence of planning for this fundamental career change is all too apparent among the many who start out enthusiastically but fail.

This guide has therefore been written with the intention of providing realistic help and advice for those who are embarking on a career of independent consulting for the first time – but more seasoned campaigners will also find its contents useful. We have intended its scope to be broad enough to encompass some of the fears and opportunities that will go through the mind of anyone contemplating a major lifestyle change in middle age, while also providing practical advice and illustrations on how to consult better. It contains a mixture of quasi-philosophical commentary along with recommendations for operational efficiency, a chapter describing tasks and actions relevant to setting up on one's own, and samples of the draft documentation that will be needed to protect one's business and earn some money.

Therefore we hope that *The Practical Guide for Independent Consultants* will succeed in its aim on different levels. We hope that it will encourage many seriously to consider entering the field, while providing a timely warning to others that consulting may not be for them, before they commit much in time and money. We hope that active consultants will find advice to help them improve their techniques and effectiveness, because we all have a vested interest in seeing the advancement of professionalism in this field. We hope also that this work will prove a continuing reference source to be relied upon in the pursuit of more effectiveness and competence among independent consultants.

Chapter 2

The rise of the self employed

Radical alterations and changes have become obligatory in the plans and expectations of most companies and across the business world in general in recent years. It is safe to say that "the future will never be the same again." Although it is impossible to gauge precisely what these changes will produce or for how long their radical nature will continue, it is nevertheless apparent that no one engaged in business activity can remain isolated from them. Terrifying as these changes may seem, it is also thrilling for the optimists among us to discover and exploit the opportunities for individual excellence and success presented in this new business world. Whether the challenge is worth accepting is largely a personal issue.

The starting point lies in how each person views the "cup of life". If the underlying belief is that the cup is half empty, effectively embracing a negative attitude that sees little in the way of expansive opportunity, or that a totally new way of living, thinking and working will not stimulate and refresh, then lay this book aside now.

On the other hand, if there is a conviction that the cup is half full and that there is still plenty (perhaps too much!) to be attempted and achieved, then read on.

Surplus people

Many of the pressures that now exert themselves so vigorously upon western society derive not from shortages but from surpluses. Substantial progress has been made in improving the operational efficiency of many processes in industry and commerce. Mechanisation has yielded to automation and this has permitted improvements in productivity levels by many orders of magnitude.

A subtle but profound change in the manner in which computers are used has accounted for much of the people surplus. Computers were originally acquired to relieve pressures on manual and mechanised bookkeeping systems caused by a dearth of suitable clerical staff in the labour market. For a significant period, people and computers at work coexisted reasonably comfortably while the latter were treated as super-sophisticated bookkeeping machines that eased the production problems of a business world with a predominantly manually orientated operating philosophy.

The transition from computerised bookkeeping to information technology was the critical point at which people were recognised as becoming surplus to requirements. Not only did the need for clerical grade staff diminish, but managers whose work centred on the supervision of information gathering and distribution were also finding that the machine could do the job better.

Concurrently, because human nature notices failures but takes efficiency for granted, the vastly improved operational standards of machine driven functions have gone largely unacknowledged. The reality is however, that notwithstanding the high incidence of fraud and the occasional systems failures, modern life would be impossible without the convenience and user friendliness of computer-led transactional systems such EFTPOS (electronic funds transfer at point-of-sale), plastic cards in their many forms, and digitised records.

Substantial increases in the number of commercial transactions have imposed the need for certain operational rigidities and for simplicity in the construction of systemic methodologies. This simplicity has achieved marvels in the level of error reduction, and thus in the need for human supervisory intervention. One may cite a story heard about an occasional difficulty in dealing with a cash dispenser. However this failure rate should be considered against the fact that in 1990, 17,000 such machines successfully handled 992 million individual transactions while by 1994 these statistics had risen to 19,500 machines and 1,292 million transactions.

While machines reduce the comparative need for people *in* work, the availability of people *for* work is reducing also. The education revolution has resulted in a diminution in the expectation that learning will be partly accomplished on-the-job. Secondary and tertiary education has become almost obligatory in most trades and professions if any ambition is harboured of gaining senior rank. This trend has trimmed 4 to 5 years off a possible working life at the front end while the average age at which formal employment is terminated continues to fall.

These phenomena imply the need for radical re-assessment of how we view work and life ambitions. In a modern society, productive economic activity is the basis on which key decisions are taken about how and where we live, how we provide for dependants, how we secure a comfortable financial future and so forth. Earlier generations lived with the reality of lower expectations and significantly less affluence, but they did have the luxury of a far greater measure of certainty than we may presently assume.

In the context of the modern place of work, we can be sure of pressures for obsolescence imposed by forces beyond the will of individual employers, industries or nations to control. This conviction is creating out of adversity, a totally new set of attitudes towards productive activity, the need for self-reliance, and the determination for career satisfaction in fresh and exhilarating ways.

Disillusionment and rejection of the conventional employment system

Social commentators have coined as a derogatory phrase "the nanny state" to represent a basically socialistic tendency for central authority to provide for all adverse eventualities which may beset the individual citizen in the course of his life. Quite why the term should be derogatory is not entirely clear as it well describes the nature of the many traditional employer-employee relationships that have flourished on essentially paternalistic criteria.

Paid sick leave, private medical cover, mortgage subsidies, company car, pension scheme, entertainment allowance, bonus schemes, foreign travel are all elements of the "nanny state" mentality by which employers have traditionally tied the marriage bonds with their employees. Often justified on the grounds of needing to match prevailing employment market conditions, they have nonetheless provided a paternalistic umbrella of security. This has extended even in cases of "divorce" where the employee has secured his "alimony" by negotiating matching or better conditions by transferring to a new employer.

There are many facets to the trauma of redundancy - for example loss of privileges, position, recognition etc – but in the aftermath, what will often be heavily felt is loss of all those perks and services. Some of them may have been rarely used but their availability was an important comfort factor for employees and a source of justification for their continuing to work under conditions that were otherwise dispiriting or distasteful.

The emotions that go with employment severance through redundancy can therefore often resemble those experienced with divorce. A sense of loss and concerns about financial hardship may be tempered by feelings of relief, release, and freedom. Though perhaps born of anxiety and stress, this chance for a fresh renewal is a gift that should be seen and valued as such.

Redundancy is an experience shared by many and discussion with others who have gone through the same mill provides therapeutic benefit – provided that it is with others who are not inclined towards remorse and self-pity. What often emerges from these sessions is the recognition that although redundancy may have been the catalyst for the actual change, adverse mental attitudes towards the ex-employer had been accumulating for some considerable time previously.

The authors have had extensive contact with middle aged, middle managers who have gone through the redundancy process. What has been consistently noticeable is the degree of dissatisfaction felt towards erstwhile bosses exhibited by individuals of proven experience and competence. Setting aside the understandable grudge factor, the repetitious message is of management hierarchies that plainly do not function properly.

This is obviously a complex subject but two factors emerge time and again. One relates to bad experiences working for senior executives with specialist backgrounds and training who have signally failed to embrace the broader, generalist responsibilities and duties of the chief executive officer. The other derives from unpleasantness in the workplace created by corporate bullies. In either situation, it is clear that the people surplus has greatly aided and abetted the behaviour of senior managers who may satisfy certain intellectual and technical criteria, but who are seriously lacking in what it takes to be effective and respected business leaders.

The result of these and other factors is measurable in the growing number of competent ex-managers who are so disillusioned with the corporate system that they will not re-enter a management hierarchy under any circumstances. They now stand outside the system, and they refer to their erstwhile colleagues as "wage slaves" – a condition to which they have no intention of ever returning.

Lifestyle change

It may well be that redundancy is the catalyst that stimulates action in response to a long-held wish for a change in lifestyle. Perhaps the individual feels that the corporate decision that invoked his redundancy was unfair because it appeared to label him personally as obsolete. Initial motivation may simply derive from the determination to prove the corporate decision wrong and the resultant label inaccurate.

Positive motives of this nature are a good start to planning a new future, whereas caution should be adopted concerning retaliatory measures against the former employer. Decisions to initiate claims based on grounds for unfair dismissal require careful and measured consideration. The attraction of possible financial compensation should be weighed against the substantial negative aspects of such action.

Whether or not the action is successful, it may consume possibly already limited resources of time and money. Re-entering the lists against an old employer can lead to the other side engaging greater legal firepower, and in any event will re-open old wounds and revive feelings of bitterness that may be better left buried and forgotten. Retaliatory action is risky also because it can be a serious distraction at a time when detailed assessment of future potential and its exploitation may be a more productive pastime.

Restraint is also advisable because the belief that nothing could be worse than the previous situation may induce a cavalier attitude towards the challenges of adapting to a new lifestyle. In fact, thorough self-assessment and planning is needed to ensure that the change is successful. Previous experience may be of only minimal help in coping with important change factors, especially if that experience has been of a limited nature, and earned through immersion in the internal focus of a corporate institution.

Sadly however, the authors have all too frequently met aspirants to self-employment who are ill-equipped or mentally unprepared to face what will be demanded of them. For example, "experience" in a general economic, legal and commercial sense may be little more than the sum of the accumulated knowledge of the standard procedures and workings of the previous employer.

Case 1. Tom, a candidate for general and management consulting work strongly expressed the view that he had no need for re-training before commencing work in the general market. His career had consisted of 25 years with an aggressive, well-run national group that demanded high standards of its executive team. For the last few years, Tom had been an internal consultant and trouble-shooter with the group. It had been his task to be attached to a department, to review operations, to identify areas for improvement, to draw up a remedial action plan, and to guarantee to the department's head the results that would be achieved following implementation of the improvements.

Tom stated that this background was quite sufficient for him to earn a good living elsewhere. He maintained that his excellent performance record was due to his own efforts, and refused to accept suggestions that his position and seniority guaranteed that his internal "clients" had to listen to him. Further, he refused to accept that he always had the tacit or overt backing of higher authority, and that the client's choice was either to comply, or to risk losing his job.

The lasting impression was that Tom had learned a way of doing things that accorded with a set of internally derived procedures and values ordained by a successful, large company. It seemed that his point of embarkation into consulting was to assume that what he had learned was so superior, he could make money by re-designing clients' businesses to conform with the sole business model with which he was familiar.

The inability of individuals to differentiate between their own skills base, and their position of authority gained while climbing the greasy corporate pole is a recurring contributor to failure in the lifestyle change. The gloss and importance attaching to a corporate appointment can cruelly mislead in the self-assessment process. It is quite a shock to some otherwise intelligent people to discover that the previous recognition and respect that they enjoyed was driven more by the position they had occupied, than by personal characteristics and attributes.

Diminution in influence induces the need for a new approach. Orders and instructions must give way to requests. Time schedules are no longer yours to command; it becomes necessary to fit in with the demands of other peoples' diaries. Proposals can no longer be imposed by pulling rank; the institution of ideas must rely on persuasion, logic and reasoning.

Case 2. Daniel for several years had occupied a senior position with a highly regarded international bank. Following his retirement, he embarked on consulting and on a pursuit of several new initiatives in the financial services sector that required liaison with government officials and others. The supercilious manner in which these parties responded to his requests and proposals continually annoyed Daniel, making him ever more agitated that this was treatment that he had not been used to receiving. He could never accept that his own voice, however legitimate its message, would never carry the same weight as his voice when it was the mouthpiece of his erstwhile employer.

Independence Maturity: the essence of success

The authors' term "Independence Maturity" succinctly summarises the personal qualities that are intrinsic to success in self-employment. Although educational background and intellectual capacity both play their part, a sustained performance level when working on a solus basis requires additional qualities. In this respect, diverse experience is important. If the individual is sufficiently composed, he should be able to acknowledge that any experience, however distressing, will have contained facets that if properly applied will add significantly to his future potential.

Effective analysis of experience is sometimes easier said than done. It is a process that can demand self-reflection and objective assessment of significant contributing factors. Maturity is evident in the ability to acknowledge objectively the beneficial influence of outside parties in success stories, and the extent of own-culpability with failures. Learning from experience is widely accepted as being a praiseworthy endeavour but it may require quite painful introspection and honesty with oneself.

Independence Maturity is a condition where strengths and limitations are well in focus, and where constructive effort is readily applied to compensate for shortcomings. Intellectually it is a rigorous condition because without the umbilical cord to a corporate body and the associated power that such a connection implies, there is a greater need to deploy effectively one's own wits, creativity, inventiveness and persuasive abilities.

This is a key facet in the state of mind that is intrinsic with those who have achieved Independence Maturity. It is readily understood that sponsorship of the concept, the proposal, or the plan in hand must include its own sustainable logic. The ability to argue the case on its peculiar, objective and quantifiable merits is a substantial strength and an intellectually rewarding exercise in its own right. This is far removed from so many managers in the corporate world who are familiar with the regime's ordinances governing the "how" but cannot sustain an argument in support of the "why", and who to justify their view will rely on corporate policy and protocols.

Apart from the greater mental challenges facing the refugee from the corporate world, there is also the matter of physical constraints. In corporate working, the supporting infrastructure and its benefits are taken for granted. Transition to working in a smaller enterprise or as a sole trader provides sharp reminders of how valuable had been the secretary, stationery clerk, input clerk and office messenger, and how important it is to accept a measure of demotion in those areas to get the job done. Independence Maturity thus induces a measure of occupational humility!

Negatives aside, the positive elements combine to create a heady and exciting mixture. Unless experienced directly, it is hard to describe how enjoyable it can be to undertake a task for its own ends and in search of the optimal solution, without the debilitating need to watch out for the bureaucratic minefield. There is real pleasure in having total discretion to follow your own judgement about those people with whom you will work, rather than succumbing to the company requirement to be part of a team in which the personal chemistry is a disaster.

The individual who is close to, or who enjoys Independence Maturity will recognise these advantages as being more than adequate compensation for the reduction in income, loss of corporate nanny state benefits, and elimination of status, all of which so often attend a lifestyle change away from the corporate executive world.

Earlier we reviewed the negative factors associated with disillusionment and a sense of rejection, which might induce an erstwhile wage slave to turn his back on the corporate system. The discovery of Independence Maturity is by comparison a far more powerful positive. It is a state of mind which offers something much more stimulating and attractive than anything the corporate world can offer, and invites lifestyle change through choice, rather than necessity.

Fresh start opportunities

Reference has been made to the social impact of surplus people, the effects of automation and the corollary of redundancy. This cycle has had most noticeable effect upon the workforces of larger commercial entities among traditional private sector companies, and in the privatised sector.

In tandem with this, however, many smaller enterprises have survived through periods of substantial market upheaval but without their own organisational structures undergoing anything like the same re-design. Generally speaking the main reason has been that minimal bureaucracies and management hierarchies have played an important role in cost minimisation. Many of these smaller companies never participated in the burgeoning growth of the ranks of senior staff that so typified larger entities in the 1960's and 1970's.

In these smaller companies, the owner is often the manager, and he habitually stands close to the pit-face of the business, rather than in monitoring from afar in the comfort of the executive suite. Short lines of communication, decisions taken in committees of one, and face-to-face contact with the customers combine to minimise the need for managerial redundancies because those additional managers were never appointed in the first place.

In terms of general operations, smaller companies often man-for-man achieve superior productivity and efficiency compared with their larger counterparts. They can only function in this fashion without the burden of heavy overheads, thereby avoiding a prime objective of bureaucracies which is to appoint staff for their self-administration rather than to add commercial value. It was Tom Peters who stated with characteristic forcefulness "that there is no way you can run a business efficiently through eleven layers of management".

On the other hand, many smaller companies are intellectually weaker than is safe in a fast moving and technologically orientated world. This is because a modestly sized management team that is fully stretched in satisfying daily commercial requirements does not have the available bandwidth to absorb and utilise new management and business concepts.

This provides a significant window for anyone seeking to make a fresh start. Large organisations habitually train their executives in a far broader range of skills and techniques than they are ever called upon to exercise for the corporate good. Indeed, it is most noticeable how often the senior management of large companies take little or no interest in the content of executive training programs, particularly where these employ the services of outside experts and speakers. From the narrow corporate angle, training courses are sometimes overtly subversive in content – ironically tacitly blessed by senior management through disinterest and neglect – but they are invaluable in stimulating lateral thought processes, and in giving exposure to alternative options and remedies.

The process of self-assessment to evaluate just what skills an individual may really command is considered later in Chapter 4. Here, it is pertinent to emphasise the point that ex-executives of large companies have at their disposal a substantial source of skills, knowledge and experience. They are frequently unaware of the commercial value of what they have to offer, or more likely they do not know how to put those assets to remunerative commercial use. Nevertheless, if marshalled and deployed properly, these attributes can considerably advance the cause of many smaller companies.

These skills do not lie in that pool of knowledge reflective of the corporate ethos, rule book and instruction manual. They are to be found in the logic and rationale that derives from an appreciation of first principles, from experience and sound judgement, and from common sense. Persuading the recipient to accept the importance of the message, or even the need for such a message, is a test of selling and persuasive skills far more intricate than anything that Tom in Case Study 1. was planning to bring to any business solicitation encounter.

Belief that fresh opportunities do await is critically important. It is indicative of a determination not to give up, that there is still something of worth to offer, and that a valued contribution can be made that will make a real difference. This statement of confidence is significant and should be most remembered at times when morale has been undermined.

However unpleasant or distressing has been recent experience, it is essential to recognise that everyone in this situation is worth more, has a broader range of skills, and is of greater commercial value than he is conditioned to believe of himself as a result of the redundancy experience.

The advantages of ageism

The modern corporate strategies that embrace de-manning or downsizing exercises usually rely heavily on ageist principles for the basis of selection. Where employment severance is the issue at hand, confrontation with the individuals so affected can be difficult for he who has to impart the message and age-related criteria (real or invented) may be employed in part justification. In this context, ageism may be used as a blunt weapon that pays little heed to individual attributes and abilities. One result is that certain executive age groups within particular professions are collectively labelled as "over the hill".

Although some economies may be gained on the premise that older personnel equate with higher average employment cost, this approach can easily be insensitive to individual qualities, and thus wasteful of talent that otherwise would be still profitably employable. As an aside, the practise is also unresponsive to the recorded comparative performance levels of individuals which in turn calls into question the purpose of the annual ritual of employee performance evaluation.

Ageism is therefore a major factor in this transitional process, and is a major negative element in the prevailing standards of the corporate scene. However, as recurs in other aspects of the lifestyle change process, what was negative can yield a strongly positive obverse, following the transition.

Case 3. Paul had spent a full career of forty years with one employer, a major multinational industrial group. During that time he had gained very broad experience in a number of different disciplines, and by working in several different countries. Following retirement at age 65, he retained his business connections and from time to time, undertook informal consulting assignments to maintain his interest in business affairs and as personal favours to old friends.

By chance, he was introduced to the young CEO of a specialised engineering company. The CEO had somewhat prematurely inherited his position from his father, now deceased, and had set about revitalising and expanding the business. He was hard working and committed, but also impetuous in his enthusiasm. As a result, ill-planned expansion had been undertaken with concomitant increases in costs and a general loss of business focus. Turnover had increased but so had bad debt levels, while profitability suffered badly. Liquidity was under pressure and the bank was increasingly restless.

Paul was asked to help out as a consultant and he quickly recognised that much of the company was fundamentally sound, that the young CEO had many good qualities, but that a hand of restraint and guidance was needed. Before long he was able to withdraw from what in the crisis period had been a full time assignment but the bank and the CEO requested his continued presence. He thus became an effective and successful non-executive Chairman of the company.

This mutually satisfactory end result was a classic example of a successful consultancy engendering real benefit, and Paul's age, demeanour and wisdom provided a perfect counterbalance to the CEO's exuberance. However, Paul had only won that recognition by his determination at the start of the consultancy to be practical in his approach and realistic in his recommendations. He had shown willingness to get his hands dirty in sorting out the mess, and in so doing had demonstrated beyond doubt the value of the experience and knowledge that came with his age.

Practical observation has convinced the authors that for those who are embarking on a new life, ageism can be a vitally important asset in the process of self-promotion. Indeed, opportunities and horizons appear to expand, not contract, with greater age – subject once again to the caveat that proper planning and preparation has been undertaken to equip oneself for the new career.

It has been said that many candidate consultants hope to succeed with nothing more to sell than their accumulated wisdom. Certainly, wisdom plays an important role but this must be combined and packaged with all the other benefits which age and experience can provide. With the right attitude, the older consultant can be highly effective in providing help and advice of both a generalist and specialist nature – as Paul so ably demonstrated in Case 3 above.

Age thus will mature and develop the range of benefits that the individual has for sale. For this reason, we have segmented parts of Chapter 14 along ageist lines. The type of work which an individual in self employment is able to undertake convincingly will be partly determined by his age, and this in turn will reflect his experience and the range of topics on which he can speak with real authority.

More importantly, clients who have not been faced with the need for significant downsizing but who do require outside executive level advice and assistance will pay no heed to a suggestion that age is any deterrent to quality. Very much to the contrary, they will recognise value in experience, in a broader knowledge base, and in the quality of management discipline that an executive career bestows.

There are many companies that do not recognise where they require help, or if they have made this recognition, they do not have the means of access to that help. What type of help an individual is able to offer is explored in Chapter 4, but first it is necessary to consider the market and environmental change factors that are placing unprecedented pressures on so many companies.

Summary points

Surplus people

- *Surpluses, not shortages, drive modern pressures for change*
- *Automation magnifies the impact of improved efficiency*
- *More sophisticated computer use exacerbates the people surplus*
- *Modern IT creates most current management redundancy*
- *Modern education techniques have replaced "learning on the job"*
- *Competitive activity drives key lifestyle decisions*
- *Lifestyle changes embrace greater self reliance and fresh career objectives*

Redundancy and rejection of the conventional employment system

- *"Nanny state" implies central orchestration of individuals' needs*
- *Generous corporate benefits create nanny states for employees*
- *Employment severance is a complex and stressful process*
- *Redundant yet able managers are often dissatisfied with erstwhile bosses*
- *Two main factors in dissatisfaction: incompetent CEO's and corporate bullying*
- *The people surplus protects unsatisfactory senior managers*
- *Disillusionment invokes rejection of the "wage slave" role*

Lifestyle change

- *Redundancy encourages efforts to prove unfairness in ex-employer's judgement*
- *Approach with care any legal action for wrongful dismissal*
- *Any gain from legal action should be balanced against:*
  time expended/ employer's legal firepower/ re-opening of old wounds/ distraction from priority of planning for the future
- *Success in new lifestyle needs thorough planning*
- *Distinguish between authority of previous position and personal attributes*
- *Lost authority requires substitution of personal qualities and intellect*

Independence Maturity: the essence of success

- *Intrinsic to success in self-employment*
- *Working alone demands additional personal qualities*
- *Self-evaluation must be objective and honest*
- *A rigorous and intellectually demanding state of mind*
- *Requires logic, analytical and persuasive skills in absence of corporate support*
- *Embraces a ready acceptance to undertake more menial tasks.*
- *Freedom and personal discretion outweigh the negative aspects*
- *Exhilarating advantages over the benefits of the nanny state*
- *Inducements to independence are stronger than incentives to escape wage slavery*

Fresh start opportunities

- *Opportunities with small companies that have avoided market upheavals*
- *Smaller companies perform better through less bureaucracy*
- *However, smaller teams are less able to absorb new business techniques*
- *Managers are more broadly trained than their daily duties require*
- *Redundant managers have a range of unutilised skills to offer*
- *Skills must rely on intellectual integrity rather than company rules*
- *Belief in fresh opportunities is vital*
- *Individuals have more to offer than rejection through redundancy implies*

The advantages of ageism

- *Ageism is one foundation of many downsizing programs*
- *Ageism is a blunt instrument that falsely labels certain age groups*
- *Financial benefits of redundancy are offset by wastage of talent*
- *Ageism in transition to self-employment can be an advantage*
- *Wisdom, knowledge and experience combine to make an attractive package*
- *Smaller companies value age more than their larger counterparts*

Chapter 3

The economics of plenty

The plentiful supply of goods and services that we now enjoy in modern living lies at the core of the most profound changes in the mind-set of business generally. The concept of "more" carries implications far deeper than merely heightened competitive forces. It affects the balance of control between consumers and producers, and it induces far greater fluidity in the nature and disposition of productive assets for business. Concurrently it creates a benign influence for those small commercial entities and entrepreneurial individuals that are sufficiently flexible and creative to take advantage of changing market structures.

Buyer power

The luxury hotels in the West End of London have always been accepted as providing high standards of accommodation and catering, and to entertain in one of these establishments may be seen as extending hospitality of the highest order. It used to be fashionable, if ostentatious, for the host to demonstrate his influence and wealth by stipulating that dessert should include every fruit that was not in season. In contrast it would today be impossible to detect the season by studying the fruit and vegetable section of any decent supermarket as those once scarce fruits are now accepted as standard fare available throughout the year. While the price might fluctuate, mainly determined by how far the produce has had to travel, ordinary people with a reasonable disposable income expect to have access to "exotic" items as a matter of right.

This change says something about the democratisation of food. It also speaks volumes for the nature of concentrated buying power, for advances in the speed and efficiency of international or inter-continental freight services, and for the potency of modern distribution technology in international markets.

The production and distribution of food is an excellent example of how a globalised industry may develop on the back of plentiful supply. Equally it can be salutary to note how some investors and existing industry players are still prepared to risk substantial sums without due cognisance of what is going on around them in an industry that they claim to know well.

Case 4. One of the authors unsuccessfully advised a grower group in a Mediterranean country on the risks and challenges facing them in setting up a new fruit canning plant using locally grown produce. The mind-set of the sponsors was directed towards maximisation of EU grant assistance to get the project underway, and to the securing of substantial export sales. It was pointed out that in that same country, a multinational fruit canner was importing oranges from Iberia and strawberries from Poland for processing and re-export. This was necessary because despite a favourable climate and plenty of fertile land, indigenous farming methods were too inefficient to provide a reliable supply source.

Despite considerable advisory effort, the project sponsors could not understand the point that any attempt at international sales would only be successful upon achievement of rigorous quality standards. In the globalised food industry, the concept of import and export is largely obsolete as an international frontier is now only a peripheral factor in the process of efficient procurement and distribution.

In the 1950's, the purchase of a new motor car could be a harrowing and frustrating business. A wait of 6 to 9 months for a standard model could be quite usual, and in that interval, the buyer had little option other than to accept any price rises which the manufacturer might seek to impose, or lose the chance of driving a new car. Then when the vehicle did arrive, its colour would be that which the manufacturer had chosen to apply that day, not what the customer would have preferred.

Compared with current conditions, such a situation seems laughable but it was a genuine reflection of the high levels of demand and shortage of supply then obtaining. Today customer power exerts pressure on the manufacturer to deliver what is required out of a bewildering range of model variations. Wily purchasers are able to negotiate substantial discounts on new vehicles, or new vehicles that have been “clocked” i.e. odometers falsely turned *forward* to represent a “nearly new” car and thus disguise the ex-factory discount that has been applied to shift surplus stock.

Case 5. Stories are legion about deals that are done in this market. The authors are aware of one case where through good judgement and timing, the offer of cash for a model that had just become obsolete resulted in a £27,000 UK new list price car being sold for £12,000. For adventurous buyers prepared to seek cars in continental Europe, or alternatively new or one year old imports originally produced and homologated for the Japanese market, price reductions running into thousands of pounds are regularly achievable.

The perception that shopping around the marketplace will produce a better deal for the canny consumer erodes traditional notions of customer loyalty. In a generously supplied world, customers seek satisfaction in diverse aspects stretching well beyond the physical characteristics of the product itself. Price, packaging, performance, functionality, delivery, availability, warranties, after sales service and value for money are all factors which combine to determine in the buyer’s mind whether the purchase represents a quality deal. Failure on just a single criterion may now be all that is necessary for the buyer to abandon loyalty, and to approach alternative suppliers or to consider different types of product.

In some sectors, brand remains a major factor in the loyalty equation and an obvious example is with the products of the motor vehicle industry. Manufacturers in other sectors however must contend with circumstances of multiple competing products, and with buying decisions determined by numerous other factors. For example the print wizard on the personal computer being used to prepare this text advises that there are forty-nine manufacturers whose various printers are compatible. In such circumstances, the selection of a new printer is likely to be driven by price, performance and the availability of local dealer support. Brand may only play a small part in the decision.

Motor cars, computers and fresh fruit are disparate products for several reasons – unit price, consumption patterns, buying psychology etc – but the same underlying trend prevails with each. The manner in which buying patterns and customer psychology now operate is quite different from that of a few years ago. In each case, the producer should be aware that customer power is paramount and that successful sales can only be sustained by due recognition of this factor. These are examples of the economics of plenty at work - in simple terms, good for consumers but tough on manufacturers and producers.

Supply competition

Competition has of course existed ever since man first engaged in economic activity but an impact of the economics of plenty has been to tip the scales further against the interests of the supplier. There are distinct strands to this fundamental movement and three that have profound implications are cost, time and delivery.

The continuing refinement of technology and its increasing accessibility has collapsed the real cost of new investment in many activities. An IT problem that a few years ago would have demanded all the paraphernalia of corporate strategy implementation (technical assessment, planning and costing protocols, budgetary approval etc) may now be solved by acquisition of standardised equipment, much of it available at the local computer superstore. Such benefits are a powerful inducement for new market players because cost as a barrier to entry is significantly reduced, if not removed.

Competitive pressures and technology have combined to instil a sense of immediacy in the minds of consumers. Industrial consumers expect just-in-time performance levels from their trading counter-parties, just as individual consumers require immediate access to goods on offer. Failure to perform leads to the instant search for supply alternatives because time is so critical. In the IT sector, the demand for immediacy is driven by the extreme pace of new technology introduction and has lead to the concept of "cyber years" which, like dog years, equal one-seventh of the standard twelve month cycle. The cyber year is a crude method of measurement but a cogent means of reminding you that even if you are not counting time in that fashion, there is a strong likelihood that your competitors are.

Delivery is in many ways the most unpredictable. Creation of alternative ways of finding a solution might mean the arrival of a new competitor who sees the whole business opportunity through a totally different set of dimensions, and who recognises different and perhaps more pressing aspects of the customer's range of needs. In a world of multiple channel delivery systems, the opportunity exists for a customer contact to be exploited for the sale of a whole range of ancillary items as is evidenced by the range of products and services promoted through junk mail "flyers". Each of these items is promoted in that fashion on the basis that the all up cost of manufacture, packaging and delivery is cheaper than through traditional means. Every such sale is at the expense of a producer still reliant on the conventional means of reaching his customer.

Our extensive observation of, and contact with smaller companies supports the contention that organisations in this category are less likely to be aware of the combined threat that inadequate attention to cost, time and delivery presents, or if they are aware, less able to cope robustly with the combined challenge. Typically, the managers of smaller companies are very much closer to their respective customer bases on a micro or one-to-one level and may feel justified in believing that they know a lot about their customer needs. Paradoxically however, because so much management resource is devoted to monitoring the needs of individuals, scant attention is paid to the "big picture" and to the nature of evolution at the macro level.

Small companies are usually owner-managed, often by the founder. The corporate ethos is centred on the excellence of those products or services that have provided the core of the income right from inception of the business undertaking. Asked for a definition of his company's aims and future ambitions, the owner-manager's frequent response can be reduced to words along the lines of "our business is dedicated to the manufacture of the country's finest widgets, and we intend to continue to be successful in that aim".

This sort of sentiment usually derives from the manufacturing or process orientation of the company, and relies on a hope that the business environment will continue to support a demand for widgets made in the traditional fashion. This belief in a business continuum may be reasonable in certain industries. A niche market situation might favour resistance to change and place particular value on time-honoured processes where the customer is willing to pay a high price for production inefficiency. It is fun to try to identify businesses falling into this category, but objective measurement of the total value of their production compared with the economic whole swiftly identifies them as being small and peripheral.

Thus for the vast majority of companies with a traditional management whose main priorities are concentrated on issues such as what happens in the plant and how efficiently can the widgets be made, the future may far be less secure than is desirable. These companies we term as being "internally focussed", and their obsession with their processes all too often distracts their attention from what is happening externally in the market.

Implications of the power shift

An interesting feature of the power shift from supplier to buyer power is that the evolving scenario is far more complex than a mere game of large versus small. Of course large established companies in control of research capacity, sophisticated marketing techniques and the ability to bargain aggressively for their own input supplies will command more raw commercial strength than the smaller competitor. Likewise the small company will enjoy volume-based advantages over the sole trader.

However, the collapsing price of technology has enabled the small organisation with dynamic operating philosophies and fleetness of foot to punch well above its weight commercially. This type of organisation may be superbly suited to operate in conditions where the usual duration of individual work opportunities is short and where reliance is placed on external suppliers by out-sourcing. Paradoxically therefore, while expanding and ever more inter-dependent markets have favoured the large players, they have also advanced in parallel the opportunities for the smaller enterprise to flourish and succeed.

Smallness carries potency and a special type of effectiveness that arises from minimal bureaucracies, short chains of command, and an understanding of what the customer expects. Conversely, the smaller organisation is often incapable of realising these opportunities because its very smallness may prevent it from accessing the broader range of modern and more complex technical skills that may be required. Additionally, a process of re-education may be needed to re-focus management practises and philosophies away from traditional to more innovative habits. More often than not, it is the existing management mind-set or paradigm that is the biggest obstacle to realising the benefits that wider, more open market situations offer.

The skills cascade

Any business undertaking intent on sustaining itself successfully in the medium and long term needs to synchronise and balance the resources under its control. Its strength will rely on the adequacy of three fundamental resource components – financial (balance sheet, fund raising capacity, profits), intellectual (know-how, expertise, technology) and social (personnel, individual skills, internal and external human relationships).

In the last fifty years, the relative significance of these components has tended to shift quite substantially. Those with memories of business conditions in the extended periods of full employment in the 1950's and 60's will recall that a persistent challenge to management was presented by shortages of sufficient personnel of the right calibre. More recently, expanded tertiary education, better employer sponsored training, and technological progress have combined to reverse the skills shortage. The modern senior manager has the luxury to select and discard subordinate personnel in a fashion (and with a freedom from labour representation) that his predecessor of twenty years ago never enjoyed.

This unparalleled freedom to manipulate human resources is directly attributable to the manner in which the economics of plenty have permitted the re-alignment of the key components of business mentioned above. Whether or not this mass displacement of human resources will auger well for future business and social stability is not within the scope of this work. However, what it has done is to create a cascade of talented and trained people whose skills are available on the open labour market in greater quantities than ever before.

This rich resource is both plentiful and pliable. The recognition that a job for life is now a rare concept has stimulated an acceptance that working diversity is a welcome addition to modern life. Flexibility and adaptability are now exploited to a greater degree than before with people prepared for, and enjoying, working styles that encompass change and variety. Work opportunities are now seriously considered that require either travel over greater distances than previously or use of an office within the home. They demand flexible working hours at weekends or overnight, and the engagement of a far wider range of skills and disciplines than would have previously been expected of stable, conventional employment conditions.

The skills cascade has been exciting in that people have been able to fashion and co-ordinate in novel ways their working habits alongside their lifestyle requirements. This has been the good, and in some ways largely unexpected, outcome of the changes wrought by the economics of plenty. On a personal development plane and in the interests of self-fulfilment, we should be able to expect a greater prevalence of balance and contentment among those who recognise and exploit the opportunities that these profound changes present.

Transportability of business assets

The newly created flexibility of attitude among more progressive and adventurous elements of the workforce exposes established businesses to new commercial risks. Just as large organisations demonstrate reduced loyalty towards their employees, so they place at greater risk many of the key assets that those employees represent. Their accumulated skill sets typically comprise high standards of academic and business education, practical experience and a great deal of accumulated know-how. Thus an individual may be the custodian of a great deal of intellectual property largely bestowed upon him at the expense of his erstwhile employer's shareholders.

Intellectual property rights (IPR) are notoriously difficult to preserve and protect once they have been shared with others. Like all knowledge, its commercial value to its owner is substantially reduced at the point of its sharing, and effectively there is little in the way of protective remedies available to prevent plagiarism and blatant copying. Patents, copyright law, non-disclosure contracts etc may look powerful on paper but in effect they are cumbersome instruments whose implementation often is too slow and too complex to have much effect.

It is quite likely therefore that the most significant and potentially damaging element of the de-manning exercises in recent times in large organisations is not so much the loss of the personnel but of the IPR that those personnel take with them. This loss need not be a matter of theft of documents or other written material, but simply that of key data being carried away in the heads of the people concerned.

Of all the modern features of business life, IPR is the one most likely to foster discrimination between success and failure, and paradoxically often its significance in this regard is barely acknowledged, or even understood, by those whose prime duty should be its preservation. IPR is a powerful weapon in the competitive marketplace and those who wield it to most effect have the ability to do much damage to established business enterprises.

If IPR is harnessed to state-of-the-art technology, the ability exists to build virtual business activities quickly and effectively, and at a fraction of the sunk cost incurred by existing players. For example, it is well known in the financial services sector that a clever new product may have a short unique lifecycle (perhaps only a few days) before it is copied and marketed by a competitor. In the same sector, it has been authoritatively estimated that to start a significant new consumer orientated financial services company in the conventional form would require capital of around $1000 million whereas to do the same thing in virtual mode using the Internet would require about $10 million. (Significant in this example means a customer base of 10 million).

Thus technology, the power of virtual as opposed to traditional bricks-and-mortar business organisations, and the disbursal of IPR offers stunning opportunities for new enterprise, and poses dangerous threats to established market participants. In this arena, the changed nature of competitive forces, driven by the economics of plenty, allows the hitherto minor operator the chance to enter competitive or symbiotic relationships with larger counterparts. As mentioned above, this yields a capacity to punch above an expected weight measured on a traditional scale.

Implications for the individual

This book pays only passing heed to these fascinating macro level developments and possibilities because we are primarily concerned with the needs and objectives of the individual who is considering life as an independent consultant. Even so, it is important background and should be understood as providing the atmosphere and context in which independent working may be considered as a feasible and serious career alternative.

It is probable that the reader of this book will have formed part of this skills cascade and we are concerned to identify on individual planes why a career termination may have been unavoidable, and how this traumatic change can yield more positive elements than might be immediately apparent. Modern commercial circumstances have created an undoubted concurrence of challenge and fresh risk for both the business organisation and the individual worker. Both must confront the continuous need for re-invention and re-direction and while leaving the former to their own devices, we explore the potential and the demands that face the individual person who is the by-product of this process of plenty.

In this context, it is readily recognised that the individual must find a new repository for his accumulated skills and abilities. Most frequently the cascade will direct him to the smaller business enterprise that has yet to engage head-on the economics of plenty but will in due course inevitably be exposed to the forces that this phenomenon increasingly exerts upon the business world. Thus the refugee from big business has much to offer the company that by design or situation has been constrained in the development of a full range of skills and management techniques. One option thus arising as available to him is to market what he has to offer through the mechanisms of independent consulting.

Summary points

Buyer power

- *Plentiful supply has helped build a globalised economy*
- *Concentrated purchasing and swift distribution aid buyer power*
- *Improved quality and service result from enhanced competition*
- *Customer loyalty demands more than just product quality*
- *Loyalty now relies on many other related and dependent factors*
- *"Good for customers but tough on manufacturers and producers"*

Supply competition

- *Economics of plenty have tipped scales further against supplier*
- *Three distinct strands to this movement are cost, time and delivery*
- *Technology and its accessibility have collapsed the cost of much new investment*
- *Competition and technology instil a sense of immediacy in consumers' minds*
- *Performance failure initiates instant search for supply alternatives*
- *Multi-channel delivery systems encourage ancillary sales promotion*
- *Every such sale is at the expense of a conventional sales opportunity*
- *Small company ethos is usually centred on product or service excellence*
- *This internal focus distracts attention from critical market trends*

Implications of the power shift

- *More than merely large versus small*
- *Resource advantages of large companies aids aggressive bargaining*
- *Technology gives small companies more business punching*
- *Less bureaucracy and proximity to customers gives potency to small business*
- *Re-education re-focuses management on more innovative habits*

The skills cascade

- *Sustained success needs resource synchronisation and balance*
- *Strength relies on key resource components: financial, social, intellectual*
- *Component weighting can shift quite substantially*
- *Education, training, and technological progress have reversed skills shortages*
- *Economics of plenty have re-aligned key business components*
- *A cascade of skilled people on labour market has resulted*

Transportability of business assets

- *Enhanced flexibility and new attitudes create new competitive threats*
- *Diminished employer-employee loyalty risks assets that employees can access*
- *De-manning threatens preservation of Intellectual Property Rights*
- *Technology aids new enterprise and threatens established players*

Implications for the individual

- *Factors enumerated are equally relevant for the individual*
- *The reader is quite possibly a participant in the skills cascade*
- *The individual continually needs re-invention and re-direction*
- *Skills cascade usually directs individuals to smaller businesses*

Chapter 4

What does it take to be a self-employed consultant?

A prerequisite to pursuit of a career as a self employed consultant is to have gained sufficient experience to have the confidence and belief that this comprises something worth passing on to others. However, if that experience has previously been entirely taken up in working for other people, it may not provide the best platform from which to launch into a new career that is characterised by fundamentally different problems and challenges.

It is a common mistake to assume that previous corporate experience is automatically transferable into the consulting arena and that this will provide an adequate personal resource base to ensure success. In fact, the move from a corporate executive position to consulting is a substantial career change, and the individual should prepare himself accordingly. Because the broad subject matter might appear similar, this can breed a false sense of familiarity that yields an assumption that the transition can be achieved simply and smoothly.

Successful consultants operate and think quite differently from their corporate counterparts. It is that essential difference which enables them to assess problems and issues from alternative points of view and so to develop creative and effective solutions. An approach that adopts the posture that consulting advice consists effectively of a pure re-incarnation of previous corporate experience has a high probability of failure.

It is vital for the new consultant to understand that he needs to be quite certain in his own mind what he has to offer his clients. Further, he needs to have a logical modus operandi to ensure that he is able to communicate effectively with the client, that he can properly evaluate the client's needs, and that he can prepare and present proposals in such a fashion that the client will listen, accept and act accordingly.

A program of self-assessment and review of personal development requirements is necessary to identify the nature and extent of the skills that can be deployed commercially.

Specialist or generalist?

Broadly speaking, all consultants may be segregated into either of the above categories but in the authors' view, consultants should always strive to assemble a portfolio of credentials that qualify themselves as generalists.

Specialists who have one or more defined disciplines at their disposal may so label themselves while generalists take the view that the overall denomination of "business consultant" or something similar is sufficiently wide-ranging to catch a variety of business opportunities from a variety of clients. There are benefits and drawbacks to both denominations, and the inter-dependence of the relative factors requires that they should be assessed in some detail.

Specialist: often ensures that a specific skill or discipline is embodied in the title, and this may greatly help the client to understand the nature of the services being offered. Indeed, quite often the client will have identified the need and will then search for a consultant who promotes himself as being a specialist in that field. Thus a company required to adopt ISO 9000 for customer retention purposes might seek out an individual who specifically promotes himself as an "ISO 9000 Consultant".

Advantages lie in clarity of purpose. The agenda between client and consultant may be easily assimilated and understood, often supported by accepted market yardsticks for the pricing of such specialist services. Accordingly, promotion of the consultancy and justification of the results is relatively straightforward as the client has already seen the need for a solution to a recognised problem.

Specialist consultants have often learned their skills in the corporate world and these may have constituted a full time task while in salaried employment. It is quite usual that successful completion of a project in the corporate environment has led to those skills being no longer required, and hence redundancy for their owner. The corporate decision not to re-train or re-deploy the individual concerned leads quite logically to his attempting to continue earning by offering his services on a freelance basis in the outside market.

Initial acceptance by the market can be favourable because the disciplines on offer have a topical quality. Further sale of the skill is not difficult for a certain period but the shelf life is inevitably limited unless the consultant makes the conscious effort to invest out of his own pocket to keep abreast of new developments. Without the backing of a corporate budget, this can involve significant sums if specialist training courses and attendance at technical conferences are necessary.

Another drawback to specialist consultancy work is that some categories by definition are of specific duration, being related to one-off problems or events. For example, during 1998 and 1999 consultancy services were in high demand in conjunction with EMU and Millennium 2000 compliance.

Of a more lasting significance is the issue of limited focus. The specialist consultant sets himself up as an expert in a particular field and is thus defining his limitations in the eyes of the client right from the start. In reality, a properly managed consulting relationship with an amenable client should offer a broad range of opportunities right across the face of the business. The specialist however suffers from the problem that he has chosen a particular field and he has no apparent mandate to look laterally into other areas where his services could be of use. Likewise, the client has no identified incentive to invite the specialist consultant to adopt a wider approach to matters outside the initial mandate.

Generalist: starts with the positive point that he will look at any problem or opportunity, and will have the ability to create a solution. Alternatively he can arrange the means by which the solution is created through the help and contribution of others. This allows him to adopt a "can do" attitude to matters that may or may not yet have been identified as problems. The generalist thus may gain the opportunity to persuade the client that no issues are outside his brief, and that in respect of matters in which he is not qualified to deal, he can always seek specialist help.

If there is a pecking order of sorts in a joint consultancy, the generalist should be the senior or managing consultant because he will be exposed to a fuller range of corporate issues and will thus be better able to review matters on a strategic plane. The wider ranging nature of the brief often permits the generalist to identify and pursue issues that were not within the original client mandate. He thus has far greater opportunity for cross-sale of his services whereas once the specialist's job is done, he has to commence the search for his next client.

Counting against the generalist is the challenge to validate properly his role and contribution in the eyes of the client. We will address issues concerning how to communicate effectively with the client when we consider techniques in practical consulting in Chapters 10 and 12. However, it is important to note here that while clients often believe that they need help, they may be uncertain where or how. This can complicate the definition of their needs, and their appreciation of how a consultant can assist.

Unlike the situation confronting the specialist, the agenda can be far from clear. In fact, there may be much confusion in the client's mind about the purposes of the exercise or what benefits will result. The fully trained and accomplished consultant should be able to alleviate the client's concerns but nonetheless the generalist has to be clear and determined in his objectives because he does face greater hurdles in negotiating a workable mandate.

The preference: as stated at the commencement of this section, the argument is strongly in favour of generalism. Consulting should always be approached with the intention of building a sustainable income base in the medium/ long term. Employment of skills that have a restricted commercial life naturally militates against that objective.

Also, it should be borne in mind that this is a highly educational activity for the consultant himself. Increased exposure to a wide variety of different companies, industries and situations multiplies knowledge (and self-confidence) at a surprising and gratifying pace. That expanding knowledge base in itself is a source of potential incremental income, as opportunities for profitable cross-fertilisation become apparent.

As a general rule, ageist principles should be an indicator of suitability for more generalist consulting efforts i.e. the longer a person has been active in the business world, the more likely he is to have accumulated skills and knowledge of a broad nature. However, there is always the chance of winning the best of both worlds by promotion of both generalist and specialist skills - but always with the proviso that generalist capacities should take pride of place.

The self-audit

The self-audit can be a radical but essential step in the move to a career in consulting because typically individuals are not good at recognising the full range of acquired skills and talents that they have accumulated over the years. Proper attention to this subject should help to identify the opportunities that the broad canvass of generalist consulting can offer, and which are frequently more readily achievable than may seem possible at first sight.

A newcomer to consulting may be tempted to measure his skills in terms of the seniority and importance of his most recent appointments in corporate life. However he will have more at his disposal to draw upon than that and it is essential for his future prospects that this value be sought out, assessed and marshalled so that it can be made commercially exploitable. This is a deeply personal process requiring a good memory, much maturity and sound judgement. It is substantively different from that applied to produce that egocentric sales document known as the curriculum vitae!

A self-audit should go right back to the days of tertiary education i.e. well before formal employment commenced. It should embrace all types of business situations experienced, and all relevant elements - contributing factors, personalities, good and incompetent managers, achievements and failures. In fact the negative aspects of a past career can often be far more educational, and of greater benefit in assembling the suite of consulting capabilities than the successes.

Success is a much more popular commodity than failure but claiming credit for it can be a dangerous exercise that may rebound to the individual's cost. The authors' experience with new consultants has revealed a noticeable trait among some to claim experience, abilities and competencies that are clearly not their own.

For example, there is a tendency to record that they have expertise based on practical experience in a particular type of work, implying that they have led or managed at least one project or work program in that field. Subsequently, it has been disconcerting to discover that the reality is markedly different. In the training process it has become quickly apparent that the previous experience claimed could at best have been shallow, and gained from a junior or subordinate level rather than as leader or manager.

The superficiality of the understanding and the failure to comprehend basic principles can be embarrassing enough within the closed and friendly environment of a training session. In the real world, such superficiality can be damaging for the consultant's chances of securing a viable relationship with his client. In addition, it is hardly good for the reputation of consulting as a whole and will give rise to regrettable conclusions that the resultant advice is insubstantial.

Commonly this situation appears as an unfortunate outcome of the ethos of the curriculum vitae where it is normal to overstate experience and abilities in the process of attempting a sale to a prospective employer. The self-audit process needs a radical move away from this mind-set because in consulting the CV is largely redundant. The client is not going to be interested in what the consultant claims he can do, but in what he can really contribute. An honest approach whereby the client quickly learns the scope of the consultants' capabilities, and also those areas where third party quality assistance will be necessary is going to win far more brownie points than fatuous assertions of ability that are later found wanting.

Honesty in the self-audit therefore makes good sense. This is why it should be detailed and deeply introspective. For example, an unhappy time perhaps long ago working for an idiot boss may be regurgitated as a useful tool in explaining how human relations (and hence productivity) on the shop floor can be improved through simple measures that are efficient in implementation. Equally, good or bad experiences at lower levels in a corporate hierarchy may provide an excellent basis on which to advise changes to an organisational structure. Lost business orders in a past job may be cited as a cogent reason for overhauling the client's management information system, and for that information then to be taken seriously in future business decisions.

The examples are endless and their effective exploitation in the formulation of sound advice is a vital ingredient in what the client is buying. If the consultant is promoting himself on the legitimate grounds of an ageist approach – because age equals experience, a feature still valued by remarkably many people – then it is access to this attribute that the client is seeking.

Experience is a commodity that must be dredged up from the memory and realistically evaluated. On occasion, you may hear a statement that someone has worked in an industry for say 20 years. However, brief interrogation might yield the impression that the claimed experience was more akin to a single year repeated twenty times. If this is the case, then it is either a sad reflection of the fruits of 20 years' of work, or an indication of a lazy and superficial approach to measurement of accumulated experience.

Another aspect of memory of use to the ageist consultant relates to work with companies that have themselves undergone widespread redundancy programs. A serious element of de-manning that is rarely factored in by those who inaugurate these programs, never valued by those charged with their implementation, and rarely recognised by the younger generation that follow is the destruction of the corporate memory. This unquantifiable, intangible asset in many cases is destroyed virtually overnight and there is good reason to believe that its absence will result in repetitious problems that otherwise could have been easily avoided. The ageist consultant who is capable of marshalling his varied and valuable experience in all its aspects has much to offer in such situations.

Experience therefore provides an excellent base on which to promote the means of implementing a corporate solution. This alone, though, is unlikely to be sufficient in convincing a manager who relies heavily on logic and who may seek a rationale for taking action. Recommendations for a specific plan may have to be supported by validated reasons. Here again, a probe into the past in the self-audit process should identify more resources than may have been immediately apparent.

Every consultant will on occasion require access to technical and theoretical works to support his contentions. His proposals to a client may be controversial or revolutionary and to convince, it may be necessary to quote from reputable third party sources. Thus theory plays an important part in helping to implement practical efforts.

Retrospection should once again identify resources waiting to be exploited. They may be there in the form of technical books used while at college or university, or in the acquisition of professional tertiary qualifications. They may lie in the magazines and publications of professional bodies of which the individual is a member. Also, the notes, pamphlets, handouts, commentaries that were distributed during attendance at corporate training courses and seminars are a useful source of theoretical and technical assistance.

Indeed in the case of the latter, there is a certain irony in putting to later commercial use the material that was distributed so freely but which may well have received only passing attention at the time. Corporate training programs are often poorly applied in a practical sense but much of what is divulged at these sessions provides sound technical assistance for the individual who has chosen to work freelance.

In summary, a thorough search and review should identify that there are more skills and capacities on offer than might be initially thought. The more care and effort devoted to the process the better. After all, in toto it represents a unique assembly of attributes that will provide the basis for maximisation of income.

Self-audit methodology

A structured approach is worth the time because it may lead to identification of additional available resources, new ideas and prospects, and alternative ways of pursuing business opportunities. The system is similar in some ways to the consequential fashion in which a mind-map process opens up additional relevant factors.

Set out below is a suggested methodology that is based on a simulated case concerning a specific period in an individual's corporate career. There are other means of carrying out an audit but this format has been proven to work reasonably effectively.

Let us assume that Michael Jones has recently been made redundant and after a varied and reasonably successful salaried career, he has decided that he would like to try his hand at consulting. Being a disciplined individual he has started with the latest version of his curriculum vitae and is methodically auditing the nature and value of the experience he has gained. This will help him to determine what he has to offer, and also to identify those weak areas in his skills base that need remedial attention. A section of his CV reads as follows:

1/2/87	Promoted from accounting supervisor to Marketing Manager, ABC Ltd. Responsible directly to the Managing Director for all aspects of marketing policy, market research, sales promotion, advertising and new client liaison. Control of advertising budget (typically £350,000 per annum). During period, sales increased at rate of 25% per annum
15/2/89	Resigned to take up position of Assistant Group Accountant, XYZ Controls Ltd. Reason for leaving: desire to broaden career experience in different industries

The self-audit in respect of this period of Michael's career might paint a slightly different picture:

Appointment: Marketing Manager, ABC Controls

Date started: 1/2/87 **Dated ended**: 15/4/89 **Period in job**: 26 months
Age at starting: 38 years

Job description: Sole responsibility for all marketing matters and sales promotion. Planning of advertising campaign. Supervision of advertising budget. Liaison with new clients and responsibility for ensuring that their needs are being properly serviced by respective operating departments.

True job content: Management of sales records. Pursuit of late payers on an irregular basis as and when required by the MD. General "gofer" for MD in respect of information needed by him in connection with competitor prices, alternative sources of supply, competitor advertising campaigns. Provision of assistance to MD in connection with sales budgets and annual sales plan. No involvement whatever with new clients as respective departments claimed "ownership" of customer relationships and resented any intrusion.

Reason for leaving: Job content was vastly different from that which had been promised with the promotion, or what appeared in the formal job description. Had reached age where real management responsibility and experience was important if career progress was to be sustained. Job was effectively little more than that of an executive assistant or PA. MD was reluctant to delegate or to allow me any initiative or management discretion. What had at first been a friendly relationship turned sour and it was necessary to find another job.

Lesson learned:

Self: Need for more patience in business relationships. Need to improve negotiating and persuading skills. Job descriptions are frequently misleading. Important differences between sales and marketing. Importance of real delegation. Need to work hard to sustain good inter-departmental relations.

About MD:	Had a background in sales. Confused sales with marketing. Was indifferent to the broader responsibilities of a CEO. Preferred to "retreat to the familiar" where he felt more secure i.e. sales. Had not thought through how to get departments co-operating and working together. Managed the advertising program directly and did not use outside expert help – thus advertising was crude, ineffective and unduly costly. Was jealous of his knowledge and contacts, and did not want to share or delegate them.
About company performance:	Consistently under-performed. Poor internal organisational structure led to costly inefficiencies. Little understanding of the significance of customer profiling, competitor analysis, market research, marketing targets and budgets.
Results for company:	Sales growth was reflective of boom conditions in market rather than company's comparative efficiency. Downturn of 1989-90 hit company hard with loss of market share, sales and profitability. Company close to bankruptcy in 1991 – owners sold out at a capital loss to direct competitor.
Benefits for self:	1. Ability to argue the importance of a proper marketing strategy from having tried and failed in that regard. 2. Recognition of practical difficulties with inter-departmental relations and need for CEO to remove ambiguities and misunderstandings. 3. To improve own performance, joined Marketing Institute in 1988
ACTION NOW	- Review marketing books owned for technical library - Revive Institute membership/ participate in events program - Use membership for affinity promotions/ networking

An important factor arising from an exercise like this is the recognition that adverse experiences can help in understanding why things are the way they are, and why plans and the best of intentions may go wrong. Although companies each face unique circumstances and environmental situations, many difficulties that they encounter are caused by factors that are fundamentally generic. In this context, it is not unusual to meet a client who forcefully states that his products, company, and industry sector are so unique and his problems are so special that it is highly unlikely that an outsider will have any real appreciation of the complex issues at stake

The self-audit process highlights the nature of the consultant's past experience and serves to demonstrate a remarkable degree of commonality among problems that affect many institutions. Of course, analysis of the contributing factors and the structuring of corrective action plans involves bespoke tactics to meet the specific needs of the case but the fundamental causes very often conform to common criteria that are repeatedly encountered.

Thus, when challenged about his competence to address what the client rates as peculiar or special circumstances obtaining with his situation, the consultant is in a position to assert familiarity with the underlying causes. This claim is sustainable by his general knowledge and expertise in how businesses should be properly run, rather than in the peculiar technical and internal matters relating to the specific business under scrutiny.

Put another way, the client may ask, "what can you contribute to my knowledge of the efficient manufacture of widgets, a business in which I have been engaged all my working life?"

Consultant "I do not claim to have any knowledge or expertise in making widgets; I am knowledgeable about how a business should be managed efficiently to manufacture widgets or any other product or service".

The individual's SWOT analysis

It will be apparent that a thorough self-audit should result in the assembly of quite a lot of information, and its summary to make the key elements more easily assimilated is thus worthwhile. To this end, it is recommended that the technique of a Strengths, Weaknesses, Opportunities and Threats (SWOT) analysis be applied.

It may seem a tall order to summarise a lifetime of education, training and employment in a single page delineation using these four categories but this is a useful and rigorous self discipline that should greatly aid objective assessment. (This parallels the standard consulting operating procedure of distilling a complex client situation into a SWOT summary).

We have emphasised above the significance of previous experience in determining what the individual has to offer to consulting and to reflect this aspect, we recommend that the strengths and weakness should be divided into at least three sections reflecting education and training, employment history, and the current situation. This type of division is slightly unusual in a SWOT but we feel it is appropriate to adopt this structure as it helps to reflect the dynamics by which an individual's talents and abilities develop and become refined over time. We set out below how a SWOT employing this format might appear.

Michael Jones: self-SWOT analysis

Strengths

Education & training:

Good grades at GCSE/ A Level
Honours degree (2.2) Leeds University
Technical training courses
(basic IT skills/ sales techniques/
office admin./ personnel relations
basic bookkeeping & accounting)
Training courses generally good

Employment history:

Reputation for integrity
Relate well to most intelligent people
Well known in plastics & light alloys industries
Worked for 5 companies over 22 years
Employers engaged in 3 industry sectors
Middle management experience (office admin./
personnel management/ sales/ advertising/
divisional accounting controls)
Broad career experience
Worked in Leeds, Cardiff & Plymouth

Current situation:

Located in Plymouth – close to 50% of
natural market
Good office accommodation at home
Well known to local trade associations
Several contacts among local accountants
Good basis general consultant to SME's
Initial target list of 50 clients

Weaknesses

Degree not used in career
No planned self education program
Relied on learning-on-the-job without
matching theoretical study
Untrained in advanced accounting
Uncertain about company law

Never a senior manager
No experience of contract reading
IT experience inadequate
Do not suffer fools gladly
Impatient with unnecessary red tape

Many potential contacts too far away
(Leeds & Cardiff)
Inadequate accounting experience
Poor IT skills

Opportunities

Dockyard closures – many SME's need help
Expand target client list beyond 50
Renew & foster trade association contacts
Call on accounting firm contacts to explain
my activities & services

Threats

Failed client = unpaid fees
Delays in getting started
Reportedly several new consultants
in area

The marketable skills base

The assembly of the inventory of skills derived from the self-audit process should yield an objective evaluation of the consultant's expertise and resources in terms of their income-producing potential. Re-definition of some terms may be necessary when describing this expertise to the target client to ensure that the descriptions are understandable. For example, in the case set out above the MD to whom Michael Jones reported had clearly made the common error of believing that sales and marketing are the same thing when clearly they are two quite separate business disciplines.

Re-statement and amplification may be necessary to accommodate situations where target clients are unable to differentiate or to understand what is entailed under a particular subject heading. This is discussed more fully in Chapters 9 and 10 where questions concerning the importance of "getting inside the clients head" and "looking at issues through his eyes" are discussed more fully. Suffice to caution at this point that situations do occur where clients simply do not understand technical words and phrases, and may therefore misinterpret the import of the message that the consultant is endeavouring to pass on.

The risk of misunderstanding is enhanced where the consultant chooses to use management jargon of the nature applied in the MBA-type environment. Nothing is more likely to turn a prospect off. It is not just a matter of body language; the glazed expression of confusion or indifference in the client's eyes can speak volumes!

The skills base is a moveable feast because active consulting is a dynamic process where new situations and industry circumstances are continually faced – particularly for the generalist who is promoting his services to a broad range of different companies and industries. Knowledge can be gathered at an amazing pace and this can be of sufficient quality to make a legitimate and valuable contribution to the advice offered in a wide variety of business cases. Indeed, a determination to maintain a commitment to self-education and to be open and receptive to fresh concepts and ideas can produce significant benefits when promoting concepts and possible solutions across different organisations.

This is where the consultant can deliver intellectual property of substantial value because company managers frequently have an internal focus about the way things should be done, based on the traditions of their own company or industry. The offer of a solution drawn from elsewhere may cut diametrically across the accepted pattern of received standards and procedures, and thereby offer remarkable results. Of course the successful delivery of a revolutionary message may be challenging and difficult, requiring skill in negotiation and persuasion. The "not invented here" syndrome is still alive and well!

The need to adopt new skills

Just as the self-audit should have produced some pleasant surprises about how much the individual has to offer of potential commercial value, so the process should also have identified shortcomings and deficiencies. It would be arrogant and self-defeating to attempt to ignore or play-down these needs, as the over-riding requirement is to be honest with oneself. There is little to be gained in covering up as at the end of the day, the self-employed consultant is principally reliant on his own abilities. Open recognition will encourage the commitment either to take corrective action, or to negotiate through collaboration agreements some form of partnership arrangement with another consultant who has complementary skills.

Some skills can be brushed up or improved relatively simply by reference to the appropriate technical publications. On the other hand, it may not be feasible to try to acquire a sufficiently comprehensive skills level in some disciplines. For example, Information Technology is developing and changing so fast that it is either a young person's game, or it is best left to specialists who have worked for many years in that arena. Perhaps exceptionally, this is an area where ageism can have negative impact for the independent consultant.

However, without exception every consultant who aspires to success needs to maintain a genuine obligation towards self-education. This is a commitment that should be evident in two ways. Firstly, it is essential to train and continually to improve performance in the art of consulting on a practical level through adherence to the standards and techniques that are enunciated in Chapter 8. Secondly, there is the continuing requirement to foster the expansion of the range of marketable skills as considered above.

A practical difficulty may lie in the fact that while the self-audit and SWOT is effective in assembling a logical inventory of what comprises the individual's skills and background, the process may be of little use in identifying those matters about which he has slight or zero knowledge. As a further step therefore we recommend that the individual should check his review by conducting the audit process again but from a different angle i.e. in the form of a summary skills evaluation as set out in **Appendix G**.

This may seem an unnecessarily tedious and detailed exercise when added to the self-audit etc. However it should not be overlooked that all this data gathering and measurement is a critical element in the design and construction from first principles of what might constitute a new business venture i.e. a new independent consultancy. We advocate that the very maximum amount of review and analysis is desirable at this stage before any decisions are taken that will lead to actions or expenditure that might otherwise be regretted later.

Additionally, if the decision is taken to go ahead with consulting, we believe that the whole process should be repeated say twice a year as a matter of renewal and review. Active consulting invokes a steep learning curve, and the discipline will measure how much more has been accumulated, thereby engendering confidence to seek diverse work opportunities on an expanding front.

For many aspiring consultants, this obligation proves too onerous. It may be that arrogance and self-satisfaction is prevalent. It may be that it is considered too demeaning to return to studies or training programs in middle age. It may be that accumulated experience and presentational techniques are considered sufficiently matured to be able to "wing it" with the client.

Perhaps these are risks that are considered worth taking. If so, the chances are heightened of being caught out and of failing in key objectives, resulting in loss of business opportunities and of benefits being delivered to clients in need.

Skills gaps and how to fill them

Independent consultants often share a feeling of camaraderie and it is a real pleasure to discover how willingly, formal or informal working relationships are formed to help each other out. The core objective of winning a client contract and of sharing in the fees earned in preference to not doing a deal is sometimes all the incentive needed to form bespoke allegiances swiftly and without bureaucratic fuss. In fact the pragmatic manner in which associations are created is enormously refreshing for individuals whose previous experience has been soured by the internecine bickering and open warfare that so often accompanies management gymnastics in the corporate world.

The ease and simplicity with which these arrangements are concluded is an efficient means of accessing skills that the individual may not have in his own armoury. Nevertheless, care is necessary to ensure that arrangements are not entered into that may prove damaging or counter-productive in the long run.

Unless the other party's capacities and abilities are already well known, it is advisable to conduct some due diligence before entering a collaboration with another independent consultant, covering:

A. Age, technical qualifications and educational background
B. Nature of previous corporate experience
C. Consulting history, work undertaken, and indicative income level
D. Daily fee and expenses rates
E. Nature of other current contracts and obligations
F. Conflicting demands; level of priority to be accorded the collaboration; is timely completion feasible?
G. References from previous clients

Where the other consultant is to occupy the role of sub-contractor, the lead consultant may be required to warrant contract satisfaction to the client. Failure in performance may invoke claims for compensation under the category of professional indemnity, but even if things do not go that far, the lead consultant's reputation may be irretrievably damaged. Accordingly, selection and recruitment of a partner consultant whether on equal terms or under a sub-contract deal should be treated as a serious matter.

Once a partner consultant has been selected, equal care should be exercised in structuring the collaboration arrangements so that nasty surprises are avoided.

Case 6. Arnold had been engaged for many years as an effective and successful specialist consultant in the agricultural field. He was technically qualified to BSc. Level, which was adequate for most of the contracts that he won. Then he was commissioned to advise on a project that involved new cultivation techniques and crop strains. To undertake this work he needed specialist research services that were available in his technical discipline but required more advanced data and techniques than were at his immediate disposal. It was therefore necessary to sub-contract these services to a technical colleague, Russell, who was qualified at PhD level.

Arnold was essentially a technician and not well versed in either financial or contractual matters. He entered into a written contract with the Russell that remunerated the latter on a daily basis but did not limit the amount of work that was to be undertaken. Russell exploited the open ended nature of the contract by producing more research data than the project could practically absorb, and involving many more days' work than Arnold had originally envisaged. Additionally, Arnold's monitoring methods were insufficiently comprehensive so that it was not until after the event that he was aware of how much work Russell had devoted to research.

When matters were finally brought under control, Arnold discovered that he was obliged to pay away sub-contract fees equal to 85% of his gross revenue under the project. After deduction of direct expenses, Arnold incurred a net financial loss on this work.

In this situation, the sub-contractor's over-performance can be as damaging as the more common example of one who under-performs. In either case, it is sensible for both parties that any collaboration agreement is evidenced in writing before any work commences, and that the terms of the agreement are carefully negotiated.

A collaboration agreement need not be a lengthy document but it should embrace a number of key points to provide adequate mutual protection, including:

I. Brief description of work to be undertaken either jointly or by each party
II. Duration of the collaboration on an elapsed time basis
III. Definition of who is lead consultant and who is sub-contractor
IV. Nature of the responsibilities of each party and professional indemnity obligations
V. Split of fees and direct expenses arising from the projected work
VI. Project milestones and deadlines
VII. Competition restriction

An example of a consultancy collaboration agreement appears in **Appendix B**. The key message is to research the prospective associate fully and to document the arrangement clearly so as to eliminate the risk of costly misunderstandings and errors later.

Summary points

- *Confidence to sell services based on experience is a pre-requisite*
- *Corporate experience alone is insufficient to consult effectively*
- *Successful consultants operate and think differently from corporate counterparts*

Specialist or generalist?

- *Consultants can be segregated into specialists or generalists*
- *Generalists have wide-ranging remit to seek varieties of clients and opportunities*
- *Advantages and disadvantages to being a specialist:*
  - *Clarity of need for, and purpose of, the consultancy*
  - *Agenda is more easily assimilated*
  - *Accepted market yardsticks for pricing services*
  - *Promotion is easier as client has acknowledged need*
  - *Shelf life of the specific skill may be limited*
  - *Specialism may limit recognition of capacity for other tasks*
- *Advantages and disadvantages to being a generalist:*
  - *Generalist may convince that no issues are outside his brief*
  - *Where special help is needed he may sub-contract*
  - *In a joint consultancy, generalist is likely to lead*

  - *He faces challenge of validation of his role in client's eyes*
  - *The agenda of the client seeking a generalist may be unclear*
- *Preference should always be for generalism*
- *Pursuit of a steady income is hard if skills have restricted commercial life*
- *Wide exposure multiplies knowledge*

The self-audit

- *Everyone has more of value than reflected in his recent executive experience*
- *Value must be explored and assessed to make it commercially exploitable*
- *A self-audit should go back to education years*
- *It embraces all types of business situation experienced*
- *Negative career aspects are often beneficial in identifying accumulated skills*
- *Self-audit is a radical change from curriculum vitae mind-set*
- *In consulting, the CV as a sales document has no role*
- *Client is not interested in the consultant's claims, but in what he can really contribute*
- *Client will appreciate honesty regarding capabilities*
- *Experience is a valuable commodity, thus it must be thoroughly self-assessed*

Self-audit methodology

- *Structured approach should lead to full identification of additional personal resources*
- *Start with the curriculum vitae as an information base*
- *Re-state the CV with honest appraisal of individual components*
- *Adverse experiences are useful in identifying causes of problems*
- *Generic commonality of business problems is often apparent*

The individual's SWOT analysis

- *Self-audit information should be summarised through SWOT process*
- *Divide strengths and weaknesses into at least three life phases*

The marketable skills base

- *Skills inventory helps full evaluation of expertise and resources*
- *Amplification may be needed to aid client understanding of subject matter*
- *Misunderstandings may occur through use of management jargon*
- *New industries and situations make the skills base dynamic*
- *Cross fertilisation of practises may be highly effective*

The need to adopt new skills

- *Self-assessment should identify abilities plus shortcomings and deficiencies*
- *Recognition will encourage corrective action or need for partnership collaboration*
- *Some skills can be improved by use of technical publications*
- *SWOT may not identify zero knowledge areas – cross-check using Appendix G*
- *Repeat SWOT etc six monthly to measure growth of knowledge*
- *Every consultant should maintain a genuine obligation towards self-education*
    - *by improving practical performance levels*
    - *by fostering the expansion of the range of marketable skills*

Skills gaps and how to fill them

- *Collaboration with other consultants may help winning a deal*
- *Before a collaboration, due diligence on partner is important*
- *Beware conflicting demands; assess mutual priority levels*
- *Structure the collaboration arrangements to avoid surprises later*

Chapter 5

Working from home

There is a deceptive simplicity and logic to the idea of setting up an office in the domestic home, making it easy to overlook the views of the rest of the family. It is strongly recommended therefore that any prospective consultant should invite his or her partner to read this chapter so as to ensure that the exercise proceeds with full understanding by those with differing domestic views. Some constructive consulting at this point is not only good training, but also makes sound business sense!

Successful consulting is deeply concerned with improving business efficiency, including the search for the best utilisation of assets under control. It follows that if principles along these lines are to be expounded to clients, those same principles should be applied to ensure that the consultant's own business is optimally managed.

It is highly unlikely that the acquisition of a separate office for use by a single independent consultant is justifiable. Most if not all face-to-face contact with clients will take place on their premises; it is always far more informative to meet on their home turf than at any other location for reasons that are explored in Chapter 9. Written work undertaken for clients – reports, analyses, and evaluations – demands little in the way of physical resources other than the normal equipment of a small office. Usually therefore it should be possible to create the space required for such a facility in the domestic home.

Other factors encourage the idea of working from home. Informality of working style and elimination of the need for commuting (except to visit clients) make the concept attractive and these are usually high priorities for someone seeking to take up independent consulting as an alternative to corporate salaried employment.

Having your office close at hand at all times can result in interesting changes in working hours and patterns. The move away from a work regime which accords with standard 9 to 5 type office hours can lead to fascinating discoveries about when an individual is most productive.

Some find working in the peace and tranquillity of the small hours to be extremely satisfactory while others prefer working in the late evenings. Working how and when one personally chooses and especially when feeling mentally attuned tends to produce much better standards measured in quality and volume than may be achievable through effort at times pre-ordained by others.

Whatever the personal preference, it is commonly evident that much higher productivity levels can be achieved while working at home. The ability to design a work area that suits one's personal style in comfortable and familiar surroundings can have a beneficial impact on office ergonomics. Additionally, the absence of working colleagues means freedom from interruptions and this factor alone can greatly enhance concentration and clear commitment to the work in hand.

Broadly speaking, the positive elements to working from home make the concept feasible in terms of daily office operating costs, of productivity levels, and of personal discretion. There is a recognised trend towards this work style and it seems likely to be a growing feature not only for the self-employed but also for corporate executives who do not necessarily need to attend the office everyday. However, some words of caution about the drawbacks are necessary before the move is taken up with gusto.

Invasion of the home

The setting up of an office in the home can prove to be a path littered with banana skins vis-à-vis the relationship with one's wife or partner. All too often the fledgling consultant sees only the economic benefits and personal comfort factors, without considering the risks he is running by his invasion of someone else's space.

In the previous corporate life, the relationship within the home will have long before settled down to a predictable and tidy pattern. There will be a tacit understanding that the breadwinner will be absent for perhaps ten hours or more every day and that whoever has responsibility for maintaining the home will have complete freedom of action there during that period. By the time the breadwinner returns at the end of the working day, circumstances will have been re-ordered to accommodate his or her presence in the house.

This may seem beguilingly obvious but at the risk of sounding sexist, it does seem that most men give little consideration to the havoc and disturbance that they cause by electing to remain at home for most of every day. Their focus is towards operational and economic efficiency, while paying no heed to the emotional and social disruption that may result.

A change in employment with all its attendant uncertainties can cause enough anxiety under normal circumstances but stress factors can be multiplied where the establishment of a home office is also involved. It is a process therefore that needs plenty of debate and discussion in advance, and wisdom dictates an exceptional degree of sensitivity to the views of others.

Case 7. When Raymond gave up his corporate employment and moved into consulting, he felt that he had made a flying start. He immediately recruited two clients who promised to pay satisfactory fees for work that would stretch forward over at least 18 months. Further, he needed no persuading about the advantages of working from home as his wife who was self-employed had done so very successfully for several years. Moreover, the configuration of the home was such that there was ample room for him to set up his office within the room that his wife was already using for her work. A perfect situation – or so it seemed.

Six weeks later, Raymond had concluded that his marriage was more important than his office arrangements and that if something was not done quickly, he would face severe problems. A hitherto perfectly happy marriage had been exposed to all sorts of fresh strains, and however good the personal chemistry, it was going to be seriously damaged through constant daily contact. Removal to another part of the house with a clear delineation of "working territory" immediately solved the problem.

Accountability to the partner

In normal corporate employment, it is quite usual for the breadwinner to discuss work extensively with his partner. This communication may be relied on as a prop, as a source of guidance and advice, and as a wellspring of sympathy when things have gone wrong. Stories about what has been happening at the office are inevitably one-way, and with a subjective message and reflective of only one point of view.

More significantly because the information is fashioned in a certain way with the intention of inviting a specific type of response, it may portray a somewhat misleading picture of actual conditions and circumstances. It is common that such information should concentrate on successes or disasters, and be presented in rather conclusive fashion with often little reference to the precise sequential nature of related events.

The result can be a fair degree of understandable confusion in the mind of the partner who is asked to receive and accept information that may be distorted and quite confusing to the lay mind. An integral part of this confusion stems from an inability to appreciate the passage of elapsed time between the inception of a project or transaction and its ultimate success or failure. The drama and interest lies in the conclusion, and not necessarily in the minutiae that will have gone before, perhaps over several weeks or months.

Thus it is quite understandable that the partner may have a totally misguided view of just how much time may be expended in the development and conclusion of a business transaction. While working *away* from home, the information flow can be tailored and censored so as to keep the partner informed to a degree that suits the needs of the breadwinner. However, once he is working full time *at* home, his partner will take a much closer interest in what is going on, and will quickly start to develop views on the nexus, or lack of it, between working effort and financial results.

Concerns arise basically because of a straightforward comparison with earlier conditions. The partner will be aware that corporate employment had ensured the receipt of a steady salary in return for events that appeared to happen fairly regularly through the breadwinner's periodic "reports". Now things have changed and the breadwinner as consultant is working hard for no immediately apparent gain.

Basically, in the corporate world with its strong orientation towards reward for success, the issue of transaction gestation may be unrecognised or underestimated. The gestation of a business transaction may take a long time, and may require much individual or co-operative effort in initiating a contact, building a relationship, establishing trust, proving competence, selling a deal, contracting the sale, executing the contract, and securing payment. It is therefore understandable that previous experience derived from modern corporate conditions may have induced in the partner at home an expectation of instant results. Thus a special effort to explain this change in the nature of the working environment and remunerative expectations is worthwhile.

Some consultants go to great lengths to ensure that their partner is fully informed on what is going on and some even employ their partner as secretary or assistant in the business. Whether living *and* working together so closely is wise may be debatable.

Case 8. Timothy had secured a reasonably steady income base by offering a limited number of services to a broad range of potential clients. To find these clients, he had to rely on his own telephone selling efforts. At the same time he had to keep his wife satisfied with daily progress reports on how much money he was earning.

Accordingly, Timothy undertook a review of his activities and calculated that:

i. *For every 100 selling calls, he secured on average five invitations to meet to present his product (all business development efforts were scrupulously planned and logged)*

ii. *He was successful in securing a contract in 20% of the meetings he held with target clients*

iii. *The average income earned from each contracted client was £900*

iv. *Typically the elapsed time between contact initiation and payment for his work was two months – but he had achieved a steady, if delayed, flow of income.*

In answer to his wife's enquiries, Timothy would thus advise that his "daily earnings" had been a specific amount, derived directly from the number of teleselling calls made that day and the predictability of his earnings. His methodology:

On average:
100 teleselling calls = 5 appointments = 1 contract = £900 gross income
Thus 25 teleselling calls will yield 25/100 x £900 = £225 in daily earnings

Therefore, if he had logged 40 promotional calls in one day, regardless of the response level because he operated in strict accordance with his prescribed averages, he would advise his wife that the day's earnings had been £360 (i.e. £225 x 40/25).

In fact, Timothy was wisely covering three separate and important issues in his home working ethos. Firstly he had developed a neat and provable method of accountability that kept his wife adequately informed and allayed her fears. Secondly, his planning and logging procedures formed an important ingredient in his daily work disciplines and habits – which will be discussed further later in this chapter. Thirdly he had embraced totally the significance of averages, which is a concept which we explore in Chapter 8 on the principles of consulting.

Office design and location

With due heed to constraints imposed by the need to respect each other's space, the creation of a comfortable and efficient office environment is important. The consultant will spend many hours in this location and he should ensure that his physical wellbeing is not jeopardised by skimping on office furnishings. Bearing in mind that working at home yields a substantial saving compared with the cost of a remotely located purpose designed office, it is sensible to invest in equipment that is efficient and properly designed for the job.

Natural light, adequate artificial lighting, heating, communication ports, filing facilities, stationery storage are basic factors that may have previously been taken for granted. These are matters for the independent consultant to address plus issues such as the occupation of space in a quiet part of the house where disruption by the family will be minimal.

Available square feet and the impact on other occupants of the home should also determine selection of suitable space. There is little point in setting up in a small box room if this will shortly lead to the need for storage facilities elsewhere in the house. The volume of files and stored information grows almost exponentially. Not only does this annoy other family members, it can also make recovery of data time consuming and difficult. In fact, a discipline that is vital to effective self-employment is proper filing systems, and without them, one quickly comes to learn just how valuable had been one's secretary in previous life.

These factors all relate once again to the general and critical issues of living and working coexistence in the home, and for the need to respect each other's space. They are essential to the necessary pact between consultant and partner in formulating a new way of living, in new approaches to domestic harmony, and in a totally different relationship between home and work.

Case 9. Patrick eventually discovered that a shed in the garden was the best means of establishing harmony for his home working needs. Located about 30 yards away from the house, he was able to install power, heat and communications at minimal cost. For the expenditure of £20 a simple intercom linked him with the main building.

Every morning he "goes to work" in his shed, and returns "home" for mid-morning coffee and for lunch. There is usually a similar break in the afternoon. Patrick's wife only occasionally visits the office (she finds the mess in which he prefers to work to be too upsetting) and any communication during office hours is through the intercom. The arrangement works very effectively with complete respect for each other's space and with a daily timetable similar to that which obtained when Patrick was in corporate employment.

A drawback to working in one's own office, well away from distractions and the rest of the world can be loss of a sense of time. Without outside factors to interrupt and remind one of the passage of the day, it can be very easy to discover that one has been working intensively for far longer than had been originally intended. Tiredness and staleness under such circumstances can inhibit productivity and quality. Hence it is desirable to develop the habit of consciously leaving one's desk for at least a few minutes in every hour to ensure a short spell of relaxation.

Electronic communications

This topic is critical in office location and design, and requires special consideration in its own right. Just as office furniture is important for comfort and effectiveness, so communications need to be properly set up as an essential means of obtaining new contracts, and of servicing existing clients. However, the authors are actively in contact with independent consultants and they are continually amazed by the number who are content to live with barriers to effective communication between themselves and the outside world.

When working on one's own, the telephone line is a vital tool of trade. Failure adequately to invest in appropriate communications equipment must call into doubt the individual's commitment to succeed in consulting. There is now a recognised level of kit needed to be effective in the distribution, and often more importantly the receipt, of business information. The low cost of additional equipment and the speed and simplicity of its installation means that there is now no excuse for not putting in place a proper electronic communications architecture. The following factors are relevant for consideration:

Single telephone line: this is really placing oneself at a disadvantage because incoming and outgoing business traffic may be in conflict, and because personal and business calls may be using the same line. It may be hard to believe but some consultants even try to work with this simple configuration while there are teenagers living in the house.

Telephone and fax on same line: the worst configuration as the chances of conflict with incoming/ outgoing, personal/ business, voice/ data traffic are maximised. Also, it is quite common to encounter technical difficulties when trying to send information to a facsimile machine that shares a line with a telephone, necessitating a separate voice call to ensure that the machine is operating properly. A hurdle like this is an active disincentive for the other party to persist in trying to establish contact.

Two telephone lines with one devoted solely to fax: the installation of an additional line is a marginal extra cost that is justifiable.

However with this configuration the fax line usage may be slight thus creating surplus unused capacity while the telephone line is still subject to most of the usage conflicts outlined above.

Two telephone lines, one with a listed number and the other for fax and telephone communications: this allows incoming traffic to be directed to the listed telephone number while the other line is used for outgoing telephone calls, and for two-way transmission of fax messages.

Three lines – listed/ unlisted/ data transmission: here the listed number receives all incoming telephone traffic while the unlisted line is used for outgoing traffic. The third line handles solely data traffic i.e. fax, electronic mail and Internet.

Fax versus email/ Internet: while fax is reasonably effective in the transmission of pre-printed or third party data, it can now only be considered as a fallback solution for self-generated data transmission. Compared with email it is slow, costly and susceptible to corruption during transmission. In cases where consultants working in partnership are creating and exchanging data, fax has no role to play as the double entry aspect is too time consuming. Additionally, the Internet yields access to the vast database sources of the World Wide Web. In summary, a consultant without an email address will not be considered a professional in his field.

The minimum acceptable communications architecture for effective independent consulting is considered to be the following:

	Facilities	**Usage**
Listed line	Office extension	All incoming telephone traffic
	One or more extensions at strategic points in the home	Outgoing personal telephone traffic
Unlisted line	Office line only	Outward business telephone traffic
Data line	Office only	Email, Internet, fax

Additionally, a telephone answering facility may be appropriate although it is recommended that this only be employed if the home is likely to be empty for long periods. Callers prefer to speak to a real person if possible and this can be a helpful element in humanising the relationship with a client.

Although mobile phones do have the advantage of convenience, they are not necessarily an incentive for inward calls because of the cost. Also, they only serve to duplicate access channels while the consultant is at his desk and they should be closed during interviews with clients. Thus in direct connection with consulting work, they are most likely to be justified only if substantial amounts of time are spent in travelling.

Working habits

Despite drawbacks, working from home has a number of attractive advantages the benefits of which can be improved further by careful planning and by controlled fixed asset investment as explained above. Indeed, a short period of work in this fashion can quickly recruit body and mind totally to the concept, and it is not difficult to appreciate the view that this style of working and living will have increasing application in the years to come.

By comparison, the whole panoply of daily dressing, grooming and commuting appears inefficient and time consuming compared with the opportunity to tumble out of bed and to set to work fresh and early in the day. Undoubtedly the sense of ceremony (?) that attends the formal presence at a place of work is important for some people. For others who value substance over form in their creative efforts, the office at home is a powerful means of contributing without the need to conform with arcane corporate rules and procedures that may have no direct positive bearing on quality of output.

Hence the arguments in favour of working from home are as persuasive as the concept might seem romantic. The sense of freedom and discretion regarding the content and direction of one's working activities can be intoxicating. Like all intoxicants it can be taken for granted – until one re-enters as a visitor a corporate working environment. Then one realises how regressive and how constrictive a return to such a world could be. It is with good reason that many who have experienced this alternative lifestyle are quite content to rate themselves as unemployable within the normal systems and controls of the conventional corporate world.

However, competence in home working is not necessarily as easy as the compatible surroundings might imply. Family-related distractions represent one facet that might detract from a sound performance. Self-induced distractions are another and the ability to overcome them is an integral aspect of the Independence Maturity that is so essential to successful self-employment.

The temptations to idle away the day are legion where no-one is looking over the individual's shoulder and he is left to make up his own rules. The daily scan of the financial press might lead to a full-scale study of lengthy and stimulating articles. A search for some specific data on the Internet may lead to all manner of tangential enquiries of interesting but irrelevant data. Fine weather may send a shaft of warm sunlight down on the fishing rod standing temptingly in the corner. Any honest home worker will admit to such temptations, and to having succumbed more than once.

Just as creation of the right working conditions is important, so is the commitment to developing proper working habits in the face of many pleasant distractions. Habit is important in helping breed success for those who have recently converted to self-employed status because revelling in freedom from the corporate employment yoke can so easily lead to self-indulgence.

Summary points

- *Working from home is not as simple as it may seem – consult fully with one's partner*
- *Home working aids productivity and reduces business overheads*
- *Acquisition of a separate remote office may not be cost justifiable*
- *Home working encourages flexible working hours*

Invasion of the home

- *Recognise the risk of trespassing on the partner's "space"*
- *Men often do not take account of the wife's feelings about the change*
- *Stress can be multiplied for all concerned*

Accountability to the partner

- *Be ready for partner taking a greater interest in the work content*
- *Work out a means by which the partner can reasonably be kept informed*

Office design and location

- *Create a comfortable office environment as it will be heavily used*
- *Study factors like space, natural light, room for expansion, filing needs*
- *Try for a location in a quiet part of the home*
- *Consider imposing "working hours" when interruptions are not permitted*

Electronic communications

- *Plan an efficient communications architecture*
- *Distinguish personal channels from business channels*
- *Install capacity for adequate telephone, fax and email/ Internet*
- *To be readily accessible for clients is essential*

Working habits

- *Informal lifestyle can greatly aid productivity*
- *Beware of distractions that can waste time*
- *Ensure compatibility with personal needs but know where to draw the line*

Chapter 6

Working in virtual organisations

The previous chapter considered the essential informality and flexibility that goes with the work and lifestyle of the self-employed consultant. These characteristics have a direct impact on the manner of working, the capacity to tackle varied tasks and situations, and not least the quality of what is produced. A condition of these success elements is the capacity to forge co-operative arrangements with other parties. In this context, the client is the most important of these relationships but others may well be necessary through alliances with other consultants or similar who have complementary skills that are needed to help get the job done.

Relationships like these can be formed, re-fashioned or broken up swiftly as time and circumstance dictate. They are effective because they are created with the sole purpose of undertaking a program of work which will be defined and agreed within a bespoke legally binding collaboration agreement or engagement letter. This contract should be straightforward, with none of the complexities and obligations that attend the more traditional way of securing the skills and services of others.

By comparison, conventional employment contracts are tedious and costly to establish, and may be painful to unwind. In a world of change where so many responsibilities and projects are finite, it is understandable why contracted engagement under specific task orientated projects should be attractive for all concerned.

Nevertheless, there is far more involved in setting up the organisational elements to working under these conditions than the mere negotiation and signing of the work contract. In each case, what will have been established is a form of virtual organisation which may also be considered a virtual company, if not in a strict legal sense at least within our broad understanding of what the term company entails for a group of employed individuals.

Virtual organisations are a relatively new phenomenon that is rapidly becoming a significant and potent force in business life. Even so, there are no legal ground rules and very little social acknowledgement of what should comprise a virtual organisation and how it should operate. However, because it is inevitable that all consultants will encounter these animals, salient features of virtual organisations are considered in this chapter.

The power of the virtual organisation

Once again, the change process forms the underlying theme and in this area it relates to the constructional cost and resultant inflexibility of the conventional corporate model. By construction, we refer to the time and money needed not only to create the requisite tangible assets in bricks, mortar and operating equipment but also the full-scale social fabric involved in finding, engaging and developing the right calibre of employees.

Often with the intense pace with which modern companies and business situations mutate, the redundancy threat hanging over existing assets – be they physical or human – argues strongly for hire over a limited, determinable period in preference to outright ownership. Outsourcing is thus an attractive means of covering for short term resource deficiencies, but even so the disciplines of selection remain as critically important as if the resource was to be acquired for the long term. After all, time is a relative factor and incorrect selection can prove costly if undue delay arises from the need to unwind a relationship and seek an alternative in substitution.

With the virtual organisation, it is possible to achieve the best of all worlds. The concept involves typically a group of people who are located remotely from each other, and who rely heavily on Information Technology for their creative efforts, and for communication with each other. Because the virtual worker only requires a computer and telecommunication access, his individual set-up costs are effectively restricted to provision of his tools of trade. Without the obligation to provide physical infrastructure, the virtual organisation minimises the burden of central cost, and thereby gains competitive advantage.

Collapsing telecommunication costs – most significantly linked with the power and immediacy of the World Wide Web greatly helps virtual working. The independent consultant has immediate and effective access to these benefits thereby enabling him to exploit the operational superiority of the virtual organisation over its traditionally structured counterpart.

These advantages are not restricted to first or capital costs. Effective use of the normal business related programs on the personal computer with electronic links to partners and trading counter-parties opens up enormous scope for business in cyberspace. Initial production costs are not substantial while the cost of replication is so low as to be virtually zero. Concurrently, use of the Internet permits efficiency in the transmission of information in a fashion and at a cost unattainable by traditional methods.

Surf the Web and it will be readily apparent that a plethora of new merchants have set up business to sell goods and services because the cost of production/ replication/ marketing/ sales is comparatively insignificant. Additionally, the World Wide Web automatically permits access to global markets thus bestowing sales reach well beyond the limits of geographically constrained markets.

The same advantages of cost, production efficiency and marketing reach are available to assist the independent consultant. Indeed it is impossible to conceive that independent consultants could have proliferated without the PC and its standard accoutrements. Thus the technology that rendered so many managers surplus in the corporate world also provides the means by which they may re-enter business cost-effectively on their own account.

Proliferation of business opportunities

With the low cost profile that attends virtual working, it is feasible to tackle a far broader range of opportunities than would otherwise be possible. The consultant is in the game of selling his know-how and business skills, and the low entry cost to a virtual business relationship means that he has less at risk. Equally, should it become apparent that the project will fail in its objectives, withdrawal becomes that much simpler.

Against the comparative ease of creation and unwinding of propositions that have been pursued in virtual fashion, a note of caution should be sounded concerning commitment levels. Commitment as a key element of successful consulting is explored fully in the next chapter but it is important to note here that the fluidity and speed of virtual operating can result in a dangerous "easy come – easy go" ethos developing.

Because a virtual business proposition requires so little in the way of physical assets and actual expenditure, the temptation is to build a portfolio of ideas and proposals. However, with so little hard cash at stake in each, the portfolio can grow rapidly but with few if any transactions actually being consummated. Email correspondence, revised plans, budgets, and targets etc may multiply because they are so easy to create. A sense of "being very busy" may camouflage the reality that tangible progress may be minimal.

Even so, the virtual organisation and philosophy is ideal for the independent consultant because it allows the development of alternative proposals and the application of numerous business planning models to help build optimal recommendations and solutions for clients. A project or a business plan in which the consultant is assisting can go through endless re-designs and modifications while it is still on paper. Once committed to physical reality, modification becomes more expensive to implement, often by a factor of hundreds or thousands.

Operating disciplines

The low start-up and capital investment costs which minimise financial and organisational barriers for new venture creation are complemented by the ease of securing the co-operation of others who are used to working in this mode. The project leader is easily able to contact large elements of otherwise redundant workers, and to mobilise their innate and acquired abilities.

The message to co-workers approached in this fashion is highly appealing. An opportunity to exercise intellectual talents in working conditions of their own design and creation, tends to free up a greater enthusiasm and desire to contribute than may be possible through conventional motivational efforts. This is an asset whose beneficial potential should not be underestimated. Working in partnership with other virtual operators can be highly stimulating and productive.

The advantages are sufficiently pronounced for the virtual employee or project partner to be an increasingly common business phenomenon. Logistical demands are simple and common to all those who have a genuine commitment to succeed in consulting. The virtual employee with his own tools of trade (acquired skills and knowledge, own working space, telecommunications, computer) and prepared to offer his services to the highest bidder has plenty of historical counterparts. Mercenary soldiers, navvies who built railways and canals, and the journeyman/ artisan class – all thrived in earlier ages on a simplistic nexus of personal self-sufficiency, desire for freedom, and commitment to the job in hand.

However, virtual working is subtly demanding in novel ways and it is only likely that individuals enjoying Independence Maturity will be fully successful working in this fashion. It has been noted that virtual organisations fail for sociological rather than technological reasons, and such an example exists in the global call centre industry. This is a cost sensitive activity that exploits cutting edge technology and which relies on focussed, high quality training of above-average personnel. Theoretically, modern communications make distributed call centres, where personnel work from home, an ideal form of virtual organisation engaging a fraction of the capital cost of a central operating unit organised along traditional corporate lines.

However, practise has shown that net cost savings are unachievable because minimised capital investment does not offset below par operating performance. Distributed call centres do not work for fundamentally social reasons including loneliness, difficulties with self discipline, outside distractions, absence of face-to-face contact with working colleagues, and a sense of distance from the corporate ethos.

Thus virtual operating introduces a range of problems which are not encountered with conventional organisations. Success demands a strong measure of discipline and self motivation in the individual, as well as care in selection of those with whom he will be working, and on whom he may have to depend to ensure that a job is completed in timely and efficient fashion.

It is physically and psychologically hard to ensure that a collaborator whose contribution is essential but with whom face-to-face contact is at best spasmodic is really productively committed to meeting common goals.

Virtual management

The virtual structure is ideal for the creative and visionary entrepreneur. It allows for the establishment of new styles of business model, often relying on a unique or unprecedented co-joining of disparate technologies. On a grand scale, the virtual organisation that fully exploits the potential of cyberspace threatens the future of the traditional model because its manufacturing, marketing and delivery costs are so vastly lower.

However, the elegance of the design sometimes distracts attention from the need to make it work properly and this places a significant management burden on the project leader. The virtual structure as an operating entity can be fatally weakened through below par leadership. Physical remoteness may be exploited as a convenient means of sidestepping awkward issues of management i.e. out of sight implies out of mind.

Modern business education and practises have concentrated on the empowerment of subordinates and this practise is a significant contributor towards Independence Maturity. Nonetheless, relatively few individuals can be safely left to their own devices to maximise their full operational effectiveness. Indeed, virtual companies are more likely to encounter change, innovation and uncertainty than their conventional counterparts thereby intensifying the demand for help and guidance of individual employees. It is paradoxical that while the virtual organisation may render the formal management hierarchy obsolete, the need for a tangible business leadership with which the rank and file can identify becomes commensurately more pressing.

The opportunities

The competitive advantages of virtual operating are so extreme as to make a properly integrated and controlled structure worth the effort. This means thorough design and implementation under the aegis of a clearly defined management culture and corporate ethos.

The temptation to go for a quick fix without thinking through fully all the implications should be resisted. The low fixed cost scenario favours design, modification and re-design many times over to achieve the optimal solution. Simplicity in and codification of procedures should ensure a high productivity factor. Once clarity and unanimity of understanding has been achieved, the variable cost / income equation will guarantee generous returns and reward levels amply to justify care and thoroughness in establishment and execution.

The essential ingredients are not unlike those needed for success in a conventional business but need re-stating here to emphasise their essential inter-dependence:

1. Simple, clear statement of business intent.

2. Strong, rational code of business standards and ethics.

3. Documented recognition procedures for IPR protection.

4. Good training and grooming of all the venture's participants.

5. Tariff and operating code for dissemination to clients.

6. Codification of standard internal and external contracts.

7. Standardised kit of tools of trade for every operator.

8. Flat management structure.

9. Heavy emphasis on maintenance of internal network relationships: Internet discussion groups, regular up-dates on progress, periodic physical meetings, quality circles etc.

10. Continuous, visible participation by the CEO.

11. Immediate response to and assistance for troubled areas.

12. All the blood, sweat, toil, passion, hatred, atavism, love, care, that goes with effective leadership.

After five years' experience of working with virtual enterprises we are in no doubt that it is the way for the independent consultant to develop. However, the model fails more often than it should because of failure in enunciating fully what the venture is about, in addressing "tedious" minutiae, and in patiently weaning newcomers to perform beyond their current expectations. These are all elements of sound management and these should be thoroughly explored before entering a commitment with a virtual organisation.

Summary points

- *Meaningful co-operation with other parties is essential*
- *Relationships can be re-formed swiftly as time and circumstance dictate*
- *They are effective as purpose is a defined legally binding work program*
- *Relationships comprise a virtual organisation*

The power of the virtual organisation

- *Comparatively very low "constructional" cost and high operating flexibility*
- *Virtual organisations avoid many pitfalls that bedevil conventional organisations*
- *Concept involves remotely detached workers who use IT heavily*
- *Set-up costs avoid the major burden of central overheads*

Proliferation of business opportunities

- *Low entry cost to a virtual business relationship reduces risk*
- *If project fails in its objectives, withdrawal is simpler*
- *Fluidity and speed can result in an "easy come easy go" ethos*
- *Minimal investment cost, encourages a portfolio of ideas and proposals*

Operating disciplines

- *Effective means of low-cost mobilisation of otherwise redundant workers*
- *Exercise of talents in own working conditions aids contribution and motivation*
- *Virtual organisations may fail for sociological rather than technological reasons*

Virtual management

- *Structure allows establishment of new, unprecedented business models*
- *Fully exploits cyberspace potential with much lower operational costs*
- *Drawback may be low cost creativity but few concrete deals completed*
- *Cost/income equation may yield high returns justifying careful planning*
- *Virtual organisations usually fail through inattention to detail*

Chapter 7

The 3 'C's: limitations on self-employment

The idea of working for oneself often sounds romantic while still suffering frustrations and annoyances as an employee. Nevertheless, there are limitations on how much can be physically achieved while self-employed and it is important to review these constraints as they form a significant part of the self-assessment process in deciding whether or not to "go it alone".

It may sound an obvious statement, but working alone is very different from working with a group of people. Work as an employee can be almost as much a social activity as a means of financial support, and in a sense it is a style of living to which we are conditioned right from our earliest schooldays. At school, we learn to work both independently for specific periods and to finish set tasks, but we also co-operate in projects with our fellows to meet joint deadlines. Concurrently we follow prescribed standards of behaviour that have been imposed by higher authority as part of the fabric of a cohesive social unit. At university, this pattern changes subtly in step with the individual's growing maturity. Greater personal discretion is permitted regarding working independence, academic objectives, dress etc but university life still offers a distinctive cohesion that is perceived as important in personal development.

Many of the key social ingredients of school and university are continued in conventional employment. Joint and individual work goals co-exist and blend within overall organisational parameters, and these rely upon the existence of a recognisable social structure. This structure may well have its deficiencies with internal politics, hierarchical orders, creative and non-creative friction but the endemic codes and rules help the individual to measure where he stands vis-à-vis the organisation at large.

Progression from school through university to an employed career rarely allows exposure to the challenges and thought processes that will be required for successful self-employment. Starting up as a self employed person calls for creation of a new business. This means the determination of a set of codes and practises by which the business will be operated, and this relies on the creation and application of a set of first principles.

For clarity, the basic factors that will underpin these principles are grouped under three categories – capacity, cost and commitment.

Capacity

The novelty of having an office in the familiar and comfortable surroundings of one's home, combined with the luxury of exercising discretion over how long to spend at the desk, and the excitement of starting anew can unleash a previously unrealised ability and enthusiasm level. The change of circumstance can revolutionise productivity, aided by the reduced level of interruptions and by the complete absence of colleagues who would otherwise initiate conflicting demands and requests for attention.

With such comparative freedom, it is easy to be heavily absorbed in the matter in hand. Sometimes quite different working habits emerge from those that previously obtained. Often the only consistent element to working long hours is a lack of predictability – an early morning start one day may be countered by a late afternoon start the next. One clear aspect is that quality of work (and of life) is often improved by being allowed to decide when to work, rather than having this dictated by a 9 to 5 regime. In this world, weekends and public holidays may lose their relevance, and it can be a real bonus to live a life that may be counter-cyclical to the usual routine.

On the other hand, the lack of any supervisory guidance can bring the flip side of not knowing when to stop. Sometimes described as "cabin fever", it can be quite shocking at the end of a long day to discover that other than answering calls of nature, a project may have engaged one's attention and total concentration for twelve hours or more.

The main external pressure to work long hours usually comes from the client. Consultants may have a lot of discretion over which hours of the day they choose to work, but they have little or no option with respect to deadlines which the client might impose.

The situation of the single self-employed person in these circumstances can be discomforting. The nature of the contract, and the fees it promises, may not allow for the recruitment of an assistant, even allowing that assistance of the right calibre can be found in the time available. Equally, failure to meet the deadline is unthinkable, as a consultant knows that his business situation is only as good as the income-producing work that he has on hand. Very often a successful contract will lead to repeat business or to introductions to other prospective clients, and nothing is more likely to alienate a client than failure to deliver on time.

Understandably therefore, flexible working hours are enjoyable but also essential. With experience it should be possible to regulate the flow of business and thus the throughput of work. Logjams can be as frustrating and as demoralising as shortage of earnings opportunities.

Case 10. Patrick found himself with a heavy workload resulting from two projects, one in England to be completed by Monday of the following week and the other in the Mediterranean, commencing rather unusually on the Sunday (i.e. the day before). The English project was complex and required preparation of a detailed viability study. Recognising a busy period ahead, Patrick concentrated on completing the English task by devoting all his working hours solely to it from the preceding Tuesday onwards.

On Wednesday he started at 0830hrs and worked through until 0100hrs on Thursday. He started work again at 0900hrs on Thursday and worked through until 0300hrs on Friday. He slept until 0930hrs that Friday morning, and then worked through until 0500hrs on Saturday morning, by which time he had despatched by email all that was required by his client. He then took a shower, and departed to the airport to catch the morning flight to the Mediterranean.

Although he was physically present for the next task on that Sunday, mentally he was in no condition to work and indeed it was another 24 hours before his contribution could be considered worthwhile. Not only had his performance been damaged by the work schedule of the previous week, he had also worked a seven day week for the last two months or so. While adrenaline had kept him going for some time, the over stretching of his work capacity eventually told against him in the eyes of his clientele.

This may be an extreme example but the story emphasises the risks and stresses that can be incurred when working without any form of back up, or support. In this case, an over-commitment towards an unreasonable deadline with a consecutive obligation to be available to work for another party ultimately placed at risk the proper completion of two separate contracts.

In some situations it may be possible to pass surplus work on to a fellow consultant, perhaps by a sub-contract type of collaboration agreement. However, this may be unsatisfactory if it is attempted when the contract is live, when time is slipping away, and when the other consultant may have trouble in co-ordinating his own availability to suit. If the services of a fellow consultant are required, then this should be identified well in advance, and his services should be engaged on mutually satisfactory terms before the obligation to the client goes live, and the clock starts ticking.

In Chapter 4, we considered issues surrounding the self-audit process and demonstrated how this could identify latent skills and abilities that may be mobilised and turned to productive use. At the same time, the self-audit should show where capacity limitations exist, and should suggest what remedial action is necessary. Capacity is partly a matter of education and additional training. It also relates work capability measured in hours per day or per week, and the mental willingness to work those hours. A further factor is the means by which one's consulting business is planned and developed – where the achievement of balance may be difficult.

Balance is important in striving to create a business with a steady workflow, and thus a smooth cash flow. Consulting can swing between feast and famine conditions and this is best avoided by attempting to maintain a portfolio of transactions at various stages of maturity. Thus as contracts come to a successful conclusion, there will hopefully be a new stream of opportunities or of fresh client contracts becoming available. To achieve balance therefore, two disciplines are needed.

The first is an honest appraisal from the self-audit of those deficiencies in one's armour that cannot be corrected through self-help. In compensation therefore, a search is needed to find ways and means of accessing complementary skills that other self-employed consultants or consulting groups may have to offer. As with collaboration agreements (see Chapter 4), caution is warranted in choosing one's consulting allies and thorough due diligence may be advisable. The rationale however that a shared fee is preferable to a fee foregone should be sufficiently persuasive to enlist the right calibre of help.

The second concerns the manner in which one's consulting business is managed and controlled. In this context balance in the business requires a mental leapfrogging where the securing of a client contract induces the search for the next successive transaction to follow that currently in hand. By recognising this iterative need, the marketing effort remains evergreen and in an ideal world would guarantee continuity and consistency in the flow of business.

Unfortunately, the real world is not so straightforward. The inability to control the workflow because of clients' requirements to conform with their own rather than the consultants' timetables means that individual working capacity must from time to time call for unusual reserves of stamina and determination.

Finally, it would be wrong to assume from the foregoing that a consultant's life is all work. However, working from home does mean that the general lifestyle is one of "living over the shop" and the temptation may be strong automatically to drift to the desk, every day of the seven-day week. The evolution of work into an obsessive habit can be damaging to the quality of the end product, as well as to lifestyle generally.

Case 11. Jennifer was successfully engaged as an independent scout contracted to a number of international headhunters. In this work, it was her job to trawl through the executive ranks of companies throughout the English speaking world, searching for individuals who might be interested in changing employers. She worked exclusively with senior executives and was able to deploy her human resources training to good advantage.

Based in the UK, apart from research into companies' published records, virtually all of Jennifer's work was by telephone, involving extensive contact with the USA and Australasia. The work was lucrative, and basically there was as much available as Anne could physically handle.

After a period of growing and sustained success, Jennifer realised that 12-15 hour working days had become normal, that she often went for days without leaving the house, and that she had become a hermit regarding face-to-face contact with other humans. Before long, her health began to suffer. To counter this situation, she had to enforce a rigid self-discipline to minimise the number of hours she worked. These were still late at night to account for time differences but she successfully established a pattern whereby she would not go into her office at certain hours and on certain days under any circumstance.

The lesson is clear – work hard but sustain your work capacity by playing hard, and regularly.

Cost

A question that often stymies newcomers to consulting is "How much does one new client cost?" This reaction is often worrying because client acquisition is the single most dominant factor in the costs that an independent consultant might incur. Difficulty in coming up with a considered figure might illustrate how rarely this question has been addressed in previous corporate life, but more importantly it can point to inadequacy in the preparation that has been undertaken in planning the career move into consulting.

It is not hard to see why the question may seem so novel. The value of the client base is not a component of a set of business accounts, despite the fact that it might be the organisation's single most significant intangible asset. Goodwill on the balance sheet may be reflective of a previous assessment of how much the customers value a business from their standpoint, but it is a historic figure and irrelevant to current conditions. Alternatively, the value of a client base might somehow show in the share price, but this is also an imperfect mechanism, given that many internal organisational factors and external elements also influence the valuation.

Without therefore a formal accounting means to measure the worth of the client base, it is easy to see how a business ethos can develop that ignores this element. This ignorance is evident in many proposals for corporate reconstruction and re-focussing where costing exercises based on allegedly scientific grounds have identified categories of customers that supposedly incur losses. This premise is then manipulated as basis for a policy that contemplates the turning away of such customers on grounds that they are too costly to service, and that better returns can be obtained in other sectors.

Frequently, the analytical process that supports policy changes of this nature is superficial. The kudos of leading a new corporate development will always outshine the more tedious task of making an existing business work better. Accordingly, the corporate thought process will focus on the greener grass while choosing to ignore both sunk cost in creating an existing client base and the true incremental cost of acquiring replacement clients that fit more neatly into the prescribed ideal. This incremental cost has several components and most importantly for this exercise, we are concerned with the amount of outlay needed to secure one new client.

Costs associated with the securing of a client may be divided into actual, notional and opportunity categories. They may include actual expenses incurred with telecommunications, mail, travel, stationery and utilities, or notional elements such as rent for office space within the home and an hourly rate for the consultant's time.

Opportunity cost is harder to calculate because it assumes a standard rate of income earned from time devoted to promotional effort, which may or may not reap positive results. It therefore usually has little practical application in independent consulting.

What is important is that an average cost figure should be computed. It will be different with each individual consultant, depending on which cost categories he chooses to recognise and on how much he prices each. Without a realistic figure in mind however, it is obvious that difficulties will be met in measuring client profitability. Perhaps less obvious is that it is a cogent means of valuing a contact that has yet to produce any income.

It is not unusual for the process of business solicitation to be a long drawn out matter. Several meetings and telephone contacts may be necessary before the consultant's services are contractually engaged. Frustration may result from a series of contacts where the consultant has established that he has something of value to offer but the potential client is reluctant to recognise his need, or more importantly to pay for a solution. During this period of extended gestation it is all too tempting to sever the relationship and commence a search elsewhere for alternative business.

In choosing this course of action, the consultant has to start all over again and the acquisition cost of the next client will accordingly have been increased. Thus it is important to be fully aware of this cost as it encourages recognition of the true worth of the contact already developed, despite it yet having to yield income.

A limit must of course remain on just how long a consultant should pursue an opportunity. In conjunction with the recognition of his costs, he should also determine what should be his walk-away criteria. These will vary in each set of circumstances and continued contact over a period will help identification of the break-even point at which the target no longer has potential as a viable proposition. It may be that the target no longer offers potential income in excess of the cost of business development effort expended thus far. It may be that the target never had any intention of paying a fee but will still try to milk the consultant for help and advice. This latter issue is considered more fully under intellectual property in the next chapter.

The reality remains however that all too often, consultants choose to ignore what they have expended and to move on to what they hope will be more fruitful areas. While a target should not be pursued relentlessly in the face of overt discouragement, there is no doubt that many contacts are established that are neutral in the early stages but which can be developed into worthwhile relationships. Thoroughness and dogged persistence do pay off; reluctance to write off expenditure incurred in starting a relationship is an encouragement to "hang on in".

Case 12. Simon was employed to help start a fledgling financial services operation in Melbourne, Australia. This was part of a multinational group and it was Simon's task during a three-year attachment specifically to undertake business development. He had to create a marketing plan, identify suitable prospective clients, and conduct a program of cold calls to initiate contact, and hopefully to develop working relationships.

The job was hard work, with a poor strike rate at first. However, over time Simon's techniques improved and gradually the success rate started to move in the right direction. Nevertheless, the market environment was intensely competitive and at the end of three years, Simon was acutely aware that there were many prospects with which a relationship had been started but which had yet to earn any income. Before moving away, he passed his sales list to his successor who simply continued the processes and techniques that Simon had initiated, focussing on the same market sector.

Two years later, Simon returned to the Melbourne office on a short business trip. He asked to see the business portfolio and was delighted to recognise that a significant number of companies which had apparently responded indifferently to his original solicitation efforts were now valuable established clients. The gestation period had been long but dogged persistence by Simon and then by his successor had resulted in a substantial income flow.

Of course the independent consultant will not have the same support and corporate umbrella to help him, and of course it is unreasonable to contemplate a 3 year plus gestation period for new business development but the underlying principles are as valid as was the case with Simon in Melbourne. The pursuit of business does take time, and can be very disheartening particularly when working alone. Nevertheless, commitment brings rewards and realistic cost recognition has an important part to play in this effort.

Client acquisition cost as indicated above embraces several different components and clearly cost management generally is important in running a successful consulting business. Working from home is a major contributor to the minimisation of operating expenses, as is also the effective application of communications technology. A consultant who has been trained in cost reduction techniques will immediately recognise that his first cost reduction client should be himself. Above all, cost is important because it is no longer a somewhat distant and therefore remote element of the corporate budget – it is now a direct charge on the consultant's own wallet.

It follows also that controlled operating expenditure will significantly lower the profit threshold. There can be noticeable psychological benefits in running a well-controlled business where there is no waste. Cost disciplines, if exploited in this fashion, can be almost as great a stimulus towards better performance, as is the production of income. The feeling of gaining value-for-money is satisfying. It also heightens awareness of situations where one's partners and counter-parties are not giving value for money ...

Commitment

There is a remarkable number of would-be entrepreneurs in the market place who have a unique product or business proposition, and who are keen to harness the co-operation and assistance of consultants. The modus operandi is fairly standard and usually requires the consultant to devote a considerable amount of time and effort in helping to structure the deal, approach possible funders, handle regulatory issues, and undertake a host of other administrative tasks.

The amount of time and effort that is required of the consultant in these deals can be substantial. Sadly it may be only after the event that he measures how much of his own direct expenditure has been incurred and what has been the price of the opportunity cost. Further, the consultant may have given away a substantial amount of his intellectual property to the project sponsor with little gained in return.

These propositions are frequently sponsored by someone who indeed might have a novel concept but who is unable or unwilling to put up his own financial resources as backing. The sponsor requires help to persuade others to provide finance and although he may be a slick salesman, he knows that he lacks the personal credibility and/ or the technical ability to promote the deal on his own. What better then than to harness the skills of a knowledgeable, willing associate who has demonstrated his determination to be progressive through the promotion of his consulting activities?

The sting lies in the compensation arrangements. The proposition is sold on the basis that it is so advanced that once operating, its superior earnings will ensure that all who hold an equity position will become seriously rich. Of course, the sponsor is not in a position to remunerate the consultant now but once the latter has found the capital required, an equity issue is planned with a suitable split between sponsor, funder and the consultant.

Looked at dispassionately, one may ask how could an experienced businessman now working as a consultant be taken in by such a story? However, 20/20 hindsight is a great source of business wisdom, and often individuals are reluctant to own up that they have been conned in this fashion. The fact does remain though that these sorts of "deals" are more common than may be thought. Prospective consultants beware. The chances are very strong that a deal based on reward through a success fee or by an issue of free equity is a proposition based on a mirage.

The underlying issue here is really one of commitment, and in particular the continuity of that commitment. The project sponsor may well be vociferous and energetic in his enthusiasm, but it should always appear strange that he is not prepared to provide financial support. By his own assessment, his proposition has matured to the point where the risk should now be so refined as to make it acceptable to outside funders. His explanation usually goes along the lines of his having devoted much time and effort to the creative process, and this represents the basis of his equity stake in the transaction. He may use the term "sweat equity" to support his contention, and indeed he will usually value this more greatly than outside funds – as usually evidenced by his proposed retention of a generous share in the funded project.

Case13. Jane and Anthony jointly controlled a derelict industrial site that had been owned by their family for many years. Being in a holiday location, they determined that they wished to convert the site into a beachside hotel complex with associated leisure facilities. Accordingly they spent a substantial amount of time in getting the land re-zoned, and in securing the requisite planning permissions. They then proposed to transfer the land into the ownership of a holding company in which they would retain a 51% share. The balance was to be offered to a hotel development group who would be given an appropriate management contract on completion. All development and operational funding was to be provided by the outside party.

Jane and Anthony were adamant that their ownership of the land provided a sufficient equity base, and that the considerable time they had spent in securing the development approvals represented a reasonable injection of sweat equity in the project.

A consultant was retained on a success fee formula computed as a generous percentage of the outside capital that he was able to raise. Several development groups were approached but all considered the whole project to be too speculative and none were prepared to become involved without an undertaking by the owners that they would inject an element of the development capital required. They felt it unreasonable that the owners should now be able to sit back and leave the project risk to the developers while expecting to receive a majority share of the profits accruing to the joint holding company once the project had been commissioned.

If the client, be he a project sponsor or an entrepreneur, is not prepared to demonstrate his continuing support and involvement, how can an outside funder or a consultant be expected to fill this gap? Putting it harshly, the sponsor is quite happy to float what may be a profusion of ideas in the hope that one will succeed to his financial advantage. On the other hand he has nothing much to lose if all these ideas fail. The exploitation of the services of a consultant may well move the odds substantially in his favour but he really has no incentive to risk his own money and time if he can induce others to do this for him. Thus his true level of belief in the proposition is minimal, and with such superficial commitment, a successful outcome is improbable.

There is also an obverse side to the whole question of commitment and this refers to what the individual is prepared to put into his own consulting business. It has already been mentioned that persistence and determination are essential to success and no apology is made for repeating this message here, in view of its importance.

In addition, he must be prepared to commit a realistic element of his capital to ensure that his business is properly planned and resourced, and that he has the capacity to research and build a client base. Thus entry requires a real capital investment, as is needed for any business start-up. A casual approach to consulting assuming that it can be set up as a pastime, or as a hobby, or can be funded on the cheap, is unprofessional and will fail to secure a worthwhile activity level.

Commitment is aided by various ergonomic factors such as the comfort of the office and the efficiency of the communications architecture. It is also aided by the manner in which targets are set and pursued. Self-discipline in this regard is essential to keep oneself involved and determined to succeed. Commitment itself does not come from one single factor or element. It is a reflection of the combined efforts the consultant makes in a holistic way to ensure that all aspects of his business venture will succeed.

Realistic recognition and understanding of all the constraints on performance – grouped in this chapter as the three C's – will enable them to be tackled with the correct level of energy. It really is in the hands of the individual consultant to determine his own level of success or failure. In the next three chapters we explore the principles that should be adopted in consulting and the best practises to be adopted when actually doing the work.

Summary points

- *Measure limitations on achievement during self-assessment*

Capacity

- *Comfort of home office can release untapped capacity*
- *New circumstances can revolutionise productivity*
- *The flip side: no supervision can induce 'cabin fever'*
- *Key pressure to work long hours is usually client-driven*
- *Backup through sub-contracting may be necessary*
- *Balance is important for steady workflow and thus smooth cash flow*
- *Consulting can swing between feast and famine conditions*
- *Transactions portfolio at varying maturities can ease work fluctuations*
- *To achieve balance two disciplines are needed:*
    - *honest appraisal of deficiencies that cannot be self-cured*
    - *proper control to ensure continuity in hunt for new deals*

Cost

- *Tough question for new consultants "How much does one new client cost?"*
- *Client acquisition is dominant factor in costs that consultants incur*
- *Acquisition cost categories: actual, notional and opportunity*
- *Actual costs e.g. telecommunications, mail, travel, stationery, utilities*
- *Notional costs include home office rent, consultant's hourly rate*
- *Average cost will depend on categories and prices chosen*
- *Solicitation can be a drawn out matter*
- *Having to start again increases the next client acquisition cost*
- *How long a consultant chases an opportunity is largely cost-driven*
- *Consultant should identify his walk-away criteria*
- *Walk-away depends on break-even point where target loses viability*

Commitment

- *Many entrepreneurs sponsoring a deal try to enlist free consulting help*
- *Much effort may be needed to set up and administer the deal*
- *Consultant risks divulging intellectual property for no return*
- *Sponsor might refuse to commit his own funds despite his enthusiasm*
- *Consultants beware: a deal based on a success fee or free equity is often a mirage*
- *Likewise, consulting will only succeed if based on a substantive commitment*
- *Commitment requires real supporting capital and realistic targets*
- *New business planning is a holistic exercise*

Chapter 8

General principles of consulting

Always a deal

Every target client that agrees to enter discussions with a consultant represents an opportunity to do work. Every business whether it is a sole trader, partnership or limited company has some aspect or feature where a consultant can help. Even the best managed and most efficient of businesses will be capable of some improving modification or adjustment, and most often this may only be obvious to someone with fresh eyes looking in from outside.

This is a basic truth and its acceptance is a key ingredient in consulting success. He who returns from a solicitation meeting with a prospective client and reports that there was no business potential is only identifying that he has failed to ask the right questions, or he has failed to conduct the meeting properly, or he has failed to enquire fully. He is describing the result of shortcomings in his own operating technique, because there was an opportunity to do business. He simply failed to find it.

Of course there may be many reasons why the deal was unsuitable, not viable or undesirable, but that is not the point. The target will always represent a business opportunity, which if not right for the consultant, may be interesting to a colleague with complementary skills and expertise.

Often the physical or financial condition may be a deterrent to the search for business opportunities, on grounds that the operation may have little life left in it. Consultants with a banking background for example may have great difficulty in coming to terms with the idea of doing business with a company that is in dire financial straits. After all, this type of situation is one that a lending banker will do his best to avoid at all costs. For the consultant however, it may be of considerable interest – with the proviso always of course that there is enough money left in the pot to pay his fee!

A company that is close to financial midnight can be a rich source of consulting work in helping with a rescue strategy, or in the search for a buyer for either the business or its individual assets. Even after a company has been wound up, it may offer consulting work from the grave. This has occurred with audits of bank charges that have revealed a liability to the receiver for refund of overcharges.

The key message is that every company offers a business opportunity for the consultant and its discovery is therefore a challenge to his lateral thinking capacity, his interrogative skills and his investigative capabilities. At this stage, ignore whether the deal is suitable or not but consider whether the search for opportunities has been sufficiently thorough.

Information gathering

Information is the lifeblood of consulting. Without it, the consultant is hamstrung and virtually ineffective. It is a priority to gather and to continue searching for information about his target client using all sources available.

Information gathering is rarely straightforward. In the first instance, it may require some effort to induce the client to divulge any data that is not already available in the public domain, although his pre-agreement to talk to the consultant will be a step in the right direction. Practise shows time and again that information will be more readily imparted in a face-to-face meeting than is usually the case in a conversation by telephone. Despite advances in various forms of electronic communication, the physical meeting with all the techniques that include good eye contact, personal charisma, a pleasant manner and so forth is still the best means of building a warm business relationship. Application of professional meeting techniques is an important topic in its own right, which is addressed in the next two chapters.

Occasionally, the target client will be reticent in talking about his business situation and this will make the consultant's task virtually impossible. On the other hand, the physical meeting may be a watershed in the relationship and provided a basis of trust is established, a substantial flow of data may result. Often there seems to be a psychological point at which the target client decides to start talking freely, and surprising items are sometimes volunteered. There certainly does seem to be something in the notion that a person may wish to talk more freely to a virtual stranger, than to a friend or relation. In the personal experience of the authors, they have felt themselves on occasions to be occupying the role of "business Samaritan".

In many cases, the information will be delivered in confused and disjointed fashion, and unless fairly strict disciplines are employed in filtering and categorising this data, the effect can be almost as non-productive as a situation where the client is reluctant to talk. The client who is prepared to talk may do so unduly freely. In these situations, his information may come in a deluge and the challenge is to sort the wheat from the chaff, and to instil order to the chaos. Equally, the information may be tailored to suit the manner in which the client would like to present it and how he would wish to see it interpreted. This is not the most objective way of describing the business and its situation, but the client is the expert on his own affairs and he will be the best source of knowledge, however imperfectly delivered.

Clients are accustomed to describing their business to outsiders, but for different reasons and with different motives in mind. In a talk with the bank manager, the topics for discussion may be rather different to those considered with the accountant in conjunction with preparation of the tax return. An obvious point of differentiation lies in the interpretation of profit figures. Likewise, the client might describe his business in different terms when negotiating the sale of some of his products as compared with his message when buying raw materials.

A client who is adept at changing his message to suit his audience may have some difficulty in adopting the frankness and honesty required for the consultant to do a good job. In fact, bearing in mind the maxim that there is always a deal, a client who tries to deceive his consultant is offering a deal that is clearly unacceptable. This phenomenon is not rare, and indeed should certainly be anticipated in situations where success fee only type remuneration is promised. There can be little basis for a proper business relationship if the client is working to some alternative agenda, but is still prepared to harvest the consultant's efforts in the event that the latter comes up with something of value. The client has little at stake financially and he can always leave his consultant high and dry should the alternative agenda look more promising.

Apart from cases of outright deception, information imparted by the client may also be distorted, obsolete, or simply wrong. This does not necessarily imply an attempt to deceive; it may simply result from the client's failure to understand the issues under consideration.

Case 14. Andrew was actively consulting to a number of small and medium sized companies with annual turnovers of £10 million and less. With several of his clients he noticed a common phenomenon which was exemplified with PQR, a vehicle workshop business owned by a sole trader and employing about ten mechanics.

The business was expanding rapidly and as is common with such situations, there was a shortage of working capital and a growing number of business management problems that were beyond the training and experience of the PQR owner to solve himself. The owner was particularly cross about what he saw as the unhelpful attitude of his bank. Overdraft usage was consistently up to or above the agreed limit, but he stated firmly to Andrew that the bank was his only source of outside borrowing.

Andrew conducted a survey of the business, and studied the books at which time he was surprised to see that in addition to the bank overdraft, PQR had outstanding financial leases on workshop equipment, and the company car used by the owner was subject to a hire purchase contract. Also, it was normal to re-finance certain contracts with a factoring house.

Asked again about the borrowing situation, the owner re-confirmed that the bank was his only source of debt. In his mind he did not consider HP, leasing or factoring as borrowing in another form, and he took some convincing on this point. Having accepted the argument, he then pointed out that even so the factoring house was far more obliging and co-operative than the bank. Andrew responded that the factoring house provided far less flexible support than the bank, and at an APR two and half times that applied to the bank overdraft. Clearly the proprietor was confused about what constituted borrowing, and had little understanding of alternative finance costs.

There were a number of situations where Andrew discovered that an initial statement about a client's level of borrowing was subsequently proved to be incomplete. There had however been no intention by the client to mislead. He simply failed to understand the implication of the original question, and had answered in a literal sense.

Information sources: cross checking

Given that data collected from the client may be unreliable, cross checking wherever feasible is an essential discipline. Verbal sources should be confirmed against written records as in the case described above.

The process of cross checking requires discretion and tact. For example, if the boss makes a suspect statement about his business, it will be unwise to seek to test the veracity of his words by checking with a subordinate later. If the boss becomes aware of what has been going on – and the consultant's techniques and behaviour may well be under the spotlight anyway – the resultant loss of trust will undermine future efforts and could destroy the relationship. If there is need to talk to subordinates, the boss should be briefed in advance on what will be the nature of the enquiries, and why they are necessary.

It is usually preferable to test a suspect statement with the client himself. With Case 14 above, Andrew could have used a verifying question such as "Let me just check that I understand what you have just said. Am I correct in assuming that borrowings are only from the bank, and that you do not raise money from any outside party through leasing or hire purchase contracts?" This should have stimulated the client to think again about what he had just stated, and also would have allowed him the opportunity of correction without losing too much "face".

It is important in information gathering with the client to adopt some humility. With respect to the company's background, history, organisational structure, manufacturing processes, product range etc, the client will be better informed than the consultant. However, although it might be apparent from early on in the exchanges that much in the company can be improved, the proffering of opinions and ideas is best left until later. It may be tactically prudent to restrain from voicing opinions until a fuller picture has been developed of what is going on. Some clients resent hearing off-the-cuff recommendations and ideas from someone who seems to have set himself up as an instant expert. The consultant may eventually prepare a series of proposals for change that are contentious and revolutionary, and it is best that these be aired at the appropriate time when the maximum amount of data is to hand. The arguments for change can then be presented in the manner most likely to have them accepted.

A thorough review might also identify information sources already available to the client of which he is either unaware, or is exploiting inadequately. With small and medium sized companies, it is not unusual for information technology to be limited to an accounting, stocks and debtor system, and for this facility to be used only to satisfy bookkeeping and accounting needs rather than to provide meaningful management information.

Case 15. With respect to PQR mentioned in the earlier case, Andrew soon identified that the business had installed a computer system that was quite suitable for its needs. However only parts of the program were being used and it was operated mainly for bookkeeping needs. At the same time, the pace of business growth meant that debtors were increasing rapidly and that those in the doubtful category were an expanding element. The bookkeeping clerk was quite assiduous in scanning individual outstanding invoices in the debtor's ledger on a regular basis and in phoning those that appeared to be slow payers.

Simple adjustments to the system resulted in the creation of reports showing aggregate outstandings in name of each debtor, and debtors ageing. A management system was then introduced based on

Pareto's Law to institute weekly reviews of those 20% of debtors that accounted for 80% of the total sales turnover.

None of these changes could be considered as anything more than very basic, but the fact remained that they were control principles that the hard pressed business manager had either not previously heard of, or had never found the time to introduce.

This case is not unusual in that often, a consultant's recommended improvements do not need the introduction of anything radical. The wherewithal for problem solution may already exist but the client lacks the time or the training to re-organise, or it requires a fresh mind to instigate the required changes.

With private companies, the amount of data publicly available is invariably restricted, and an informative dialogue with the proprietor or a senior manager is essential. There is more information readily available on public companies but this does not necessarily mean that pre-emptive proposals may be welcome. Inside information about what is going on is always going to be superior to what may be divined from an outside viewpoint.

Case 16. A financial consulting group in Sydney, Australia developed a revolutionary financial instrument that had special monetary and fiscal advantages for certain categories of highly geared publicly listed companies. Having developed the product, they then conducted a search of suitable companies through the Sydney Stock Exchange publications and identified what appeared to be a suitable candidate in South Australia. Rather than travel inter-state to make a call on the target company on a speculative basis, it was decided to prepare a full-scale proposal in advance. Then a meeting would be set up with the Managing Director in order to solicit a mandate to introduce a new funding strategy for the company.

About ten man days of work went into producing an impressive and professional proposal, and a meeting with the MD was held as planned. His response was that the consulting group had done an excellent historical evaluation of the company, and that the proposed strategy was interesting and indeed could have provided a feasible way forward. However since publication of the last set of annual accounts, discussions had been held with an investor who had (subject to Stock Exchange clearance which was imminently forthcoming) agreed to inject additional capital through a private treaty transaction. These funds would reduce gearing, and place the company's finances on a sound footing.

Thus although the consulting group had done a good job, and their interest in the company's situation was very much appreciated, no business opportunity existed. A short advance visit to the company, or perhaps even an exploratory telephone call, could have avoided ten man-days of wasted investigation of public records, and the preparation of an elegant but unnecessary proposal.

The golden rule therefore is to gather the required data straight from the horse's mouth, and to hold one's peace as long as possible. It is easy of course to want to defer indefinitely on the basis that always more information can be gathered but at the end of the day, consulting is like much of the rest of business. Success often derives from firm commitment based on incomplete knowledge.

Intellectual Property Rights

A contract between a consultant and his client embodies a bargain regarding the exchange of information. We have discussed in broad terms the nature of information and how it may be imparted by the client, and in the next two chapters we will look in more detail at the specifics of meeting practises and how that information is acquired on a practical level.

It is now appropriate to review how the consultant keeps his side of the bargain, having learned as much as he thinks he needs about the client's business and its situation. In so doing, let us first consider the following hypothetical scenario:

A consultant has been contractually engaged to analyse a company and to make general recommendations about how it may be improved. After having spent two or three days in detailed analysis, he then meets again with the Managing Director. He reports that he has carried out the analysis, that everything looks fine and that he has no recommendations to make because nothing can be improved. Nevertheless the consultant presents his invoice for the time spent in executing the analysis.

In this most unlikely situation, the MD may be fully entitled to feel that he is getting nothing for his money, perhaps not even peace of mind because the consultant must surely have overlooked something of importance. Further he will feel entitled to refuse to pay the account because the consultant has given him nothing in return.

So what in generic terms does the consultant actually produce that justifies his charging of a fee? A way of defining his product in a simple, figurative sense can be through the parlour game of nine dots. It goes like this. Take a piece of paper and mark on it nine equally spaced dots:

```
*        *        *

*        *        *

*        *        *
```

Now with a pencil try to join up all the dots using only four straight lines, without allowing the pencil to leave the paper, and without going back along a line already drawn. You may though allow one line to cross another.

In a group of people, unless someone has played the game before and thus knows the answer, almost invariably the unanimous response is that the task set is impossible. However, the answer is as follows:

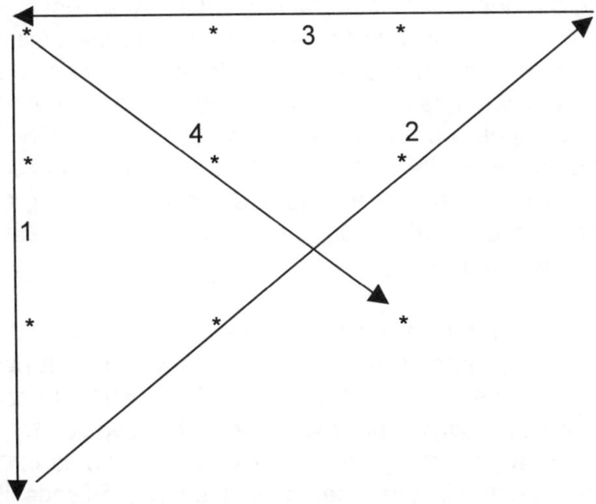

Once demonstrated, this solution is obvious but usually the viewer will only see the nine dots and attempt an answer within the boundaries that they prescribe.

This is a simplistic analogy relating to the consultant and the bargain that he strikes with his client. The latter, like us all, is limited by his knowledge, experience and senses, and because of those restrictions he is unable to envisage or enact solutions that fall outside those parameters. Quite understandably, when asked to join the nine dots with four lines on the terms and conditions imposed, a short analysis may persuade him that the problem cannot be solved.

The client and his business problems are clearly far more complex but his capacity to solve problems is finite – his own personal set of nine dots. The transaction that is tacitly struck with the consultant is one in which the latter agrees to take the client mentally somewhere new, and show him a totally fresh approach or new knowledge or a new way of looking at things that makes the hitherto seemingly impossible now possible. The consultant figuratively takes the client outside the boundaries of the nine dots to join them up with the four straight lines.

In Case 15 above, Andrew helped solve a pressing business problem with the debtors' management of PQR by essentially undertaking the nine-dot exercise with the management of the business. Firstly, he demonstrated that the requisite information was in-house already and that it only needed a new way of looking at the reports, and of asking the computer a question to improve the quality of management information. Secondly, he introduced the notion of Pareto's Law to ensure that scarce time was directed at monitoring those factors that could seriously threaten the business while safely relegating the unimportant dross.

Analysed in this fashion, it all seems so simple and so obvious, and that is the paradox of the value of knowledge. It has power right up until the time that it is shared with others, when it becomes a common commodity which all exploit but few value for its own sake. Generically speaking this knowledge is known as Intellectual Property and its control is a key ingredient in successful consulting.

Certain categories of consulting activity by their nature provide natural protection for intellectual property. For example, work in the area of Information Technology may be technically complex and too esoteric for clients to understand and appropriate, thereby providing its own protection. Elsewhere, intellectual property protection is harder to achieve as in cost reduction work, where particular techniques may be necessary to ensure that the client pays the pre-agreed fee for validated savings. For example the program may be of substantially reduced earnings potential if the consultant prematurely advises the name of a competitively priced supplier.

Understanding therefore the need to exercise strict stewardship over intellectual property is an essential facet of consulting. It is an asset that needs to be nurtured, preserved and valued in its own right. Proper respect for intellectual property will enhance consulting performance standards, and its sharing at the appropriate time can bring enormous benefits. For instance, in the courting of a prospective client, the giving away of small items of intellectual property might underline the consultant's potency and capacity to do good things. Exploited adroitly in this fashion, it can provide a strong inducement for the client to engage his services on satisfactory terms.

At the same time it must be noted that there is a class of prospective client that can be very dangerous with regard to intellectual property. This person is adept at milking the consultant for his knowledge but never has any intention of paying a fee. Much in the same category is the success fee only transaction where the consultant is bound to disseminate intellectual property but with an uncertain promise of recompense later. As mentioned above, knowledge shared loses much of its recognised intrinsic value and in these circumstances it is difficult to get the recipient to pay a fair price after the event.

Passing on intellectual property, recommendations and proposals

Assuming that the bargain to exchange information has been mutually struck and is to be satisfactorily honoured, the manner in which the consultant passes on his recommendations and proposals needs careful thought. A successful assignment will involve the creation of quite a close rapport with the client, largely because the consultant is offering dispassionate help and advice where none is available from other sources. The building and maintenance of relationships in consulting is an important topic, which is explored more fully later in this book.

In the initial stages, the review and analysis of what is going on in a business, and preparation of the related report is largely a passive exercise so far as the client is concerned. He will be asked to provide a lot of data and to answer many questions, some obvious while others will appear obscure to him. There is though a point at which a subtle and important change in the relationship will take place – the point of transition from analysis to implementation of practical actions.

Thus the transmission of considered proposals to the client may be a delicate issue and it may be the manner of their presentation rather than what they contain that will be the key determinant in what happens next.

Consider the situation where in spite of numerous organisational problems and a series of external pressures, a business has survived and is reasonably viable. Many small and medium sized companies operate under these sorts of conditions over surprisingly long periods, and with survival largely due to the extraordinary commitment and determination of the owner-manager. He will be under continuous pressure, which is about to be intensified by a series of recommendations for change and business modification at the behest of an individual who has been studying over a few days what may have been his life's work.

There is a major challenge therefore in passing on what could be received as an iconoclastic message. If rejected, the consultancy effort will have been in vain, the company and its owner-manager will be in no better condition than before, and the consultant may have scotched his chances of securing further fee-earning work from the same source.

A report, which proposes a number of changes to be instituted by an overworked man, could produce a number of different unfavourable reactions. One may be to see the report as a personal slight and to reject it out of hand. Another may be to accept the recommendations in their entirety, and to attempt their immediate and concurrent implementation thereby creating yet further problems and resulting in a series of half completed tasks with no individual or aggregate benefit achieved. A third might be a decision to cherry-pick those proposals which are easier to adopt while leaving harder and more threatening matters unresolved.

Any one of these outcomes may be equally unsatisfactory for the consultant because he will inevitably bear a large measure of the blame, and in a way this is not unreasonable. The client will have paid for good advice and a significant ingredient of this is that it should be practicable. The world is full of theorists with plenty of bright ideas, but it is doubtful whether they can be the equal of a good idea that has been practically designed and successfully implemented.

Thus the consultant needs to think very carefully about how to get his proposals across. Usually they should be embraced within a structured program, with priorities set and a plan laid out for the sequential and controlled implementation of changes. The actual style of presentation will depend on the peculiar circumstances of each case, and on the recognised ability of the client to absorb the recommendations.

Also, the actual method of report presentation should be appropriate for its expected audience. For example, a consulting task that has addressed technical issues and has been undertaken for a large organisation may require a report that will be read by different people in different locations. This document may be lengthy and self-contained with its own supporting data, bibliography etc, with the intention that it should be a reference work as well as an action plan.

For the busy owner-manager of a smaller company, the amount of time he has to read anything may be limited so written brevity linked with cohesive verbal explanation will be more effective. In general consulting in this market sector, a report of two or three pages consisting of bullet points, key milestones, nominated responsible persons and brief supporting comments may be as much as the client can be expected to absorb. **Appendix E** contains a sample of such a report.

Confidentiality

A successful consulting task should lead to significant disclosure of information in a two-way flow between client and consultant. Sometimes business secrets are discussed which are of a nature that the client would not normally share even with his accountant, banker or lawyer. Reasons for this are reviewed later but the main point to bear in mind here is that usually in relationships of this quality, the client views his consultant as a close confidant and ally who is sharing his hopes and fears for the sustained success of his business. At the same time, the consultant offers none of the standards of confidentiality that would be expected of participating members of one of the acknowledged professions. It is not that we do not consider consulting to be a profession because indeed it is. However, there is as yet no governing body on whom a client may rely for assurances regarding confidentiality and general codes of practise.

It is not always the case, but from time to time clients do ask for protection concerning the manner in which their confidences may be treated. The point should be made that a consultant would be spiting himself by openly discussing his client's business activities with other parties. Even if the client does not become aware of such practises, this behaviour will not be well received by others who will have noted that the consultant has a loose mouth, and should therefore be treated with circumspection.

Verbal assurances may not be sufficient however, in which case the consultant should be prepared to offer a confidentiality agreement as protection of the client's interests. These agreements take many different forms and typically they are in the form of an undertaking. However, in cases where the consultant's role will include the disclosure of information to third parties, or where complex issues of two-way preservation of intellectual property are involved, a more detailed mutual non-disclosure document may be necessary.

For ease of reference, a suggested code of practise, three different forms of confidentiality agreement and a mutual non-disclosure agreement are set out in **Appendix C**.

Summary points

Always a deal

- *Every target that talks with a consultant is a work opportunity*
- *Every business has some aspect that a consultant can improve*
- *Even ultra efficient businesses can still be changed for the better*
- *Lack of identified potential shows consultant's search failure*
- *Opportunities beyond own skills may be valuable to a colleague*
- *Discovery of the opportunity is a measure of the consultant's skills*

Information gathering

- *Information is the lifeblood of consulting*
- *Priority is to gather information on target using all sources*
- *Client must be encouraged to divulge data not in public domain*
- *Physical meetings are crucial to building trust and information flow*

- *Information has to be filtered and categorised*
- *Client as expert on his own affairs is prime source of information*
- *Client information serves his own agenda and may be deceptive*
- *Also information may be distorted, obsolete or simply wrong*

Information sources: cross checking

- *As client information may be unreliable, cross checking is vital*
- *Confirm verbal sources against written records when possible*
- *Cross checking requires discretion and tact*
- *Suspect statements are best checked with client himself*

Intellectual Property Rights

- *Consultant/ client contract is partly about information exchange*
- *It is imperative that the consultant keep his side of the bargain*
- *Information is power until the point that it is shared with others*
- *Some activities yield natural IP protection e.g. Information Technology*

Passing on intellectual property, recommendations and proposals

- *Skill is needed in passing on recommendations*
- *Proposals should be structured with implementation priorities set*
- *Report presentation tailored to expected audience*
- *Clarity and brevity in reports to ease assimilation by audience*

Confidentiality

- *Success should yield significant two-way information disclosure*
- *Client may view consultant as a close confident and ally*
- *Client might ask for legal protection re information disclosure*
- *Consultant should advise that reputation for discretion is crucial to his continued activities*
- *If verbal assurances are insufficient, confidentiality agreement should be offered*

Chapter 9

Best meetings practise: before, during and after

Meetings, meetings, meetings!

Anyone with experience of modern management in a corporate organisation will be familiar with the ritualistic nature of meetings. They form an integral part of company life and are considered irreplaceable in the efficient discharge of the organisation's activities. They are a key means by which companies try to foster internal communications, but they can satisfy criteria and motivational objectives separate from the ostensible agenda and business in hand.

Meetings are exploited for a variety of individual and group objectives. For example on an individual plane, he who can afford to arrive late or last will use this practise to demonstrate power or seniority. His subliminal message to other participants is "my time is more valuable than the aggregate of yours", and accordingly he is signalling that the main business of the meeting cannot commence until he is present.

Group behaviour is exploited for many complex purposes. Intra-tribal hierarchies may be re-affirmed, and inter-tribal rivalries re-defined for the purpose of marking and protecting the tribal turf. All manner of behaviour is used to display friendship or hostility, enthusiasm or scepticism, interest or disinterest. Body language, eye movements, even the choice of sitting at the centre of the debate or at the periphery is all intended consciously or unconsciously to deliver a range of messages in parallel to whatever is contributed verbally.

Most conventional business meetings in their content and structure must owe as much to the ebb and flow of internal office politics as they do to the need to solve problems more effectively, or to make the business function more efficiently. From a cynical standpoint, meetings can provide the detached observer with much wry amusement in witnessing the creation of collegiate wisdom, or perhaps just as frequently, group stupidity. Also he will have no difficulty in identifying those individuals for whom the form of meeting rather than its intended substance is an exercise of paramount importance, and the whole stuff of corporate life. For those same individuals, the elegance of their contribution and the political dexterity of its delivery is what management and climbing the corporate ladder is really all about. In the same forum, others who are less interested in stylistic form but who are committed to the substance of doing good business will find boredom and frustration.

The lesson to be drawn from extended experience of meetings in the corporate environment is that they may well not provide a suitable training ground for what will be demanded of the independent consultant when he is face-to-face with his client. The disciplines that should be engaged have little to do with the political arena of the corporate world but are much concerned with developing mutual trust and understanding. The consultant must marshal and deploy those skills that will enable the creation of a forum for exchanging views that will quickly add value. These are skills that may well require priority in the re-training and self-development program to enable effective transformation from the corporate to the consulting worlds.

The meeting agenda

In the circumstances of the typical corporate meeting, there is usually a fair degree of clarity and understanding concerning its purpose and the general intentions of those present. As indicated above, there will also often be unstated or hidden agenda to be pursued by sub-groups or by individuals intent on scoring points, or on pursuing specific objectives, or in attacking the ground of others, or in defending their own.

This scenario of clarity of agenda is broadly repeated in most other forms of encounter whether it is with friends and colleagues, with passing acquaintances, or with total strangers. There is a mute understanding between both sides regarding the reason for the approach and what the ensuing discussion should be about. There will be certain tacit rules of behaviour and social decorum that apply to the particular circumstances and situation. Thus it will be with the job applicant in front of a prospective employer, with the boy who asks the girl for a dance at the disco, or with the car driver before the magistrate in connection with a driving offence. In every case both sides will have more than an inkling about what will ensue and how they intend to behave.

The consultant facing his potential client for the first time confronts a more rigorous challenge. Firstly, he may be there on a wrong pretext and he may have to correct that misunderstanding and re-focus the debate before progress can be made. Secondly, regardless of the strength of the introduction, the consultant may have relatively little time to present his case and to establish a bridgehead of trust. Thirdly, he may quickly have to initiate a program of questions to gather information which is essential to his work, but which may border on the impertinent or unduly intrusive in the mind of the target. Further, he may have been allotted perhaps only half an hour or an hour in which to achieve his objectives.

The structural difficulties of such meetings commence right at the point of the first contact, or during the process of introduction. For example, a third party may have been instrumental in getting the consultant and the potential client together. However well intentioned, that third party may have mis-interpreted the target's problems and needs to the consultant, while concurrently mis-describing or incorrectly promoting what services the consultant has to offer. Thus the opening discussions to what may need to become a confidential relationship to be in any way effective will be hampered by the necessity to explain intentions and eliminate doubts.

Equally, the involvement of third parties is not the only cause of such difficulties. If the consultant himself has undertaken the pre-meeting promotion – say by telephone selling or mail shot, the recipient may well have misread or misheard what the consultant is trying to offer, thereby again making necessary the opening corrections.

Once this barrier has been overcome, there is the challenge of winning the target's trust. This may be a complex process engaging all the human senses and relying on intuition, judgement and any number of other factors that may come into play in determining the calibre, reliability and suitability of the consultant as a trustworthy confidant. An experienced negotiator may well be able to capitalise on any opening misunderstandings in the meeting while individuals with less developed skills can flounder and fail at this point.

Assuming that this stage has been passed successfully, there is still difficult ground to cover in the process of interrogation of the target. This may seem an extreme summary description but it accurately describes what is really involved, even if the target is unaware of the fact that he is being interrogated. Efficient assimilation of the required information is essential if the consultant is to attempt to do his job competently, and obviously the more freely the information flows in a relaxed atmosphere, the better.

At this stage in talking with trainee or prospective consultants, questions frequently arise such as "What do you say?" or "How does one go about seeking business from a total stranger?" The response that one must develop style and mannerisms that are natural and relaxed, and with which the individual feels most happy often sounds trite and fails to convince. However, a genuine approach is always the best way of going about the task, but do bear in mind that a meeting requires strategy and planning, and that success will depend on reliance on quite a large number of details. The best way in which to advise is therefore to go step-by-step through the solicitation and conduct of a meeting in pursuit of a new relationship.

The first meeting: before and after

The number of factors set out below may seem unduly detailed, or in some respects insultingly elementary. However, the authors have witnessed that failure frequently results at meetings through one or more of lack of preparation, inattention to detail, inappropriate interview techniques, incomplete information gathering, and badly controlled follow-up.

It may be asked which of the elements set out below are critical to ensuring high standards of performance; our reply is "all of them".

The target client

For the independent consultant, it is a statistical probability that his clientele will be found exclusively within the Small and Medium Sized Business Sector of the economy (SME's) which includes sole traders, partnerships and limited companies whose annual turnover is less than £20 million. Predominant features of this sector are considered more fully in Chapter 12, but suffice to note at this stage that SME's are invariably family businesses where usually the chief executive officer is also the owner or part owner.

Unless a unique or highly specialised service is on offer, it is unlikely that an independent consultant will be engaged by larger organisations. These will either perceive that they have the requisite suite of management skills in-house, or they will have the budgetary capacity to hire teams from larger consulting groups to meet their requirements.

The consultant's skills base

In approaching SME's as potential clients, the trained and experienced consultant may well have a lot to offer, but also faces the problem that the target may fail to appreciate that he is in need of what help the consultant can mobilise. The opening gambit by mailshot or telephone selling will have concentrated on a specific product or service to catch the target's interest. In reality, it may only represent a part of the full spectrum of the consultant's skills but it is a means of taking the first step towards a meaningful and broader based discussion.

Concurrently, the consultant assesses the target's possible needs in other areas, and with experience this process will become second nature. Certainly the establishment of rapport opens up opportunities for a broader review of what is available, by using the techniques enumerated below.

Opening client solicitation

The agreement of the target client to grant an appointment will have been the result of a planned promotional campaign by the consultant. Alternative promotional techniques are discussed in Chapter 11 but broadly speaking, these encompass mail shot, telephone selling, affinity group marketing and networked referrals

Each method has relative strengths and weaknesses, and some offer a chance to get alongside the client faster than do others. For example, a telesold single product will leave the consultant in a more "remote" situation vis-à-vis his potential client than a referral through a trusted third party.

However the appointment has been secured, the interval between the agreement to meet and the meeting itself may be critical. If for example, a time and place has been set which is more than three business days forward, then a short letter thanking the target, and confirming the meeting will help to keep the contact "warm". Equally, do not telephone to re-confirm the meeting as the interval may have yielded second thoughts and the telephone conversation will afford the target an opportunity for a graceful exit from his commitment, which he would find much harder in a face-to-face encounter.

Alternatively, the target may use the telephone conversation to seek further explanation from the consultant about the need for and purpose of the meeting. This may place the latter in the defensive situation of having to justify himself in advance, but in a less convincing way than is possible face-to-face.

At this stage, only the briefest of information may be available on the target (name, address, contact details, name and title of contact man, and a basic understanding of the business activities). Some additional information may be available from trade directories, but for SME's this is likely to be sparse and out-of-date. Desk research capacity before the meeting is therefore minimal and not worth much effort.

The business from the outside

In comparison with desk research, a swift survey of the outside characteristics can sometimes be quite informative. If time does permit, a short reconnaissance of the business and its immediate environment may reveal factors that could be of significance in the meeting, or in follow up work. Thus environmentally, matters such as complementary or competing businesses in the locality, adequacy of the site, room for expansion, access, suitability of available services, distance from population centres are all factors which may emerge later, but about which the consultant may be able to gain a pertinent view in advance.

Regarding the business itself, the external condition of the building, the type of motor vehicles parked outside, whether or not the grounds have been maintained, evidence of industrial waste and rubbish will say something about the business and how it is run. This may sound basic, but the consultant should have a feel for some of the things he may expect, even before he has set foot in the premises.

The business from the inside

The theme of the business saying things about itself will continue in doors. The ambience of the reception area, the condition of the sample products in the display cabinet (including the layer of dust!), the behaviour of the receptionist, and other similar factors will all help in the developing view as to whether or not the business is well run.

Dress and punctuality

It is essential that the consultant be present at least five minutes before the appointed time. Lack of punctuality is a display of bad manners and incompetence at any time, and even more so in respect of a meeting that has been initiated by the consultant, rather than the target. Never ever be late, regardless of the plausibility of the excuse.

Take care also in the mode of dress. Meetings in the corporate world are media for the display of all the paraphernalia of power dressing – intimidating dark suits, red braces, yellow ties and associated clutter.

Where you are seeking to establish a working and hopefully lucrative relationship with the busy and hard pressed CEO of an SME, your objective is to win his friendship rather than to scare him with the notion that he is in the presence of some corporate superstar. Dress smartly but quietly, using muted colours. A suit is preferable on the first meeting but it may become apparent that semi-formal wear (jacket and slacks) will be better received on later visits.

Also bear in mind that the size of one's briefcase can impart all sorts of psychological messages about seniority and temperament. For example, a large case may signify a relatively junior person, over-burdened with work and under pressure while a modest document case implies seniority and a more relaxed attitude.

Case 17. James dressed smartly in a suit for his first meeting with the proprietor of a small manufacturing business. The meeting went well, but he came away with a distinct feeling that he had over-dressed for the occasion. The proprietor was a hands-on business leader and his management style included spending most of his time on the shop floor. His daily mode of dress was oily work stained overalls whose colour and texture was matched by that of the carpet on the floor of his office.

From the outside, the business looked a shambles because the buildings were in similar condition to that of the carpet. Nevertheless the shop-floor equipment ("this is where I make my money" said the proprietor) was in excellent condition, and the business was profitable.

The relationship seemed to improve in direct proportion to the extent that James chose to "dress down" for subsequent meetings – to the point where it became a standing joke with the proprietor that he always wore his oldest and dirtiest clothes when visiting this client.

The receptionist

Sometimes the receptionist, or perhaps the telephone operator or secretary, can make the CEO far less accessible than he would wish to be. The receptionist may assume a custodial role towards her boss and getting past her can be a challenge in itself.

Reception areas are usually the receptionist's own "space" which she (or he) usually guards quite jealously. Visitors are tolerated provided that they accord with behaviour patterns of which the receptionist approves. Thus they are normally directed to a sitting area (usually with very low and comfortable couches or chairs) and offered a cup of tea or coffee. Both should be refused politely for the following reasons.

By remaining standing, the visitor is "untidy" and is thus invading the receptionist's space. This continually reminds her of the visitor's presence, and encourages her to try to move him on by periodically passing reminders to the boss that the visitor is still waiting.

The offer of a drink can be a real trap, should the CEO himself come out to greet the visitor. The latter has the task more or less simultaneously of climbing out of a low chair, straightening his clothing, picking up his brief case, shaking the CEO by the hand, and imparting that first initial and critical impression of easy competence. He will be trying to do all that while his main concern is whether he is going to spill hot beverage on the carpet or over his potential client!

How staff behave and appear to work

The process of scrutiny of the business continues on the short journey from the reception area to the CEO's office. This will provide further vignettes on issues such as staff attitudes, working conditions, tidiness, cleanliness, age and usage of IT equipment. Much of this will be little more than fleeting impressions but with experience of a number of clients, the act of looking around will enable the consultant to see and to recognise more.

None of these observations should be treated as in any way conclusive, but they all have their part to play in helping to build a picture of the business and what makes it tick.

The client meeting

It should be noted that eight discussion points, all of which are germane to the contact process, have been reviewed so far and it is only at this stage that we start to consider the content of the meeting itself. This emphasises the significance of the pre-planning and observational methodologies, which if addressed thoroughly will shorten the odds against the discussions leading to a successful outcome. Further it is apparent that this pre-meeting process is far more intricate and demanding of close attention by the consultant than would necessarily have been the case with most meetings that he attended in his earlier corporate life.

Typically, the opening meeting with the potential client will go through a number of stages.

The purpose: A remarkable number of fledgling consultants start out on a meeting without a clear objective in view. They may use terms like "courtesy call", "introductory meeting", "exploratory meeting", "marketing call" and so forth. Vacillation and uncertainty at this level is an unacceptable waste of the consultant's own time, an even greater waste of the opportunity, and a potentially disastrous waste of the target's goodwill (and time also).

There can be only one objective and that is to do business, which means either the engagement of the consultant's services by the end of the meeting or, second best, tangible progress towards building a fee producing relationship later.

This may seem rather obvious but, sadly, it is not apparent to many consultants in practise. They are so obsessed with being nice and pleasant (and there is nothing wrong in that) that they lose the plot. Conversation may turn into a convivial and pleasant meander with a failure to adhere to its key purpose. In so doing they forget that they are there to do business – which is to consult in return for a fee.

The opening: If the last section gave the impression that we are advocating a hard sell, this is most certainly not the case. The consultant bound on business solicitation may be trembling with urgency and determination but he should not be showing this to his potential client. He starts with the hope that the client will engage his services for a variety of sound reasons including trust and reliability, rather than in response to a slick and polished style. Integral to this intent, the consultant must demonstrate his commitment by setting out a quasi agenda and the following steps best achieve this:

- Thank the target for sparing his time to see you (after all it may be a considerable achievement to win an hour of a busy CEO's day)

- Remind the target of why you are there – by reference to the third party introduction/ mailshot/ telephone conversation

- If the contact has been made on the back a specific product or service promotion, briefly describe its advantages, and quote anonymously examples of how benefits have been achieved previously

- Relate the product or service to the broad range of skills which the consultant has to offer

- Explain that either the specific product or the broad range of consulting assistance on offer will not be effective unless there is a better appreciation of the business environment into which it is to be introduced.

- Invite therefore the target to talk about his business so that a better understanding may be gained.

Note also that all this should be achieved in not more than say five minutes. The point is that the consultant has a better chance of winning a contract by hearing about the client's problems than he ever will by espousing his product range at length, however superior this may be.

Build rapport: Interwoven with the opening, it is essential to build personal rapport with the target. This forms another and equally important sub-agenda in the early stage, and it may be conducted prior to, concurrently with, or immediately after the formal meeting opening. Rapport can be established relatively quickly through a number of different means, and will often derive from observations made on the journey to the CEO's office. Traffic delays; admiration for the CEO's car (it will have been readily identifiable in the company car park); praise for the size and condition of the premises; interest in the company's display cabinet in the reception area; comment on the bag of golf clubs in the corner; all these are examples of a basis for a casual comment or query that might lead to the building of rapport.

If the consultant is really lucky, the potential client will have that wonderful American invention in his office, an "ego wall" which typically depicts the major achievements of his working career. What is so helpful about the ego wall is that the target advertises what is important to him. His tastes, values, ambitions, plans, motives etc are of so much interest in information gathering, that an ego wall is manna from heaven to the skilled practitioner. More canny prospective clients reveal nothing of themselves on the walls of their offices, although it is hard for them not to reflect their self-esteem and success in the business that they have built around them. Hence the importance of the journey from the company car park to this stage.

In any event, ego wall or not, the process of rapport building should not take more than say five minutes. If you have been granted an audience of thirty minutes, there are only twenty remaining.

Read the office: Although the walk from reception to the CEO's office may have given only a fleeting impression of what the company is all about, the office itself may have a lot to say about the CEO as a man. His sense of judgement and discretion may be evident in the amount of material, confidential or otherwise, which he leaves on his desk to risk it being read upside down. The man in proper control may work with a messy desk but then he will clear it in advance, or take the visitor to a featureless interview room, rather than risk secrets being leaked to a visitor who has yet to prove his bona fides.

Material factors can be significant also. A comparison of the quality of the CEO's office accommodation with that which he feels to be suitable for his subordinates, and for the shop floor can say a lot about business acumen and a sense of reality.

Case 18. Jonathan was asked to undertake a review of a family owned, new venture manufacturing company in a Mediterranean locality. The company's business was unique to the area, was located in a modern purpose designed factory using equally state-of-the-art production equipment, and was designed to produce a high quality end product. Considerable capital (equity and debt) had been expended on business creation and this had resulted in a high fixed cost. Local sales had always been expected to be minimal, and exports were to form the major part of the company's sales turnover, and hence profit base. In the interim, lack of profits and of cash flow had placed the company in a somewhat precarious position.

Jonathan was taken on a tour of the plant by a subordinate manager who demonstrated the high quality of the end product, the advanced nature of the equipment, and the adequate space for future expansion of the business. At the same time, Jonathan could not fail to notice that construction of certain parts of the factory had yet to be completed, that part of the production equipment had not yet been commissioned, and that personnel seemed to be under-employed.

At the conclusion of the tour, Jonathan was invited into the CEO's office suite, which appeared to be the only part of the entire complex that had been finished off properly. Even before asking for his impressions of the visit, the CEO proudly showed Jonathan the carved boardroom table, the splendid marble fireplace and the oak panelling on the walls.

Jonathan concluded that the company was in desperate need of his help if it was to survive, but that the CEO's ego and self-esteem presented major obstacles to substantive improvements. He declined to pursue the mandate.

Small details in an office can be revealing also – the number of cigarette stubs in the ash tray; the half hidden bottle of spirits; the computer terminal that is there for show but is clearly never used.

Case 19. Mark had been having a hard time in business solicitation, and this opportunity was proving to be no easier. His prospective client displayed all the signs of aggressive competence, and Mark was having difficulty in regaining control of the meeting, or in trying to match his "opponent's" apparent superior grasp of monetary and fiscal policy. In desperation, Mark looked around and tried to "read the office". He noticed a bookshelf, scanned the titles and saw that prominent among them was a beginner's level teach-yourself book about basic economics.

Mark failed to win a contract but was cheered by the feeling that perhaps the prospective client was not all that he had pretended to be…….

Meeting follow-up

Following the closing of the meeting, maintenance of control over the relationship is essential. A full meeting report should be prepared immediately, as deferral will impair the memory of what was discussed. Brevity in the report may be warranted but do bear in mind that it may be a point of reference for later use by others, or for oneself so a complete picture is usually preferable.

Consecutive to the report, a letter of thanks should be despatched to the client, using similar terminology to that adopted in the meeting so as to stay on the client's wavelength. The letter should list the areas of mutual interest, enumerate the advantages that the consultant can deliver and evaluate the resultant benefits for the client. Linked to this there should be a clear statement of the next action to be pursued so that the client's interest remains current, and so that he is left in no doubt that the consultant will initiate whatever remedial action has been agreed upon.

Finally and most importantly, the consultant must retain control of where the relationship will go next which means that he must retain the contact initiative. For example, at the meeting close and in the follow-up letter he should state how and when he will make the next contact, in precise terms. "I will phone you next Tuesday morning to discuss the contents of this letter" is much to be preferred over "I will get in contact with you sometime next week". It follows also that the consultant should not leave matters open-ended by agreeing that the potential client will call him back. Practise shows that leaving initiative to the potential client in this way means that nothing more will eventuate.

Diary power and the rule of seven

It should be obvious that a well-run diary system is essential to good consulting. It is important that follow up contact should take place when it has been promised, just as it is essential that the consultant does not over-commit his personal resources and so risk upsetting promising client contacts by failing to deliver on schedule.

Wide experience in general business consulting has shown that on average, the rule of seven applies with respect to the number of contacts necessary before a client will sign a letter of engagement. As an example, the history of a client solicitation might appear like this:

1st Contact	-	Mail shot
2nd "	-	Telephone selling call
3rd "	-	Letter confirming appointment
4th "	-	Visit to target client
5th "	-	Follow up letter after visit
6th "	-	Follow up telephone call to set second visit
7th "	-	Second visit - engagement letter signed

Some conclusions may be drawn from this scenario. As the rule of seven refers to an average, and bearing in mind that some contracts will be won at say the third or fourth contact, success in pursuing other business may require a dozen or more individual approaches. Further, different marketing methodologies may bring results faster (as discussed in Chapter 11) but the average does prevail. Some types of business will require longer gestation periods and will possibly invoke greater frustration in the solicitation process.

Also, the pursuit and execution of consulting contracts should be an iterative process so that there is not, for example, a preponderance of contracts nearing completion with a dearth of new business in prospect. Thus existing business execution should be blended with solicitation of new business opportunities for a smooth workflow.

In this situation, even a small consulting business can present some quite complex management issues, and given the importance of planned and effective performance at client meetings, the maintenance of an efficient business diary is an important tool towards this end.

Summary points

- *Consultant-client meetings differ from corporate-style meetings*
- *Consultant-client meetings should focus on mutual trust and understanding*
- *New meetings practises are integral part of transition process into consulting*

The meeting agenda

- *Consultant in potential client meeting faces a rigorous challenge*
- *He must correct any misunderstanding re purpose and potential*
- *He must present case and establish a trust bridgehead quickly*
- *Consultant must quickly gather information which is essential to his objectives*
- *He may have only an hour or less in which to achieve his key objectives*

The first meeting: before and after

- *Statistically probable that client is SME with turnover below £20M*
- *Target client may not appreciate the scale of what the consultant can offer*
- *Mailshot or teleselling may have concentrated on one product or service only*
- *Rapport is needed for broader review of what is available*

Opening client solicitation

- *Solicitation will involve one of: mailshot, teleselling, affinity, networked referrals.*
- *If more than three days to meeting, send confirming letter*
- *Do not telephone reconfirm as this offers target chance to postpone/ cancel*

The business from the outside

- *Reconnaissance of business and environment may be relevant*
- *Complementary / competing businesses, site adequacy, expansion potential, access, available services, distance from population centres may be relevant*

The business from the inside

- *Decoration and ambience, staff behaviour etc. may all be relevant*

Dress and punctuality

- *Always arrive at meeting at least five minutes early*
- *Dress smartly but quietly, using muted colours*
- *Do not adopt the corporate superstar style*

The receptionist

- *Be aware of the gatekeeper's function*
- *Exploit use of her space to your advantage*

How staff behave and appear to work

- *Gain impressions from staff working conditions, attitudes, equipment usage etc*
- *Impressions are indicative rather than conclusive*

The client meeting

- *Purpose is to engage consultant's services or progress to a fee earning relationship*
- *Avoid niceties that waste client's time or the opportunity*

The opening

- *Do not let client become aware of your anxiety*
- *Remind the target of why you are there*
- *If contact is for specific service, briefly describe the benefits*
- *Relate service to full range of skills the consultant has to offer*
- *Invite target to talk about his business*

Build rapport

- *It is critical in first five minutes to build a rapport with target client*
- *Exploit whatever the office has to offer e.g. an "ego wall"*
- *Remember always how little time may remain for meeting purpose*

Read the office

- *The office can tell much about client's style, taste, ego*
- *Information which the office displays may be valuable in forming judgements*

Meeting follow-up

- *Do not forget the follow up process – maintain control of contact*
- *Thank you letter should reiterate main meetings points in consistent vein*
- *Assert firmly date and time of next contact*

Diary power and the rule of seven

- *Efficient follow-up relies on well-run diary*
- *Remember the rule of seven governs average response rate from potential clients*

Chapter 10

Best meetings practise: interview techniques

Questions and answers

The process of question and answer is at the very core of the client meeting and it is apparent from advising new consultants that this area gives ground for much concern. While some anxiety may be understandable, this can be averted through proper preparation and by attention to detail. With practise it should be possible to recognise and pursue the opportunities divulged during the discussions (the "hooks"), and to exploit the observations made thus far about the business, as described in the previous chapter.

At commencement of the meeting, the client is in total control because he commands all the relevant information about his business, and the consultant has the task of winning ground by proper and effective interrogation. This should follow a line of enquiry ideally in the mode of informed discussion, supported by questions and counter-questions commencing with those aspects of the business about which the interviewee appears at ease to discuss. An approach that adopts an overtly inquisitorial attitude is likely to receive short shrift.

Initial impressions through pre-visit contacts and in what has been observed to this point will help but from here on, it is the consultant's skill in asking the right questions that will decide success.

Stages of privacy

Assuming that the target client is an SME, the nature of areas to be explored through a series of questions should recognise the degree of intrusion with which they will be interpreted. In broad terms, it may be assumed that the CEO (who is usually the owner or part owner of the business) will view requests for information as falling into one of the following categories:

Public domain
Private domain
Personal

In most circumstances, the typical CEO will consider most of the information about his company to be in the private domain, other than the brief data revealed in trade directories and published accounts. Gaining his willingness to talk about what he considers to be private matters may take some skill.

Usually a question such as "How is business going?" is a good way of starting the discussion. It is a bland enquiry that may bring a response about the company, its industry, or the economy at large. A follow up question about why business is doing well, badly or indifferently may invoke a similarly bland response of minimal value. However the ice should have been broken, making the way clear to present a more pointed enquiry such as "How is your business doing in relation to others?" Then, further focussed questions may follow.

Unfortunately it is not feasible to prescribe what falls into each category (public, private and personal), or how one may move smoothly from one category to another. Business circumstances, the innate character of the individual, his attitudes and feelings at the time all make the combination and order of questions, and the responses, as complex as human nature itself.

It is important though to remain alive to the fact that some subjects are more sensitive than are others, and that one should be prepared to retreat gracefully if a line of questioning shows evidence of giving offence. There is no predictable pattern, however. The "how's business?" line of opening may cover most eventualities but not necessarily all.

For example, the client may be an SME whose CEO has started to plan retirement, and who has turned to a qualified Independent Financial Advisor (IFA) for assistance on pension planning. The IFA, mindful of his regulatory constraints, may turn to an independent general business consultant because the capital that the CEO needs to fund a pension plan is locked up in the assets of his business. Thus the discussions with the consultant may open with the traditionally sensitive areas such as personal capital, management succession, life expectancy, ambitions for retirement etc. In more usual circumstances, these are areas that the consultant would prefer to leave until last.

Types of questions

In a well-ordered meeting, there should be more words spoken by the client, than by the consultant. It is difficult to be specific but the consultant should consider that he is doing well if the ratio is something like 15 to 1. If the ratio exceeds 20 to 1, he may be in some trouble – which we will consider later.

To achieve a favourable ratio, it is important to ensure that questions are structured in the right fashion, and in this respect they should be "open", rather than "closed". A closed question will invite a monosyllabic reply that merely confirms or denies a supposition made by the questioner in the framing of his enquiry.

These are examples of closed questions that could bring a single word response:

- Are you happy with your rate of staff turnover?
- Do you consider your expenditure on new equipment to be sufficient?
- Are your relations with your main suppliers satisfactory?

Whereas, the same topics approached through open and more complex questions will force the recipient to qualify his response, perhaps justify his view and so elicit more information. Thus:

- Does rising unemployment have an effect on staff turnover, and is this good or bad for your company?
- What is the underlying trend in new equipment investment?
- How long have you done business with your main supplier and what do they represent as a proportion of your total procurement?

Sometimes, a single question or even just the opening comments will unleash a torrent of information that may or may not be relevant. Either way the risk is information overload that could confuse the consultant and so prevent him from proffering help to what may be an already confused client. Drastic steps may be necessary to stem the flow, such as for the consultant to hold up his hands in front of him and to interrupt clearly and firmly with a statement such as:

" I am sorry, I wish to go back to (that point) which you just mentioned and ask the following..."

This should take the conversation back to a significant fact on which the consultant may wish to elaborate, and bring the client down to earth. Behaviour like this may seem drastic but the client with verbal diarrhoea can be as difficult as one who is tight-lipped. Sorting out what is relevant and important wheat will be essential for the consultant to do his work properly. Exceeding the 20 to 1 limit suggested above can be time wasting and confusing.

The number and content of possible questions that may be directed at a client is of course an infinite variable. However, in **Appendix D** we have drawn up a pro forma list of general enquiry categories and subject types within each that could be employed as a basis for framing focussed questions. Our health warning here is that the list is incomplete and is presented to suggest ways of structuring individual questions, or of following lines of enquiry. Also the list should NOT be used as a questionnaire; there is no quicker means of discouraging a client from frank discussions in a relaxed atmosphere.

Finally, there is always the case of the party who is deliberately terse and secretive in response to a direct question, and where a complete lack of information will prevent any progress being made at all. In this context one is reminded that for many years Rolls Royce Motors famously refused to disclose the rated brake horsepower of their products. Eventually, a customer reportedly had the temerity to ask a company executive what was the official bhp of his car, and received the comforting but uninformative reply "enough".

Three can be a crowd

So far we have considered meetings with a one-on-one format. Different disciplines may be needed if more people are involved, and this can be evident for example where the consultant is dealing with two or more principles in a partnership. Difficulties may be encountered if the probing nature of questions leads to trespassing on sore points that involve individual agendas or partnership disputes.

This situation may be frustrating as being time consuming, but it might also be informative. For example, in bickering and arguing, the partners may disclose unconsciously valuable information that can greatly assist the consultant in his task. Also, his presence may act as a catalyst to reactivate disputed, and so stalled, corporate strategies. He may ultimately be acknowledged by the partners as essential to a delayed process of re-organisation, which should enhance his earnings prospects.

Family relationships can also make the interview difficult, and it is sometimes hard to determine who exercises power and control, as well as complicating the conduct of the meeting.

Case 20. George established through his telesales efforts a contact with a firm of travel agents. His initial meeting was intended to promote a specific service, but with the hope of providing general consulting at a later stage. His appointment was with the Managing Director (who claimed to be the CEO) in his office. Just after the meeting commenced it was joined by an older gentleman who was introduced as the CEO's father and Chairman of the company. "Dad" took a seat at another desk immediately behind where George was sitting facing the MD.

The meeting went reasonably amicably, supposedly lead by the MD, who every so often referred to Dad for guidance. Dad would then lead the conversation for several minutes before allowing his son to continue. This was uncomfortable for George, as he had to keep reversing his seating position to keep abreast of the main thrust of the debate, and to maintain some form of appropriate eye contact. Also, it was readily apparent that the real powers of the CEO were effectively split between father and son, and that neither could function in a business debate without the presence of the other. As George was unable to convene a follow up meeting where both were present, the business opportunity failed for lack of a decision making quorum in the company's senior management team.

However, confused management responsibilities and dissent among peers can present opportunities for the skilled consulting practitioner and allow him to consolidate a valuable and effective advisory role.

Case 21. Matthew found himself in a business solicitation meeting with the three ageing joint owner-managers of an engineering company. While the business was fundamentally sound, problems were clearly emerging with management succession and in the difficulty that the three principals experienced in agreeing policy and so in forming any sort of recognisable business strategy.

By force of personality, Matthew was able to regulate what was threatening to become a confused and interminable debate by effectively refereeing the discussions. He insisted on each point of contention being hammered out and unanimously agreed before permitting the discussion to move on to the next topic. Having gained an agreement, Matthew resisted any attempt at backtracking i.e. each agreed stage represented a firm commitment from which to move on to the next point.

The meeting ran for about four hours, and was a painstaking and difficult process but at its conclusion, a way forward had been agreed that satisfied everyone and which could be clearly documented. Although the whole saga had been hard work, in a comparatively short space of time the presence of the consultant had been enough to help iron out several long standing areas of disagreement that would otherwise have festered on, doing nobody any good and threatening the business. This had been an exercise in consulting at its very best, and Matthew had deservedly won his mandate

Consultants working together to interview one or more client representatives concurrently can also present difficulties. Unless a high degree of sensitivity exists between the two consultants, a rigid pre-set level of discipline may be necessary to prevent one consultant from commencing a tangential series of questions which might destroy or interrupt a line of enquiry being pursued by his colleague.

Catch the hooks

Study of trainee consultants engaged in role playing exercises has consistently indicated a failure to pick up on facts and comments disclosed by the client which on cross-questioning could lead to further lines of enquiry and investigation. If these opportunities are overlooked in the comparatively relaxed and stress-free atmosphere of the training environment, it is reasonable to assume that they will be missed also in real life encounters with real clients.

In practise, once clients have warmed up they often prove willing to talk extensively about their businesses. After all in many SME's, the business is the creative life's work of the CEO and understandably he will be more than willing to talk about his achievements and to show off what he has built up.

This is a situation where the consultant should be careful in how many words he uses, relying mainly on succinct questions to direct the flow of information and to clarify points that are unclear. All too frequently the consultant is more concerned with what he is going to ask next than in listening closely to what is being said by the client. This can have a negative effect should the client sense that he is talking to someone who is not really concentrating on what is being said but is more interested in something else i.e. the content of the next question. Therefore being a good listener, and actively demonstrating this skill forms an essential part of effective communication.

Very often, what is being said can naturally point the way towards inconsistencies, unresolved issues, and unrecognised but impending problems where the consultant may have something of real value to offer. Termed "hooks", these are opportunities for the consultant to gain ground quickly as they may represent chinks in the client's armour. The ability to capitalise on a hook by identifying a pending problem and offering a way to an effective solution may present a ready means of building a fee producing relationship that much faster.

With practise the identification of hooks becomes progressively easier, and as the consultant becomes more accomplished in the collection and retention of information, he will be the better able to decide whether the hooks should be exploited immediately, or stored away for use at a later encounter.

Never is the value of extensive practise in role-playing and in real life better demonstrated than with hooks. So often they will lead to identification of real needs as the client perceives them, rather than what the consultant has in advance chosen to believe that the client requires.

Recording information

Good eye contact is essential to creating rapport, and this presents the consultant with something of an organisational problem. How to look the target in the eye and record information accurately and fully at the same time? The simple answer is do not try to do both, eye contact is more important.

This may seem tough but consider the matter from the client's angle. He needs to know that he can trust the consultant, and hence he needs to read the latter's expressions, and to receive the comfort that what he is saying is being treated with the respect he feels it deserves. This will not be possible if he finds himself talking to the top of a head as the consultant is bowed down taking voluminous notes. Also, he is likely to feel intimidated and less willing to be free with his words if he sees that everything he says is being noted down.

Obviously information has to be recorded in some manner but this should not be allowed to impede the flow of discussions. One way is to develop a memory that can retain a lot of facts but only for a short period. Then, after the conclusion of the meeting the information gathered is downloaded either to hand written notes, or is recorded on a dictaphone. There is only one way to learn this skill (which is not as difficult as it may first appear) and that is to try it for real.

A compromise between no notes and a verbatim account of what the client says is to use a small note pad perched on the knee. On this note pad is entered either brief bullet points regarding the main topics, or specifically significant statistics. The odd glance down to the pad as the bullet points are noted will not impede the information flow.

If it is apparent that a lot of information is being offered which cannot obviously be committed to memory e.g. detailed statistics, then the client should be asked if he objects to the consultant taking detailed notes on that topic. A return to good eye contact should be made as soon as possible.

Exercising the vernacular

The final aspect of behaviour in a meeting is the spoken word. In Chapter 12 we will talk about the importance of relating to and communicating with the client as contact develops and broadens over what will hopefully be the medium term. An important step in that direction is the opening client meeting when the consultant and the client mutually sound each other out and form preliminary judgements that may prove significant for the future.

What is said is important, but so also is how it is said. The management teams of SME's, including the CEO, are often self taught and their organisations reflect the results of years of hard, practical work. They are unlikely therefore to respond favourably to messages which smack of the theoretical or, worst of all, are couched in the management speak that reflects a business school education. This is not a denigration of MBA's; it is a reminder that so many of the sound principles that comprise that qualification need to be toned down and simplified to make them acceptable to the CEO who is wrestling with a myriad of real life stresses and problems. Management terms can be received as "power talking", and can be as disconcerting and intimidating as is "power dressing" – again to the detriment of the consultant's own mission.

The process of simplification should not be a matter of being patronising, but it should be a genuine effort to talk to the client in language that he will understand. It is the client who should set the tone and the standard, and the consultant should seek to match this. Put another way, the consultant is entitled to swear but only after the client has sworn first!

Closing

However well a meeting has gone, there often appears to be a marked tendency to allow it to fizzle out towards its close. It is pertinent to remind at this stage that the objective (see Chapter 9.) is to convene a business discussion with a view to securing business that will produce tangible benefit for the client, and real income for the consultant.

The temptation may be to shy away from gaining firm commitments from the target. This can often develop during the meeting rather than at its close. For example, discussion on a particular point (where the consultant may have missed some hooks) may conclude with the consultant saying something like: "perhaps I could look further into that some time?" or "do you have further information which you could provide for me later?" or "perhaps we could consider that at another meeting?"

What is happening is that the consultant is deferring a matter that is of immediate relevance. In so doing he dispels the sense of urgency, and undermines his own proposition that he is the right person to assist with immediate remedial action. In the interim, the client has been alerted to the issue and may initiate his own action without further reference to the consultant. Not only has the intellectual property been given away but also the chances of securing a fee-earning mandate have been substantially reduced.

If the client suggests or half way offers the availability of additional documentary information during a meeting, the consultant should ask for a copy there and then. If the client suggests that help may be needed in a certain area, then reference should be made back to this at the meeting's close and a commitment to action sought. If the client indicates possible interest in a specific service, then refer back to this before the end of the meeting and ask him to sign an engagement contract before leaving.

In closing the meeting it is vital that the consultant is in command. Having come to the end of discussions, he should ask "Where do we go from here?" and then proceed to answer his own question by listing the areas of mutual interest, and reiterating the benefits that a consultancy contract will bring.

There is nothing to be lost in asking the client to complete and sign a standard form engagement letter (see **Appendix A**), a blank copy of which the well prepared consultant will always have available.

If a signed contract is not immediately in prospect, there should at least be a stated series of follow-up actions, such as time and date of the next meeting, or date of the next telephone contact. Specific agreement should be sought on the next action by the consultant, not by the prospective client. A statement from the consultant such as "I will wait for you to call me back" is tantamount to acceptance that the contact will die because it must be assumed that the client will never keep the relationship alive on his own volition. That is the consultant's task.

The shop floor

Regardless of how the meeting has progressed, one further adjunct is to ask the CEO to show the consultant around the shop floor, if it is conveniently close to his office. This is an invaluable means of learning more about and understanding the business, and of seeing how the boss interacts with his subordinates. Usually the CEO is more than happy to show off his empire, and a genuine expression of interest will be a further means of consolidating a relationship that hopefully will already be showing signs of blossoming.

Improving interview techniques

There is no doubt that performance during an interview has a direct bearing on the results achieved. Accordingly, the more practise the better, and one way is to engage in role playing exercises before facing a potential client in a real business search. Role-playing is most effective where there is a third party present to observe the techniques adopted and to comment afterwards on shortcomings. In particular, practise is useful for identifying poorly phrased or structured questions, for providing guidance on how best to develop a line of enquiry, and to highlight hooks that might have been missed.

Another useful method of instruction is to follow discussions and interviews in the more serious radio and television debates. These can be instructive, particularly when the interviewer addresses penetrating questions to an evasive interviewee e.g. politician or trade union official.

However it is pursued, the achievement of competence in this area is important to enhance the client's attitude towards the consultant, and will have a beneficial effect upon the relationship.

Summary points

- *Question and answer is the core of the consultant-client meeting*
- *Practise eases recognition of opportunities divulged i.e. the hooks*
- *At meeting start, client is in control as he commands the information sought*
- *Consultant must win ground by proper interrogation*

Stages of privacy

- *Neutral questions are a good way to start*
- *Some subjects are intimate so retreat gracefully if questions seem offensive*
- *Be prepared to tackle sensitive issues later from another angle*

Types of questions

- *A 15-1 ratio of client to consultant words is a good target to aim at*
- *If client is too verbose, consultant must re-assert meeting direction*
- *Open and structured questions encourage informative responses*
- *Closed questions are more likely to induce monosyllabic answers*
- *Information categories: public domain, private, personal*
- *Information overload can confuse both consultant and client*
- *To re-assert control, re-start from earlier point in discussion*

Three can be a crowd

- *Consultants may have meetings with two or more partners*
- *Consultant might trespass on sore points of conflict between partners*
- *Argument might lead to disclosure unconsciously of valuable information*
- *Dissent among peers can affect advisory opportunities*
- *Two consultants working together must ensure they respect each other's ground*

Catch the hooks

- *Consultants fail to pick up comments which offer other lines of enquiry*
- *Consultant might be too focussed on next question to listen properly*
- *Client must feel that consultant is a good listener*
- *Client might accidentally reveal unresolved issues where the consultant can help*
- *Hooks are opportunities for the consultant to gain ground quickly*

Recording information

- *Good eye contact is essential to creating trust and rapport*
- *Eye contact is more important than immediate information recording*
- *If written notes are essential, restrict them to bullet points*
- *After the meeting, download information to notes or dictaphone*
- *Develop a memory that retains many facts for a short period*
- *If much data is being offered, consultant should ask permission to take full notes*

Exercising the vernacular

- *Talk to the client in language that he will understand.*
- *Avoid messages which sound theoretical or use management speak*

- *Clients are more interested in real problems than in untangling MBA-type terms*
- *Simplification process should not be patronising, but a real effort to communicate*

Closing

- *Seek to gain firm commitments from the target*
- *Never defer a matter that is of immediate relevance*
- *Deferral undermines proposition that consultant is the best help source*
- *If client suggests availability of written information, ask for copy now*
- *Nothing to be lost in asking client to sign an engagement letter*
- *If no immediate contract, advise before leaving the nature of the follow-up actions*

The shop floor

- *Regardless of meeting outcome, ask client for shop floor tour, if nearby*
- *Usually client is happy to oblige, and genuine interest will help relationship*

Improving interview techniques

- *Practise will improve interview techniques*
- *Use role playing exercises before facing a live potential client*
- *Study interview styles in more serious radio and television debates*

Chapter 11

Clients: where are they?

It has been estimated that in the United Kingdom, there are approximately 3.5 million active businesses in the small and medium sized sector with annual turnovers of £20 million or less. It has also been estimated that for every 100 businesses which start life in any one day, 98 or 99 will have radically changed their structure or will have failed, closed down or been sold within five years. On the basis of these broad statistics, there appear to be ample opportunities for the independent consultant.

However, despite the fact that SME's comprise an essential part of the total UK economy, the absolute number of potential clients is substantially less than these figures may tentatively suggest. Many enterprises are simply too small to be able to afford third party management consulting assistance (e.g. small retail establishments) or would not be naturally in need of this type of help (e.g. professional partnerships). Nonetheless, there remain a significant number of businesses that stand to benefit from advice and help from someone who has had corporate business experience.

Many of the SME's that flourish beyond their first five years retain the temperament and operating styles that suited their owner-managers at the time of their creation, despite the fact that success has resulted in an expanded business which may now be throttled by out-moded operating methods. Other businesses are in a fragile condition because they are run by entrepreneurs with vision and flair but whose general management skills are wanting. Still others that were created on a conceptually sound basis may fail to change radically and quickly enough to match evolving market conditions.

The evidence consistently indicates that many SME's are failing to realise their full profit potential or are failing to earn sufficient profits to sustain themselves in the long term. Many face problems, the solution to which does not necessarily require the application of rocket science, significant new capital or recruitment of additional personnel.

Often the answer lies in the re-organisation or modest augmentation of existing resources. Often incumbent managers sit too close to their problems, and may have re-configured themselves to meet the demands of their environments, rather than to modify their surroundings to satisfy their needs. It is in this arena that the independent consultant has so much to offer. He can form part of the cascade of skills no longer needed in the large corporate world, but which up until now elements of the SME sector may not have been able to afford.

In this chapter we will look at ways of finding the SME client, and in the next we will consider how to deliver real value to him, and thus earn an acceptable consulting fee in return.

Beware the "natural market"

Anyone who has spent some years in business and who has achieved a reasonable level of seniority will have established for himself what we refer to as a "natural market". This consists of a circle of friends and acquaintances built up through the normal flow of social contact associated with representation of one's employer, and through mixing socially in connection with work. The natural market will comprise past and present working colleagues, clients, competitors, business associates plus other people encountered at the golf club, or on the cocktail party and business convention circuits.

This range of contacts is built on friendship, esteem and respect, and it can be a rich source of help at the point at which one's life is changing from the predictability of salaried employment to the uncertainty of self-employment. This watershed will differentiate the true friends from those who had valued the acquaintance on the basis of what it could do for them.

It is common for those true friends to offer tangible advice and assistance, and included may be the offer of short term consulting contracts. These offers should never be rejected because they are a valuable prop to what may be wounded self-esteem and damaged pride at a traumatic period.

Nevertheless, there are significant limits to what one's natural market can provide. Those kind offers from friends may comprise partly an acknowledgement and thanks for past services and help, plus an expression of sympathy. However, the services sought of the independent consultant thus newly formed are more reflective of what he once was rather than what he is about to become. It may have been recognised that accumulated influence and knowledge has an immediate economic value, and that this should be procured while it is still fresh.

The trap that the natural market presents is a belief that this marketability is sustainable, and that it is a genuine reflection of one's ability to attract continuous work in this newly acquired freelance status. The reality is that everyone's natural market is finite in terms of both time and earnings power. It is hard to be specific about earnings levels but as a general rule, it should be good for about 12 months of contractual opportunities. We have heard of people who have enjoyed up to five years of a full work schedule through exploitation of their natural markets but these have been exceptional cases, driven by unusual knowledge and expertise, or through unique market circumstances.

The key warning note is that everyone's natural market wears out eventually, and it is recommended that this be pre-empted by attention to a program of self-training and development as advocated in these pages.

The ex-employee as consultant

There is a tendency with some organisations to announce large-scale de-manning programs with less-publicised concurrent re-engagement of selected personnel as consultants from among those redundancies. Under present conditions, no doubt stability in some salaried employment may be almost as uncertain as consulting work. However, it would be a delusion to believe that a consultant created under these circumstances would be any better equipped to engage in independent work once the contract with his ex-employer expires.

In fact, a misleading belief may result about the ability to find work, and while the cushion of the natural market may still await, the need for a program of re-training etc. will remain.

Client search: the importance of generalism

Many SME's operate with slim budgets for any unusual type of expenditure, and may be reluctant to consider engaging a consultant who offers a specialised service and who has little capacity to provide anything beyond that. It is often the case that the smaller business, perceiving a pressing problem that lies outside the scope of its immediate skills and experience, will resort to tried and tested sources of help.

For example, a problem deriving from changes in compliance standards or new employment legislation is more likely to cause a referral to the local chamber of commerce, than an approach to a specialist in the relative field. In turn, the chamber may levy a modest charge for attendance at a specialist seminar or for provision of the services of an advisory unit. The chamber's own publications may also provide as a service to its members, information about the prevailing issue in which case the assistance from that source is likely to be regarded as virtually free.

By comparison, to use a consultant can be viewed as an exotic and expensive course, with uncertainty over the quality of the results and a residing doubt about value for money, unless the problem is so large and complex as to make recourse to outside expert help inevitable.

For these general reasons, we hold the view that the independent consultant should not risk sole reliance on his specialities for his income. It may be feasible to lay emphasis on specialist skills as an introductory gambit, but he should be trained and prepared to respond to a broad range of matters that the prospective client may choose to raise.

It follows that as a generalist he should be prepared to tackle any challenge thrown his way, and to refer matters outside his range of expertise to suitably qualified consultant colleagues through collaboration agreements and, where stipulated by the client, under the umbrella of a confidentiality agreement.

Determination to develop as a generalist can have pleasing and stimulating results. Experience of different industries and companies should result in an exponential growth in knowledge. This in turn will lead to greater self-confidence and assurance, and to an enhanced ability to ask sensible and penetrating questions of the clientele.

It is noteworthy how clients can respond more favourably to enquiries from someone who is a layman but who is obviously to some extent informed on the types of problems that the client habitually encounters. Clients do like to share their problems with someone they feel they can trust, who is genuinely interested, and who wants to learn more. Equally, clients can readily detect the layman who pretends to be an expert, with predictable results for the relationship.

At the end of the day, this is an area in which the consultant has very little choice; he really has to address issues as a generalist, as an integral part of his continuing program of self-education and development.

Defining the market geographically

The local approach: Assuming that the decision has been taken on a generalist course, the next issue is to define the market, principally in terms of geography. It is preferable wherever possible to select a specific area - say within a ten-mile radius of one's home. This may sound modest but there are good reasons for being so selective.

Firstly, by concentrating on pursuing business close at hand, travel and time costs are minimised. Secondly, many SME's service market sectors on a parochial basis and the independent consultant tends to do better in his marketing if he similarly localises his promotional efforts – this will be reviewed later when we discuss networking and affinity marketing. Thirdly, careful study and investigation should reveal a surprising number of candidate SME's quite close at hand.

On this latter point, it should be noted even in locations that would normally be considered as predominantly residential, there is invariably an infrastructure of locally based service and manufacturing companies. Many of these organisations are hidden away in side streets in town centres, or are found on purpose designed industrial estates intended for small companies and light industry.

Another factor that favours a localised geographic segmentation of the market is that this will help to build up a store of local knowledge, and improve the chances of new business referrals from existing clients. In situations that are non-competitive, clients may be happy to recommend the consultant's services to their trading partners. It is possible to augment this process of cross-referral by participating actively in the affairs of local associations – for example the chamber of commerce.

The national approach: There is growing evidence that independent consultants can successfully find work by promoting their services through the Internet, which appears to be far more efficient than the costly and less measurable means of printed media advertising. We are aware of one consultant who has established a Web Page and is receiving over one hundred enquiries ("hits") per week. While a large number of these are either time wasters or of no commercial value, a significant core of genuine enquiries does result. This consultant is able to achieve this level of response because he promotes at least two specialised services of topical interest, in addition to his general consulting activities.

Promotion through the World Wide Web of course means promotion on a national, if not global, scale and thus is the antithesis of the localised posture described above. However, this can be an effective weapon in cost management, as reviewed in Chapter 7. Provided that there is a willingness to travel for work, and to spend perhaps prolonged periods away from home, a Web Page may be a simple but powerful means of finding suitable clients.

Building a database

Returning to the theme of a localised marketing effort, it is important to build up a database of target names within the pre-determined geographic limits. Time and effort expended in this exercise is thoroughly worthwhile, as the process of search and of recording names will help to build a fuller picture of what is going on locally. Database preparation is not difficult but it takes time.

There is a plethora of information sources readily to hand and in the spirit of cost recognition, virtually the only expense in searching through them is the consultant's own time. Every home receives a copy of the Yellow Pages and sometimes other trade telephone directories, and although it may sound a daunting task, it is quite possible to plough through and record the name, address, telephone number and declared activity of potential targets

Local newspapers and free press are invaluable information sources in that they often have something to say about local businesses that are expanding or contracting, or are in the process of being established. The appearance of a newspaper article can almost be treated as a direct invitation to make contact. After all, someone (usually the CEO) is keen to talk openly about himself and his business, and he wants the world to listen. A telephone approach is worth trying along the lines of "I was fascinated to read about your company in the recent article in *The Chronicle*. You are engaged in activities which are of real interest to me, and I wonder if you could spare the time to meet and tell me more….."

Not only are direct announcements and articles relevant, but also the classified employment advertisements will indicate organisations which are expanding and seeking new staff. The consultant is always interested in the process of change and the local printed press can be an excellent means of monitoring this phenomenon.

If further research is felt necessary, then the reference section of the local lending library should be well stocked with the latest editions of the standard business directories. Several of these are segmented geographically, and this feature will greatly assist the tedious but valuable process of searching out those businesses located within the immediate vicinity. If there is an interest in searching for suitable targets on an industry wide scale rather than simply locally, then once again these business directories can meet the search criteria.

The actual process of recording the information gathered is a straightforward task with a personal computer. It is nonetheless essential that care be taken to keep the information contained therein up-to-date. Thus the database should be treated as an ever-expanding reference source in daily use. Active consulting creates an exponential growth in the flow of information, some for immediate use, but a lot of which is stored away for later reference. For example, in talking to one client the consultant may pick up gossip and speculation about another company in the market area. This should be entered against the appropriate name in the database for later possible use in developing new business in that quarter. An example of a database appears in **Appendix F**.

Collection and storage of market intelligence is continuous and so important that a fixed part of the daily or weekly routine should be allocated to conducting the task properly. Much of the information may have to be filed for later use, and experience soon shows how important it is to devise a filing system that actually works. When information has to be recovered quickly, it often proves to be elusive unless a disciplined approach has been adopted.

Sales promotion: telephone selling (or telesales)

Having committed resources to market definition and to creation of the database, the issue arises of how to set about finding suitable clients. A popular method is to undertake a program of telephone selling, a process that fills many new consultants with trepidation.

The idea of telephoning a total stranger to sell a service or to set up a meeting to sell a service is understandably anathema to many people, unless they have had direct training in and experience of sales. It is a great pity that selling seems to be so often unfairly downplayed by many businessmen. This is evident in the efforts taken to label oneself anything but a "salesman", resulting in titles such as "business development executive", "customer relations manager" and "marketing executive". The latter is particularly dangerous in helping to fuel continuing confusion between marketing and sales, a lack of distinction that can cause difficulties for many businesses. Even in consulting, the term telemarketing is used when the proper term should be teleselling.

If selling as an activity had a more prestigious reputation then perhaps consultants would have less difficulty in telesales. Nevertheless, with good preparation and practise, selling by telephone can be successful and satisfying, as well as being a relatively low cost means of finding clients. A well-planned telesales campaign should involve the following:

1. Review the product or service that will be promoted. Identify its main competitive advantages, and calculate what typical benefits will derive from its successful implementation. Identify also how it may replace or improve upon any existing facilities that the target client may be currently employing. Set out the key features and benefits in a purpose designed brochure or flyer. The artwork may be prepared by use of the PC, or it may be necessary to refer to a local printing firm for assistance.

2. Study the market database and flag those names that by their declared activities would appear to be possible users of the service on offer. If the details are not already on the database, telephone the client and ask for the CEO's name.

3. It is quite likely that the target list of names has been approached in telesales campaigns for other services. Typically campaigns start at the letter "A" but some fizzle out at some point in the alphabet. There is thus a statistical possibility that names later in the alphabet will have been canvassed less frequently and will therefore put up less sales resistance. To counter this effect, other campaigns may well have worked backward from "Z". We have the view that the best results are possible by starting at "M" and working backward and forward from that point!

4. Through the mail merge function on the PC, prepare and despatch a solicitation letter addressed personally to the CEO, with the brochure or flyer attached. Never address the letter to the "Managing Director" or the "General Manager"; always target a named individual. The letter should be short and concise. It should clearly identify what is being offered, what benefits can result, and it should conclude with a mention that the consultant will telephone shortly in follow up.

5. Allow an interval of say five business days after despatch and then telephone the CEO. If the receptionist or secretary (the "gatekeeper") refuses to make the connection, or wishes to know what the call is about, explain politely that it is in relation to correspondence entered with the CEO. Sometimes even this does not work, so it is worth trying to phone before 9 a.m. or after 5 p.m. as the boss often works longer hours than does his gatekeeper.

6. Once actually speaking to the CEO, briefly remind him of the letter and its contents, and once again emphasise in a few words the benefits on offer. The tone of voice should imply warmth and commitment, without appearing either "glossy" or over-enthusiastic. The actual structure and content of the words to be used are a matter of personal choice; adopt whatever terminology is natural and comfortable to use. Remember that the mission is briefly to describe what is on offer so as to capture the recipient's interest to the point where he agrees to a meeting.

7. The target may claim that he has not received the original letter in which case advise that you will send a replacement and call him again at a specified time and date – thereby maintaining a measure of control on development of the relationship.

   Another response may be to ask for further details there and then; keep the explanation brief, and re-emphasise that a meeting would be preferable to explain further. Sometimes the nature of the offer is misunderstood and if this is apparent, the need for a meeting will be all the more important.

Sometimes, the target will seek merely to defer the matter, in which case advise that you will make a further contact at a specified future time e.g. two weeks forward and diarise to act accordingly.

8. In the majority of cases, the target will refuse to take the matter any further and that will be the end of the contact. It is easy to get downhearted when efforts to promote a service that could bring real benefit are rejected out of hand. However, it should be remembered that unless the consultant takes the initiative, the chances of doing business are that much reduced. Also, persistence and practise will improve one's technique and confidence in telephone selling, which is a significant factor in achieving better response rates.

9. Where the mailing effort and the telephone call does secure an appointment, all the principles of meeting preparation and interview techniques as described in Chapters 9 and 10 should be employed.

10. During the interview, the first topic for discussion will obviously be the service that was promoted by mailshot and telephone call. However, if the consultant is intent on pursuing a more general relationship with the target client, he should ensure at the appropriate point that the service is set within the context of the full range of facilities that he has to offer.

The search for clients through mailing and telesales programs is, like much of successful consulting, quite hard work. With experience, rejections are accepted as an inevitable component to the whole process, but there is no doubt that success when it does come more than makes up for the disappointments.

Also, experience shows that many fruitful and beneficial consultant-client relationships start out in this fashion. In the next Chapter, we will be reviewing how such relationships are nurtured and expanded.

Sales deriving from affinity marketing programs

Although telesales can be very successful in the hands of prepared and experienced operators, it cannot be denied that there is an element of roulette in this form of approach. Also it is not wise to rely on a single method for finding new clients, and the main alternative way is to operate an affinity marketing program.

Starting once again with the database, it is recommended that an analysis be conducted of what activities predominate on the local commercial and industrial scene. For example in the Birmingham area, traditionally metal working in its various forms and components manufacture for motor vehicles have formed two important elements to industry. Reference to relative trade magazines (perhaps available in the local library) will reveal the main industry players, those where major changes are occurring, and the identity of representative trade associations.

Having some understanding of the industry structure in this fashion, a contact program with the officers of trade associations may prove beneficial. Often they will have a more objective view of what is happening on a broad strategic front in their industry sector, and they will welcome the interest of independent advisors who could help solve pressing problems for their membership.

In some circumstances, associate membership may be available, or a list of members forthcoming, or it may be possible to attend, and even better speak at members' meetings. Being involved and showing interest in this fashion will help develop an affinity relationship with the association, and with its membership. This can lead to the consultant gaining recognition and a profile that will reflect well on his reputation, get him talked about, and lead to business referrals.

Taking on board the concept of affinity, it will be apparent that it can be pursued in a number of other ways. Chambers of commerce can be an excellent source of contacts and of introductions. Better-run chambers will produce comprehensive and informative directories of members. Contact with the chamber's officers is recommended, and if the consultant has a unique or topical service to offer, he should consider writing a descriptive article for publication in the chamber's journal.

Chambers typically conduct a program of dinners, lunches and cocktail parties for the purpose of bringing people in business together to generate more business. An excellent innovation is the marketing breakfast where for a nominal sum, one is invited to sell one's products and services to a small group of often complete strangers, or perhaps to the assembled company at large. Two or three minutes' hard sell of what one has to offer to a group of one or two hundred business people for a nominal cost can be an excellent means of self-promotion.

In the follow-up attempt to secure a meeting with a target there is the starting point of the nature of the affinity i.e. mutual membership of or involvement with the relative representative body. This is an effective means of breaking the ice and of establishing a platform from which to move on to specific matters of business interest.

There is also an important and beneficial spin-off to affinity activities for the consultant, which relates to remaining "in touch". Consulting can be a lonely existence with client contact on a one-to-one basis, and with long hours working in solitude. All this may be very different from the social aspects of working conditions in corporate life. Hence the opportunity to mix socially with other business people at these functions is a welcome antidote to the hermit life, as well as being an informative and educational pastime.

Third party promotion

This is a variation on affinity marketing and sales techniques, and relies on third party introductions. Being a more passive means of promotion, the results are likely to be less directly measurable as once contact is established, any resultant business opportunities depend entirely on the goodwill and judgement of the intermediary. Nevertheless, the same broad principles of developing a market profile obtain.

Basically, the technique relies on the development of relationships with members of those professions who provide services in their specific fields to potential clients who fall within the parameters of consultant's own database. Introductory meetings are sought with the principals of the relevant firms at which the specific and general services available are described, and where possible are supported by distribution of relevant literature.

Business referrals rely on those principals identifying clients' problems where they have no immediate expertise or where it would be unethical for them to offer help and advice. For example, an Independent Financial Advisor (IFA) is regulated regarding what advice he may proffer, and he may refer to an independent consultant if he encounters issues outside his legal remit.

Similarly, accountants or lawyers may become aware of business clients who are in need of help in a specific area, e.g. cost reduction, and a referral to a consultant who had made his skills and capacities known in this area could result. In such situations, the lawyer or accountant would take measures to respect the client's confidentiality and interests, and of course the consultant must act similarly with competence and professionalism.

Self-education

An area for business opportunity search that is often overlooked relates to self-education. In corporate life, business education is often endemic and taken for granted because the employer conducts continuous training programs to ensure that employees are informed of technical and commercial developments. Once on the "outside", access to this support ceases and there is a risk that the independent consultant's knowledge will age and become obsolete quite rapidly. There is thus a concomitant need to remain up-to-date with important changes in one's chosen disciplines.

Self-education is therefore important and may be best achieved by reviving participative membership in professional bodies. Their meetings and publications provide ways of staying informed on key changes, as well as maintaining one's profile with people who may lead to business referrals.

This process of self-education has also been exploited by innovative consultants in expanding their skills base into new areas, and thus enabling them to promote services on a broader front. This has been particularly evident in the field of compliance auditing (e.g. ISO 9000, EMU, Millennium, and with employment law). In a world of burgeoning regulation, this can be a valuable area for consultants to develop.

Balancing the work demands

The foregoing identifies that successful consulting relies heavily upon a number of differing promotional techniques, and skill is necessary in ensuring that a reasonable balance is maintained between searching for new clients, and executing the mandates of existing clients. Generically and collectively known as "networking", the methods outlined above should ideally be pursued in equal measure but not so intensely as to threaten contracted client deadlines. Consulting is an iterative activity with some contracts drawing to close as others are in the early stages of execution. There will always remain the need to search for the opportunities that have yet to crystallise into income producing relationships.

This chapter should have shown that the opportunities are limitless, and that if the target client list has been fully expended (a most unlikely event), then opportunity lies in its expansion or in starting the promotional effort all over again with the same names. In any event, the fully committed professionally orientated independent consultant can never claim that he has nothing to do!

Summary points

- *3.5 million active SME's with annual turnover below £20 million*
- *98/ 99 out of 100 new businesses change radically within 5 years*
- *Many enterprises are too small to afford consulting assistance*
- *Many SME's fail to realise profit potential or to earn enough for long term needs*

Beware of the "natural market"

- *Comprises past colleagues, clients, business associates etc*
- *Significant limitations on what natural market has to offer*
- *Marketability is not sustainable solely from this source*
- *Natural market is finite, hence need for self-development program*

The ex-employee as consultant

- *Some organisations re-engage redundant personnel as consultants*
- *These people are not adequately equipped for independent consulting work through this experience*

Client search: the importance of generalism

- *Need for consultant is usually driven by complexity of problems*
- *Consultant should not rely solely on his specialities for his income*

Defining the market geographically

The local approach:
- *Preferable to select a modest area close to one's own home*
- *Travel and time costs are minimised*
- *Many SME's serve parochial markets*
- *Investigation should reveal many candidate SME's close at hand*
- *Good local knowledge improves chances of local new business*

The national approach
- *Work may be found by promoting services through the Internet*
- *The World Wide Web is effective in minimising promotion costs*
- *May lead to work away from home over long periods*

Building a database

- *Important to have a database of targets in pre-determined area*
- *Local newspapers/ free press are invaluable information sources*
- *Database should be an expanding reference source in daily use*
- *A fixed routine is needed to conduct this task properly*

Sales promotion: telesales

- *Review the product or service to be promoted*
- *Study market database for possible users of the service*
- *Dispatch solicitation letter to the CEO with brochure attached*
- *Allow 5 business days after dispatch, then telephone the CEO*
- *Remind CEO of letter and try to arrange a second contact*
- *Often target will not take the matter further, ending the contact*
- *When appointment fixed, apply best practises for meetings*

Sales deriving from affinity marketing programs

- *Do not rely on a single method for finding new clients*
- *One method is to operate an affinity marketing program*
- *Concentrate on activities predominant in business scene*
- *Establish affinity through relative representative bodies*

Third party promotion

- *Relies heavily on third party introductions and is unpredictable*
- *Uses mainly contact with professions which provide services to potential clients*

Self-education

- *Consultant risks his knowledge rapidly becoming obsolete*
- *Need to remain up-to-date with changes in chosen disciplines*

Balancing the work demands

- *Need for balance between new client search and execution of existing mandates*

Chapter 12

Consulting is about building relationships

Independent consulting is a personalised activity in which success relies on the ability to establish a working relationship with the client on a one-to-one basis. For the independent consultant, this will usually be with the CEO of an SME i.e. a company with an annual turnover of £20 million or less.

Many consultants have spent some part of their earlier career in large corporate organisations where a figure of £20 million might represent the annual turnover of a branch, department or division, and where the group's consolidated trading figures were substantially larger. The temptation can be strong to downplay the importance of the issues facing an SME because the numbers are so much smaller, and also because the business is likely to be structurally simpler in its operational activities and its administration.

It is easy (and the authors have made this mistake more than once in consulting practise) to listen to a prospective client's list of woes and to make a mental, or even worse a verbal, comparison. For example, the consultant in his previous corporate career may have achieved a management level where he was responsible for more people and a larger set of business figures than are engaged in the SME that he is now studying. Against that background, he may feel that the issues are trivial, and that solutions are easy to identify and implement – if only the client is willing to "gear up" to the consultant's level of thought and analysis.

Of course, the reality of the situation demands the reverse. While a successful relationship should result in improvements in the way the business is run, the establishment of a credible dialogue will require far more adjustment (or "gearing down") on the part of the consultant.

What is faced in many situations is a culture clash, and it is the consultant who should yield ground to enable effective communication to take place.

Initial obstacles

Having decided to seek assistance, the client may in the early stages get cold feet about the nature of the commitment that he is taking on. Practise has shown that clients commonly express concern about a business problem, and expect the consultant to wave a magic wand and to put in place a quick fix with minimal disruption to the business at large.

What the client has identified very often are the symptoms, or the effect of the problem rather than its cause. Thus the quick fix may provide temporary relief only to allow the undisturbed cause to manifest itself in another part of the business later. When it becomes apparent that rather more is involved in terms of investigation, re-organisation and so forth, the client may well try to convince himself that the exercise is not as necessary as first thought, and that cancellation or deferment is preferable.

Another difficulty can arise because the client is reluctant to disclose information in the depth that the consultant requires. He may feel that the enquiries are too intrusive on areas that he regards as either private or personal. He may have concerns that the information divulged might be unwittingly disclosed to outside parties to the detriment of the business. He may object that the recovery of the information will be too difficult or time consuming. Because he is ignorant of certain modern management techniques and standards, he may simply fail to understand the need for the information and thus be reluctant to co-operate.

Some CEO's are naturally bad communicators, or through a lifetime in sole command of their businesses are not accustomed to sharing their knowledge with peers, much less outsiders. Another problem may arise through the expectation that the consultant should match or at least complement the CEO's own level of technical knowledge about what the company produces. It may be felt that technical ignorance disqualifies the consultant from being competent to do the job.

Another difficulty arises where there is delayed or slow response to requests for written or verbal information, due to business pressures. This can produce problems with discontinuity and with data that is confusing or apparently contradictory, which may lead to annoyance in the process of re-validation and counter-questioning.

The prime source of information will always be the CEO, as it is he who has the prime authority in the business. However, where the information flow is too slow or in some other way unsatisfactory, recourse may be necessary to other members of the management team. Such action may be fraught with problems and should only be attempted with the knowledge and concurrence of the CEO. At a later stage when a broad basis of trust has been established, enquiries on a wide front throughout the company may be quite acceptable but it should not be attempted too early.

Having gained acceptance that discussion with subordinates may take place, it is wise for the consultant to insist on a regular program of short briefings with the CEO – say at the end of each day – to advise him of the nature and content of the meetings. SME's are prone to internal conflicts and disagreements as much as are large companies and the risk is great that the consultant may be drawn in to take sides. Certainly, if the CEO at any time suspects that the consultant is going behind his back, or withholding information divulged by subordinates, the future and security of the relationship may be jeopardised.

Where it is essential and agreed that the consultant must talk to a number of different personnel, it is not unusual for a CEO who feels insecure to rely on a stool pigeon to keep him informed of the nature and extent of the discussions. Thus regardless of how comparatively more friendly or co-operative some of the subordinates may seem, the consultant should never forget that his mandate stems from the CEO to whom he owes the prime loyalty of frankness and honesty.

Every company and every CEO is of course unique and the consultant's style and approach should be adjusted and adapted to get the best out of each situation. It can be assumed however, that in virtually every case the CEO will underestimate the amount of information that is needed and the length of time its assembly will take. It can be anticipated that he will often underestimate the nature and complexity of the problems to be analysed. Accordingly he will expect neatness and completeness in solutions within unrealistic time frames, and this could frustrate the development of a proper working relationship.

Circumstances may dictate the need to work with incomplete data, thus necessitating a process of interpolation, estimation or just guess work. This may be unsatisfactory and the consultant should make it clear that resultant recommendations are limited by contingencies stemming from insufficient tools to do a full job.

The importance of history

If the early stages are hampered through inadequate information, the adoption of a tangential approach may be worth trying whereby the CEO is encouraged to describe the history of his company, rather than immediately concentrating on the current situation. In the long run this may consolidate a position from which good advice can be disseminated.

In many cases, the business will have been created by the CEO himself or by a member of his family – perhaps an earlier generation – and for good or bad, his mark will have been indelibly inscribed upon the company. Often he has some difficulty in distinguishing between himself and the enterprise for which he is responsible and thus in hearing about the history of the business, one will learn much about the nature of the man himself.

This process of learning the history is invaluable. It very often quickly identifies strengths and weaknesses in the man and in the business, and because habit and tradition often play an important part, it will be apparent how experience has fashioned the development of the enterprise.

Most CEO's are happy to talk about the past because it reflects what they perceive as the key ingredients of their personal triumphs and successes. When discussing history in this fashion, it may be important to say very little and to allow the client to exceed the notional 15 to 1 rule about exchange of words, to which we referred in

Chapter 10 when considering interview techniques. In a way, this is a process not dissimilar to the phenomenon of "self-unveiling", which is what the ego wall in the CEO's office is all about.

This delving into history will also be informative about the good and bad management habits that the CEO has built up. It may be tempting to criticise the CEO who is of the second or third generation of a family that has owned a business for having had a silver spoon in his mouth. Having identified this however, it may be apparent that he deserves sympathy for being beset with problems stemming from the curse of a burdened legacy, or from a narrow background of training and experience, or from family circumstance that restricts the institution of radical change.

Knowledge of the history gives an essential insight into how the whole enterprise started, the original investment rationale, and subsequent changes. The consultant is not yet at the point where he can form balanced and informed judgements about what should be done next, but he will have gained an understanding of the "why" of it all. Also, he will better appreciate how the institutionalisation of the business has developed, and from that he should be sensitive to those aspects that will be considered sacrosanct.

This may seem a quaint term but however much a CEO may subscribe to the urgency for radical reform, there will always be part of the business that he will think of as being a constant. It may be an operating practise or a product that has become time-honoured, or it may be a pet project or activity that he has sponsored. Whatever it is, human nature will have ensured that there will always be some aspect of the undertaking that is considered immutable, but which may have an unhealthy appetite for capital, expertise, time or some other scarce resource that could be more productively applied elsewhere.

Becoming well informed on the history will be instructive about the size and nature of these sacred corporate cows. Unless they are so problematic and so substantial that they threaten the immediate viability of the enterprise, they are better left in peace until a later stage in the evolvement of the relationship when it may be more tactful, and productive to consider their elimination or re-deployment.

It is fascinating how these distractions can develop. Time and again, it is apparent that some quite abstract or disconnected activities are inserted into the mainstream of a company's business. Their presence has no immediately apparent logic, and no synergy results. It is only an understanding of the history of the business that will show why they are there, and also indicate how valued they are by the owner/ manager.

Case 22. Tony developed a useful and fruitful consulting relationship with a medium sized company in a European country. The business was traditional in its policy and outlook, profitable and well run. The amount of consulting help that the company needed was limited, given the stability of market circumstances and the management competence.

The composition of the company's trading turnover was unusual. Some 80% comprised the importation and distribution of whisky and other alcoholic spirits. This was a competitive business sector with trading margins under pressure. There was a continuing need to ensure that the right mix of manufacturer representation was maintained, and that promotional and advertising policies would ensure retention of market share. The resource base of this part of the business required good warehouse facilities, state-of-the-art stock control systems, a good marketing strategy and a sound selling team.

The remaining 20% of turnover was attributable to the printing of high quality labels for use on consumer items e.g. small cosmetic bottles, pharmaceutical products, home care products, foods and beverages containers. Some of the production runs were limited but the demand for accuracy and good printing quality was critical because the end consumer product sold into premium market sectors. Print runs were invariably bespoke and the company enjoyed a virtual supply monopoly within its geographic market sector. The resource base involved a large team of specially trained printers who operated modern, sophisticated production line type printing machines.

How and why did two such disparate activities come to live together under the same roof? Enquiries into the history of the company revealed that in times past, governmental fiscal and monetary policies had traditionally been more benign for manufacturing industry at the expense of import-driven trading activities. Thus expansion of the alcohol distribution business had been helped by bank finance theoretically provided to aid the diversification into printing. Also, and perhaps more importantly, the CEO had a deep love of machinery and engineering. It was almost his hobby to involve himself whenever time permitted in what was happening in the printing repair workshop where the mechanics maintained the production line equipment.

It was apparent that the printing business took up the lion's share of the company's resources, but generated a minority of the trading turnover. It was a largely self-contained business that could be quite logically sold for a handsome price. However this was only a theoretical possibility in view of the CEO's personal attachment, and fortunately the question never had to be addressed because the overall operation was profitable and well managed.

There is a further valuable aspect to the study of client history and this relates to evaluation of the corporate memory. We have discussed elsewhere the significance of this facet of a business which is a rather obscure asset, comprising knowledge procured at a practical operating level about customers and their demands, about market traits, and about operational and administrative curiosities.

The temptation may exist to copy the modern practises of large organisations to jettison the custodians of the corporate memory in favour of younger replacements who are armed with contemporary, even "scientific" skills. Recognition and retention of those resources connected to corporate memory may be an important element in the consultant's task. An understanding of the history of the business will greatly assist in this important aim.

Worth recognition

Regardless of how strong or well managed is an enterprise, there never has been a perfect business that could not stand improvement by engaging the services of an outside agent or advisor. Whether a newcomer whose opinions may be influenced by previous corporate employment, or a hardened practitioner who has had substantial experience, the consultant usually has little difficulty in identifying aspects of a business that require attention. In fact, the identification of serious shortcomings may be so easy that a quite unbalanced view of underlying stability and soundness may result.

It is therefore important to ensure that the search for problem areas be complemented by due acknowledgement of the organisation's strong points. These are important because the independent consultant should be practically orientated i.e. an advisor who not only makes creative and valuable suggestions, but also ones that can be feasibly and reasonably implemented. There is little sense in marshalling a whole series of proposals that look theoretically splendid but lack the wherewithal to carry them out. The consultant has to work with the tools at the client's disposal, or which the client can reasonably acquire, and hence recognition of worth within the enterprise is an essential ingredient to consulting.

The actual principles of effective corporate analysis, particularly in the SME sector, comprise a topic for a separate consideration and review. However, there are broad areas which need to be considered here, and which play an important role in the process of building a sound working relationship with the client.

The CEO's leadership qualities: The chief executives of smaller companies tend not to practise management skills, or to have been educated in them, in the technocratic sense that is associated with the work of Business Schools. In the modern management terms and methods that typify larger and more formalised business undertakings it is quite usual to find the CEO of an SME to be deficient in these disciplines.

On the other hand, it is more than likely that he will display qualities of business *leadership* to a degree that would be unusual elsewhere. Here again the knowledge of the history of the business is so helpful. Many successful SME's have sprung from humble origins that the CEO is not embarrassed to describe. It may be he, or his father, or grandfather who started matters in a shed in the garden, or a rented railway arch, or similar. The story of growth and survival may well be an epic, and in any event will be an unusual one when compared with the high number of SME's that do not survive, much less succeed.

To have brought the company to its present condition will have been a major achievement in itself, and hardly due to modern management systems. It will have been a story based on above-average business leadership entailing not only long working hours but also personal risk in the commitment of private wealth through guarantees and/ or mortgage of private assets.

Recognition of this commitment level is important because time and again the leader of an SME will have proportionally much more personally at stake in the continuity of his employment than will many of his large corporate counterparts.

Further, this commitment will also entail other responsibilities that are rare in the corporate world. The CEO occupies a position of *command* in a way that is uncommon in the mutually protective corporate world of committees, organograms, divisional management structures and so forth. The CEO is the boss and employees, customers and others will all hold him virtually totally accountable if things go wrong.

He may prefer to be a specialist, and the burdens he carries may encourage him to retreat to the familiar i.e. to focus on those matters that he likes and understands, and to ignore issues with which he feels less comfortable. Regardless of how well or badly he manages the totality of the enterprise, the all-embracing nature of his responsibility nevertheless remains clear and unbridled.

Thus while it may be easy to criticise his shortcomings, the CEO will nonetheless have demonstrated significant leadership qualities. Those energies supported by whatever skills and assistance he needs from his consultant may combine to provide a potent formula for success and progress.

The management team: SME's often have the appearance of autocracies with all authority and inspiration stemming from the man at the top. Certainly an organisation chart usually implies such a situation, but the reality may be slightly different. SME's are often characterised by significant staff loyalty, and by substantial respect for the boss in a paternalistic family-like situation. Additionally, it is not unusual for substantive authority to be exercised lower down the command chain to a greater degree than might be implied by the modest job titles of those concerned. They may feel that they belong to and identify with the company in a special way. Thus they find it natural to commit something extra to its continued well being, beyond that which might usually be expected of their position and ostensible seniority.

Also, lack of formal business training, or of promotion prospects does not necessarily mean that there is a lack of potential. One of the exciting things about consulting to SME's with the right calibre of support from the CEO is the manner in which latent talent can be uncovered and motivated. Enthusiasm may be readily translated into a thirst for self and company improvement, into a keenness to know more, and into a joint determination to improve productivity and efficiency.

It follows that without upsetting the CEO, the recognition of worth should include dialogue with and assessment of what potential waits to be unlocked among subordinate staff members.

Internal strengths v. external elements: The elements of success can be complex and may in significant part be due to superior internal features of the company and its leadership. However, the external market situation can also obviously play a significant role and it is always relevant to review success against how the economic environment has evolved. The last twenty years have witnessed profound changes in the structures of many industries, with the disappearance of some activities that would once have been considered stable and immovable.

The SME under consideration may be just holding its head above water, and earning only enough to survive without yielding to its owner anything like a satisfactory return on investment. However, the company may be located in a depressed area or in a declining industry sector where survival in itself represents a success story. The beaten and battered sections of any economy present a daunting prospect but it is in these areas that the independent consultant's services are needed and where he can do most good.

There are consultants who revel in helping hard pressed enterprises. This sort of specialisation may require determination and commitment of an order not far short of that shown by the management. It also needs a refined ability to identify the hitherto unexploited worth that will help the enterprise into better days.

The contra to an excellent, committed management team fighting for survival against the odds is the situation of a company with mediocre management that has been fortunate to be in the right place at the right time. In this case, results may exaggerate the quality and commitment of the internal resources – both physical and human.

The nature of the assets: This is another topic which forms an important part of the full-scale analysis process but also one of key importance in the search for worth within the client's business. Broadly speaking the concern is to distinguish assets (tangible or intangible) that are truly unique from those that may be easily replicated. Every company will have an inventory of assets that are more or less "standard". They can be replaced, purchased and sold through the operation of market forces, and hence they can be protected, insured and preserved through conventional means.

Then some SME's control other assets that may be physically unique, or special in some intangible way that imputes worth far beyond that which can be feasibly safeguarded through normal means. One example is the specialist sports car industry of the United Kingdom. Although there are now no major British owned motor manufacturers, there are very likely more independent specialist car makers in the UK than in any other country. Why? These companies respond to a particular manufacturing tradition and to a niche market demand both at home and overseas. Nor is this an old fashioned phenomenon for in the same genre of wheels, the design and manufacture of Formula 1 racing cars, with one notable Italian exception, is an almost exclusively British industry.

Again, recognition of the contra is important. For example, there are some industries where much of the technology is largely generic, and where skilled employees are habitually mobile and fully capable of taking their knowledge and the concomitant competitive advantage with them when they change jobs.

Pattern of growth: The story of the company's growth will often be informative about the causes of current difficulties. Typically, SME's often experience broadly similar problems stemming from success. In the early days, expansion of sales would have been the key to achieving enough critical mass to help preserve the enterprise. Early traumas often impose a paradigm in the management psyche that dictates that sustenance and expansion of turnover is essential to continued success.

Turnover is of course vital to the security of any business, but the risk is that its pursuit results in other critical factors being relegated to positions of secondary importance. It is not uncommon for a significant company failure to be announced at a time when "the order book had never been fuller". Over-trading is a common downfall of many businesses, and it is a depressing fact that many over-ambitious CEO's believe that they can succeed in strategies where failures are well known and well documented. Time and again, the resultant strains on physical, human and capital resources are under-estimated until it is too late.

Achieving balanced growth is not easy and many success stories include times when corners were cut, or where margins were run far too finely for comfort. The nature of the growth therefore that has brought the SME under consideration to its present condition is often indicative of substantial embedded worth – but also should highlight the nature of any unacceptable risk which is being incurred.

Nurturing empathy: A CEO is unlikely to respond favourably to a litany of criticism but he should amenably accept adverse comments if the consultant has demonstrated interest in acknowledging the good as well as the bad. Thus the process of worth recognition is valuable and important in building the right sort of relationship. The intention is not to flatter but more to identify strong points (some of which the CEO sometimes fails to recognise himself) and to initiate a debate about how these may be threatened if shortcomings are not addressed expeditiously.

It should always be remembered that the consultant and his client are likely to be the products of different industry backgrounds, experiences, training etc, and that the onus remains on the former to bridge whatever culture gaps may exist. A determined effort to identify the positive through conscious recognition of worth will help persuade the client that he really does have an ally. With this sentiment in mind, the development of the working relationship will be that much easier.

The client's priorities

The final element to be considered in the building process, before we move on to matters of relationship maintenance, concern how the client prioritises the issues that he confronts in his daily schedule.

It is not unusual for the decision to engage a consultant to be taken at a time of extreme pressure when the client is desperate for help, any help, in coping with a multitude of imminent tasks. This is quite common in over-trading situations where the CEO ends up trying to do an unrealistic number of tasks (most of them very likely inadequately) in covering for over-stretched or non-existent resources. In the process of fire fighting, the consultant may receive a confused or abbreviated brief about what is going on, and then be left to fend for himself.

This can be an invidious situation where the client is close to panic, is desperate for quick-fix results, and has totally unrealistic expectations of how fast and effectively solutions can be delivered. Useful communication may be nigh to impossible, and the future of the relationship may be threatened before it has begun to develop because the consultant is perceived to be failing to provide what in the reality of the circumstances would constitute a miracle cure.

Effectively, the decision was impulsive and taken in a moment of weakness, without due consideration of what would be needed to ensure that the best is extracted from the consultant's services. It is not hard to see therefore why the consultant may occupy a low position on the client's priority scale at the outset. This may be an extreme example but even in less stressed cases, a similar challenge awaits in consolidating a position where the consultant is able to command the attention of his client whenever this is necessary.

The situation may demand firm handling and an insistence that the consultant's time (for which the client is paying) is a scarce resource and should not be wasted while the client continues to fight on all fronts. Even then, a firm stance might result in only a fleeting response in which case the debate must be continued at some location remote from the business, very likely out of office hours, and certainly with mobile phones switched off.

Recognition of the need to climb this priority ladder is important, and progress may be measured by the manner in which the client changes his behaviour patterns when dealing with the consultant. The move to first name terms; greater spontaneity and informality in meetings; dress codes; more punctuality in meetings or in response to phone calls; these are signs which should indicate that the relationship is becoming closer, more frank, and more effective.

Ultimately, the aim is for the client to consider his consultant to be the first port of call for advice and guidance on any significant new strategy or planned development. If that is the case, then the consultant may be confident that he has really got to the heart of the business matter.

Summary points

- *Independent consulting is a highly personalised activity*
- *Success relies on a good relationship with client*
- *Do not underestimate client because his figures are small*

Initial obstacles

- *Client might get cold feet about his commitment*
- *Clients often expect a quick fix from the consultant*
- *Cause and effect of problems can be confused*
- *Quick fix may only provide temporary relief*
- *Reluctance to disclose information can cause delay*
- *Consultant's lack of technical knowledge may be viewed as a disqualification*
- *CEO may be slow in providing data needed due to interruptions*

The importance of history

- *Encourage CEO to describe company history*
- *History of business will be informative about the CEO himself*
- *In need allow CEO to exceed the 15-1 rule about words in describing the history*

Worth recognition

- *Every business can stand improvement through services of a good advisor*
- *Search for problems but acknowledge organisation's strong points*
- *Worth recognition is essential to effective consulting*
- *It is assessed through analysis which inter alia considers:*

The CEO's leadership qualities:

- *He is unlikely to have had formal business training*
- *He is likely to display qualities of business leadership*
- *He may have an extraordinary commitment level*

The management team:

- *SME's are often autocracies with all authority stemming from one man*
- *High staff loyalty and paternalistic management are common factors*
- *Lack of formal training does not mean lack of potential*

Internal strengths v. external elements:

- *Success elements may be in part due to superior leadership and internal features*
- *Market situation is relevant to comparison of success against environment*

The nature of the assets:

- *Important in assessing worth*
- *Distinguish unique assets from those that can be replicated*
- *Note human assets that are mobile and at risk of loss*

Pattern of growth:

- *History of growth may directly relate to current difficulties*
- *Balanced growth is hard and corners may have been cut*

Nurturing empathy:

- *CEO will respond favourably if consultant takes account of both good and bad factors*
- *Consider how shortcomings threaten strengths*

The client's priorities

- *Be aware how client prioritises daily issues*
- *Client often under extreme pressure when he asks for help*
- *Consultant may receive a confused or inadequate brief*
- *Consultant might have to climb the ladder of client's priorities*
- *Aim is for client to view consultant as first port of call for advice*

Chapter 13

Maintaining a client relationship

Evolution

A successful consulting relationship will go through different phases as each party gets to know the other better, and to appreciate their relative strengths and weaknesses. We have already considered some facets to the manner in which a growing knowledge of the background and nature of the client's business will aid fruition of the requisite rapport. As mentioned, it is not unusual in the early stages for the client to misinterpret why the consultant is there and what can be done for him. However, careful explanation and attention to detail should relatively quickly assuage doubts or confusion over the consultant's mandate and terms of reference.

To become really effective, it is important to gain an understanding of the CEO, as well as a detailed knowledge of his business. With SME's the business vision and energy mainly stems from the CEO, and an understanding of what is going on inside his head may be critical to achieving tangible progress in the relationship. This may require discussion of a social nature where the client airs his worries and fears in a more stress free atmosphere.

Case 23. Philip had made contact with a prospective client engaged in light engineering activities. The company had been established for many years, having been set up by the CEO's father. At shop floor level, there was a solid skills base; relatively modern manufacturing machinery ensured a range of products of suitable quality and price.

Despite these positive aspects, the company's profit record was mediocre. There was little understanding of marketing, effective sales promotion, and cost management. The CEO attributed his problems to difficult market conditions, and aggressive foreign competition. He claimed to know all that there was to know about his company and its industry sector. His general attitude was listless and disinterested, and he fobbed off Philip's suggestions about areas where he could provide tangible help with clearly facile and superficial comments.

The second, unsuccessful, business solicitation meeting was drawing to a close after about half an hour when Philip happened to pass a casual remark about family matters in general. Suddenly the CEO became animated in a way not previously evident, and he proceeded to confide his concerns about one of his children who for various reasons had become a source of deep personal anguish.

What followed was an hour of general and specific discussion about the problems of raising a modern day family. There was no further talk about the business at that meeting but Philip learned a lot about the man and his worries i.e. what was the main focus of his mind. The CEO clearly felt better for having some one to talk to on a sensitive topic. By providing a sympathetic ear, and some simple comfort and advice, Philip was in a much improved position to understand his prospective client.

The company health check

Usually, agreement to retain the consultant to undertake a company health check is the lynch pin in the establishment of a relationship. Although the client might have pre-conceived ideas about what help he needs and where his business faces difficulties, he has the common problem of standing too close to the situation, and therefore being unable to distinguish the wood from the trees. As a precursor to more focussed work, it is wise to promote the health check concept as the means by which the consultant is able to assess the complete operation from an objective and dispassionate point of view.

The health check comprises an analysis of the company's structure, activities and environmental situation, using enquiry techniques as described in Chapter10 and addressing subject matter through the style and type of questions set out in **Appendix D.** The health check may require two days or more to complete, and even then it may not cover all the points appearing in the Appendix. Nevertheless it will invariably uncover issues and risk areas of which the client had hitherto been unaware and this in itself should amply justify the exercise. Concurrently, the consultant is far better briefed to set priorities for what happens next, and to lay out a logical program for more detailed and focussed work.

The great promotional value of the health check is that it is a service whose purpose most CEO's will readily understand and appreciate. Thus it forms a comparatively easy concept to explain in preference to more technical or esoteric services where the client may have difficulty in relating what is on offer to his specific situation

The health check is also valuable because it sets yardsticks and terms of reference to which both the client and the consultant can easily relate, and which proves the foundation for continuing communication. Above all it provides for a basis of trust and understanding between the two parties.

Finally, a key selling point to a health check is that it is self-financing as its cost (i.e. the consultant's fee) will be more than covered through the economies and improvements that enactment of the resultant recommendations will yield. This raises two important issues – implementation of recommendations and pricing policies – both of which we debate later in this chapter.

Effective reporting

Most would agree that good communication is essential to effective consulting yet paradoxically, an appropriate reporting style as integral to communication is often overlooked.

There is a body of opinion in the consulting world that believes a beautifully bound, professionally typed and elegantly phrased report that is suitably heavy will warrant the charging of a fat fee. We hold the view that the independent consultant, particularly if he is working with SME's, should be rather less exercised about the production of stylish reports and rather more committed to the fashioning of reliable and realistic proposals. The purpose should be to create a set of conclusions and recommendations that have practical application, engaging resources within the existing scope or immediate access of the client. Thus the report must be comprehensible for the client and persuasive in its practicality.

Occasionally a detailed report may be appropriate but in most instances, the busy CEO may do little more than scan such a document, note a minority of its contents, file it and, before long, forget it. The alternative is therefore to report verbally but again the client may have limited retentive capacity, and may have difficulty in absorbing the key points and recommendations.

Our preferred compromise, which practise has shown to be the most effective, is to report clearly and concisely through a series of bullet points, sectionalised to respond to particular areas of the business that have been reviewed. The client may have difficulty in connecting all of the arguments that support a particular recommendation but this will be no more a problem than would have been presented through a verbal report, or a lengthy and unread tome.

As we discussed in Chapter 8, effective reporting is an important element in the consultant's armoury, and it is vital in the developing relationship that the CEO is provided with a document that he can really use. The consultant will have written the report principally for the CEO, but it may cover issues with which the latter is not fully familiar. However, the CEO may have to retail those views to others (e.g. members of management or perhaps the bank manager) so clarity and brevity should help him greatly.

Appendix E provides a sample report in the bullet point format derived from the health check of an SME client.

Remedial consultancy: the follow-on from the health check

The work so far will have done little more than provide an overview, albeit quite a detailed one, of the company's internal condition and relevant external factors. At this stage, the client who is confident of his situation and competent enough to enact changes may thank the consultant for his work, pay the fee and terminate the relationship.

More common though are situations where having been informed, the client does not know what to do next and therefore chooses to re-engage the consultant to undertake more detailed analysis or to assist in the implementation of corrective strategies. At this stage the consultant should think carefully about the nature of the health check results and the complexity of implementing necessary changes.

If he does not have the skills himself to undertake all aspects of the remedial work, he should identify suitably qualified sub-contractors. This may of course complicate management of the relationship as conflicting messages or contradictory requests can result. Much of this risk may be eliminated through a well-structured collaboration agreement, but the managing consultant will have the additional responsibility of policing the situation on the ground. After all, he has initiated and nurtured the relationship, and he should not allow it to be jeopardised by the ill-considered actions of a newcomer.

The reporting cycle for remedial work needs consideration. By this stage, it is likely that the consultant or his sub-contractor is dealing mainly with subordinate staff rather than direct with the CEO, but a program for keeping the latter advised of progress will be necessary.

Remedial consultancy may follow the project format that was used at the health check stage but it may also mature into a combination of tasking company personnel to undertake specific projects and then monitoring their progress on a regular basis. Life can become busy at this stage if different departments and personnel at varying levels of seniority are required to co-operate to help bring about changes. Before long, the consultant might find himself embroiled in internal politics and demanding delicacy with respect to individual areas of responsibility, relative seniorities, and other sensitivities. It is often a matter of being involved but detached from individual jealousies and disagreements.

Whereas a health check is a comparatively "clean" and discrete exercise, remedial consulting can take up a lot of time, not so much in the pure technical aspects of the task but in addressing human and organisational issues that may result. It is not unusual for a CEO who is confronted with complex and demanding staff issues to exploit the presence of the consultant as the catalyst of change. Thus the consultant (who is hopefully sufficiently thick-skinned) becomes the fall guy, whom everyone may tacitly agree to blame thereby directing the flack away from the real sponsor of the change process i.e. the CEO himself.

This may be satisfactory for the CEO who gains a generally accepted result that would have been impossible without the consultant's "sacrificial" contribution. The relationship between consultant and CEO may remain steadfastly warm but contact quality with subordinates thereafter may be quite another matter. This can be an uncomfortable position at the time, but should be acceptable providing that a suitable fee has been exacted for the work!

Client loneliness

The use of a consultant to sponsor or supervise contentious tasks is indicative of another aspect of the client situation often prevalent with SME's, but frequently overlooked – loneliness.

A CEO who has been in business for say twenty years or more will have started up in a simpler, slower and more predictable world. In the interval, not only has his business expanded thereby adding to the number of daily problems, but also the market will have generated a growing range of fresh challenges, many of which will require instant responses. Against this scenario, where does the CEO who is under extreme pressure turn for help?

Traditionally the local bank manager would have been considered a source of useful advice but banks are increasingly viewed as counter-parties in business for their own profit as opposed to the old perception of a High Street friend and ally. The banking system has undergone its own wide-reaching re-organisation in recent years, in pursuit of better use of resources and improved profitability. While it may be argued that these changes were also in the interests of improving customer service, there is a view among many SME's that banks have become less accessible and have lost their appreciation of conditions on a parochial level. Whatever the cause, the bank manager is no longer the free source of business advice at the beck and call of his customer in the fashion of years ago.

Some professional help may be forthcoming from the accountant but this is more likely to focus on sound bookkeeping and control practises, audit requirements and taxation matters. The company lawyer may also be able to give some assistance on specific legal issues. However, it would be unreasonable to expect either source of professional services to satisfy the need for constructive advice on the strategic and evolving dynamics of the business.

Closer to home there may be no better source of help. For example the SME, in a strained and difficult market, may have a chance to inaugurate an innovative opportunity that will require extraordinary commitment for success. The vision and effort that this will demand may be viewed as unduly risky by the CEO's spouse, or as incurring too much additional work by subordinate staff. Thus it may be hard to enlist objective and determined support from these quarters.

With companies that grow through the efforts of a single person, it is quite common to find that he lives and works in a form of seclusion enforced by visionary and intellectual superiority over those immediately around him. These qualities may provide the keystones to the success story but company growth, increased complexity of the business, or diminished energy with the passing of the years are factors that may distort vision and judgement. The resultant vacuum can be damaging to the security of the enterprise, but to whom can the CEO turn for business counselling?

His individualism and personal drive will have been a major contributor to previous achievement and it may be an unacceptable admission of weakness to turn to one of his immediate circle. In this scenario the outside consultant, with whom there may have been no previous contact, can come to fill a position of intimacy in helping to concentrate thought processes on issues that until now have been "bottled-up" in the CEO's mind.

Multi-level relationships

We have already warned against the dangers of prematurely approaching subordinate members of a client's staff where the CEO may be offended that the consultant has gone behind his back. However, as the relationship matures, and as the CEO realises just how time consuming is the consultancy process, it may be expected that direct contact with other staff will be encouraged.

This is an important step which if managed properly will greatly enhance the ability to gather vital information to help make the whole consultancy process more effective. The risk as always lies in disclosing the chance view or remark that will get back to the CEO and be misinterpreted. Discretion is thus the byword – eyes and ears should be open and alert at all times, with the mouth deployed sparingly perhaps to venture opinions and ideas, but not to express them emphatically.

Penetration at differing seniority levels can be valuable because the CEO may believe that he has knowledge of his staff, their views and their performance levels that might prove inaccurate. As always, the consultant's allegiance is to the CEO – who after all is paying the fee – and feedback about the real attitudes and loyalties of staff might contribute an important ingredient in his recommendations.

Multi level relationships also give a useful insight into inter-departmental communication and liaison difficulties. The CEO who perceives his problems as being mainly externally driven and thus perhaps beyond his control can be surprised and relieved to discover that the root causes are closer to home. An example would be sub-standard internal organisation that has caused two departments effectively to work against each other rather than in co-operative harmony.

Another aspect of multi level relationships involves family members and here the consultant can be playing with fire. The CEO may be filling two distinctly separate roles that are prone to confusion. In addition to being the business leader and main decision taker, he may be the head of a family whose members are to varying degrees involved in the business. By his nature, he may well interpret the latter role in a fashion rather like that of the traditional patriarch, and by scratching below the surface of the company, the consultant may reveal all sorts of frustrations and conflicts.

The CEO's wife, for example, may have a board seat and a shareholding in which position she gains a certain level of knowledge about what is going on. The patriarchal CEO may not be above trying to disseminate business information in a sanitised or censored form but it is amazing how often his wife is far smarter than he thinks, and has a quite objective understanding of the broad issues at stake.

Again in patriarchal management mode, it is not unusual for the next generation to work in the business. Being younger, a common assumption is made that they are less responsible, committed, hard-working etc than had been the father at that age, and so less able to assume any position of authority.

The arrival of the consultant may be seen as a golden opportunity to enlist an ally to pursue individual aims. The wife may want the CEO husband to reduce his responsibilities at a time when he is looking to expand and make more profit. The next generation may want the consultant to persuade the CEO of their true worth, and of their competence for senior management, if not to take over the business completely. Getting to know the family can be helpful in better understanding the background, history and potential of the business but make no mistake, it is also a minefield for the unwary.

Economies of scale

It will not take long for a consultant who has had dealings with a number of SME's to identify a certain consistency in the nature of the problems and challenges that they face. Analysis of these issues is outside the scope of this work but it is worth noting that some recur frequently. These are examples:

Working capital shortage through intemperate business growth

Increasing profits (absolute terms) matched by decreasing profitability (percentage return on capital employed)

Turnover increase not matched by profit increase due to poor financing and inadequate cost management

Under-performing asset portfolio

Focus on manufacturing excellence at expense of proper marketing

Strained management structure with inadequate delegation

Management succession problems

The regularity with which these issues crop up is perhaps surprising but also demonstrative of the inability of many CEO's to recognise factors that present common threats to the well being of smaller businesses. However as identified above, CEO loneliness can be a significant element and within that information vacuum, it is understandable how he can miss what is obvious to others. It follows that despite the uniqueness of every business, there is a strong probability of commonality in many of the issues that the consultant will uncover.

Consulting is labour intensive, and the client will be mindful of its cost. Hence a broad awareness of the types of issues that arise in particular categories of companies offers one of the few opportunities to engage scale economies and thus improve the monetary return on the consulting contract.

This feature is also beneficial to the client's interests. The capacity to quote parallel examples of problems that the consultant has encountered before will lend weight to his authority and recommendations. Further, the client entombed within the knowledge vacuum of his position may be comforted in the awareness that others have made similar errors.

Of course, the existence and possible impact of a commonly recurring problem will need particular treatment in the individual circumstance of each client, as well as the inter-action of each problem area with others. In this regard, the opportunities for economies of scale may be diminished because each CEO requires approaching in the fashion that will uniquely stand most chance of eliciting his swift understanding and acceptance.

The injection of scale economies wherever possible links directly to the theme discussed in earlier chapters which is the preferability of general as opposed to specialist consulting. By canvassing company problems on a broad front, the consultant's knowledge is vastly enhanced and he is thus better equipped to tackle a broad range of issues. By sustaining his ability to cope with variety, he exercises more control over the relationship with reduced risk of this being dissipated through the employment of sub-contractors.

A related benefit accrues also in those cases where the client has responded to the consultant's offer on a personal basis – i.e. by buying primarily the consultant's trust and friendship rather than the specific services on offer. Such a client will be happier knowing that the sharing of confidences can continue on a one-to-one basis, without the need to involve others.

The mature relationship

Years ago, the perhaps apocryphal story was told of the old-fashioned bank manager who, entirely properly, would hear about all sorts of intimate problems from customers who would not share those matters even with their doctors. It is hard to imagine any modern bank manager finding himself in that sort of position but it is reflective of the nature of some relationships that flourish between consultant and client.

Obviously many contacts do not develop anywhere near that extent, and some are of quite short term, being related to fulfilment of a single, clearly defined task. However, it should be the aim in every case to develop a relationship that is closer and superior to any other that the client enjoys with outside agencies. How achievable this will be is dependent upon the skills and ability of the consultant. Sometimes, if the client's business is in a state of acute crisis, the maturing of the relationship may happen very fast whereas in less stressed times, it may take patience and care over many months.

The modern trait to assume that money can be made out of a purely transactional business posture is blatantly ludicrous. Any business transaction relies on the establishment of some sort of relationship recognition, however tenuous or fleeting. If that relationship can be developed and expanded, then the capacity to generate benefit for both sides is greatly enhanced.

It follows therefore that two other key aspects need to be considered in consulting relationships – pricing of services which is addressed below, and the transitional nature of consulting which is reviewed in the next Chapter.

Pricing strategy

In a live transaction, pricing would have been addressed and hopefully contractually agreed much earlier than is implied by leaving this topic until the last section of this Chapter. However, while initial pricing should be settled at some stage between business solicitation and commencement of the company health check or equivalent, its consideration is best addressed in the context of what an ultimately mature relationship might offer.

Pricing for consulting is not an easy subject. Unlike banking, legal and accounting services where there is a reasonable pre-conception about the content of the service to be provided and the probable parameters of the price, consulting assistance is harder to define in advance.

The client may know that he needs help, but not in what form. He may not know the cause of the problem or the nature of the technical services that should lead to its solution, or the capacity and the skills of the consultant making the offer. He will be understandably concerned about buying something for which he has no ready yardstick of measure. Hence the importance of embracing totally the factors set out in Chapters 8, 9 and 10.

However well the consultant has performed in the opening solicitation phase, the quotation of a price is likely to come as a shock to the prospective client and to invoke his spoken or tacit response that it is too high. Thus before, during or after the price quotation, it will be necessary to draw the client's attention to certain points that will help to establish a context within which the latter can make some form of quality judgement. For sake of clarity these points are enumerated separately although during a client meeting, it will be more effective to emphasise them in the course of discussions rather than to produce them as bald selling points:

1. Determine in advance what is the maximum fee rate. This may be an hourly rate although it is likely to be more digestible if it is quoted on a daily basis, assuming an eight-hour working day. Alternatively, a flat rate might be considered although this can be open-ended and thus unduly risky if the job takes longer than was estimated during the solicitation meeting.

2. Make sure at some stage before a specific quotation is made that the maximum fee rate is disclosed so that the client is aware of the ballpark costs and thus will hopefully be more amenable at the crunch time. Also, this will dispel any early illusions that the consultant is there on some sort of charitable mission.

3. Be prepared to be flexible with the fee rate quoted provided that one's pricing structure is not completely compromised. For

example, expectation of a fee x for an anticipated three days work may be mitigated to say 60% of x if the client undertakes to provide the requisite information in easily absorbed format, thereby necessitating only one and a half days for the work to be completed.

4. To help validate the price quote, be ready with references from previous clients (subject to their advance approval, of course). These may mislead in the sense that previous work completed may be quite different in content to the contract now under consideration but subject to this caveat, this tactic might help to allay the client's fears that he is "buying a pig-in-a-poke".

5. Emphasise that the consulting fee is self-financing i.e. that it will be more than covered by the monetary equivalent of the savings/ improvements/ commercial advantages that the work will yield. This concept is at the core of all consulting. What is the point ever of engaging a consultant unless it fits into a clear strategic aim of the client to achieve a net advantage through the exercise?

6. Recognise that market circumstances will bear on the fee that may be levied. A well set up and profitable company that is seeking a health check solely for management's peace of mind will expect to pay much less than an organisation struggling under crisis conditions.

7. Avoid quoting absolute numbers in isolation and always try to relate to some measurable yardstick with which the prospective client will be immediately familiar. For example, if the consultant's target earnings rate is £1000 per day, he may seek to justify his formula for two days' work for a company with £10 million in sales as being the equivalent of 0.2% of annual turnover. Alternatively, a similar job for a £5 million turnover company may be equated with 0.4% of sales. The objective is to demonstrate how small is the fee in relation to annual sales and thus to underline in relative terms how modest is the cost compared with the resulting benefit.

8. Always relate the fee quoted to an assertion concerning related benefit and/ or improved profit for the client. This may be supported by negative persuasion in the form of how long can the

company afford to (or will) survive without attention to specific identified problems?

9. Be willing to show latitude in price at the consultant's "voluntary" discretion before being demanded by the client. For example, having quoted the maximum price, be prepared to add something along the lines of "but in your specific circumstances, I feel that a price of *y* would be more appropriate for the following reasons...". Never ever offer a discount as this demeans the quality of the service on offer.

10. To help validate what the consultant can provide, it may be worthwhile disclosing some intellectual property by way of a partial solution to or a suggested way of solving an identified problem. This tactic should be exercised carefully as a bargaining tool. Too much disclosure may result in the consultant's knowledge being milked without tangible return.

11. Emphasise that the consultant will provide recommendations for improvements and that he will warrant their practicality by being available, if required to assist in their implementation.

12. If remedial consulting is to follow, the contract should be re-negotiated at that point before such work commences. A fundamental change in the charging formula may be appropriate e.g. replacement of a daily rate with a monthly retainer, but again ensure that this will not result in an over-commitment of scarce time for inadequate return.

13. If requested, always enter into an arrangement with the client to provide progress reports on a staged basis. This will extend a sense of comfort where the client fears that fees may otherwise escalate out of hand for little measurable benefit.

14. Always be prepared with a draft engagement letter so that the client may be invited to contract with the consultant promptly in the course of negotiations when all the outstanding issues are clear.

Above all, never forget that the world is full of theorists with lots of bright ideas that never show tangible results. Independent consulting involves direct dealings with people who have built achievement on the back of hard work and practical commitment. In the price quoted, clients will be often seeking real and effective recommendations that will yield measurable benefit, and in this respect they may look to a contingent commitment from the consultant to help make sure that everything happens as promised.

Summary points

Evolution

- *A successful relationship will mature through several stages*
- *It is essential to know and understand the CEO*

The company health check

- *This is often the lynch pin of the relationship*
- *It is the means to gain a detailed understanding of the business*
- *Its purpose is usually easily understood by clients*
- *It is a self financing service i.e. paid for by resultant savings*

Effective reporting

- *Good communication is essential to effective consulting*
- *Write in a fashion that client can assimilate and understand*
- *Avoid elegant stylish reports that look good but are not read*
- *Unless detail is specifically requested, be brief and use bullet points*

Remedial consultancy: the follow-on from the health check

- *Often requested after health check is completed*
- *Results from need to buy new skills and knowledge*
- *Care may be needed with reporting cycle*
- *Often remedial consulting follows a project format*
- *Consultant may be used as catalyst for contentious change*

Client loneliness

- *Many CEO's are intellectually isolated from subordinates and colleagues*
- *They cannot confide freely in family and subordinates*
- *Sound business advice from professional community is limited*
- *Consultant can become confidant and ally*

Multi-level relationships

- *Remedial consulting broadens contacts in client operations*
- *Avoid company politics; beware subordinates' separate agendas*
- *Exercise care with family relationships*

Economies of scale

- *Not common but some business problems are generic in nature*
- *Consulting is labour intensive – hence streamlining where possible can improve returns*
- *Performance is improved where generalism avoids reliance on sub-contractors*

The mature relationship

- *A deeper relationship than any other party enjoys*
- *This will depend on consultant's skills and client's condition*
- *Transactional based consulting is a fallacy*

Pricing strategy

- *Sense of consulting "quality" is hard to impart in advance*
- *If client is unclear about his own problems, he will be unable to value the solutions offered*
- *Price invariably perceived as too high*
- *Several factors affect price validation, requiring discernible yardsticks and context setting*
- *Client has right to expect practicality and implementation assistance as part of the price*

Chapter 14

Consulting: a transitional activity

Change is intrinsic to consulting. Clients seek consulting services because they have a need for improvement or to explore something new, and they see consultants as useful agents or catalysts to make changes happen efficiently. In turn consultants must be flexible and adaptable to meet the variety of fresh demands that a mixed and varied list of clients will present.

To some degree, effective consultants are chameleons in their need continually to re-invent themselves to satisfy the demands placed on them. One day they may be advising a manufacturing client on the benefits to be achieved from tighter stock controls and "just-in-time" procurement techniques. The next day they could be advising a vehicle rental company on alternative computer systems to improve sources of customer information.

As we have repeatedly emphasised, we believe that variety in client and industry type and a preference for generalism over specialism, stimulates wider work opportunities and aids competitive advantage through a broader skills base. In this, self-education runs parallel with the expansion of horizons and experience, and forms an important element to one's personal development program.

With all the profound changes occurring in the structure and nature of business, self-education is a constant requirement for the individual who is intent on staying in step with new techniques, and hence in maintaining his marketability to clients and employers alike. With more fluidity in the labour market and in employment conditions than has ever been witnessed previously in modern times, variety and lack of predictability are now characteristic of, and endemic in, modern business conditions.

It follows that the active consultant stands very much in the forefront of change and through the broad range of his client base is in a privileged position to see change elements at work, for good and bad. Provided he can take in and learn the lessons of his observance role, he should be advantageously placed to predict future events to far greater degree than the company CEO who is typically embroiled in the burden of daily business routine and responsibilities.

Sometimes this ability to see and understand a broad range of pressing issues can have surprising and gratifying results. A reputation for a certain category of skills and knowledge may lead to introductions to business opportunities from unexpected quarters, as well as from some that with the benefit of hindsight may have been reasonably predictable.

Client as employer?

In the previous chapter we explored issues relating to the evolving nature of a successful relationship between a consultant and his client, and we concluded with the emphasis on the importance of workable solutions. In reality, the consultant who has been successful in selling a solution to his client may be effectively buying his way into work of a new type entirely.

In a situation where a wide-ranging review of a company's business has lead to a series of revolutionary and iconoclastic recommendations for change, it is understandable that the CEO, particularly if he is of a traditionalistic mentality, may exhibit significant resistance to what has been recommended. The promotion effort required of the consultant may be substantial, but it does happen that in the nature of some human relations, acceptance of revolutionary change can be sudden and total.

This may lead to a concomitant challenge for the consultant in the sense of:

"OK. I accept the need for radical change in my business and I accept that it needs to be carried out quickly. However, while I will do all that I can to support this exercise, I still have to keep the business running throughout the change process, and as you have pointed out, there is no one available among the existing staff with the necessary vision and ability. So, who is going to do the job?"

In other words, the consultant is hoist with his own petard! The obvious conclusion is that if these radical ideas, which the consultant has dreamed up have been accepted, then there should be no difficulty in his implementing them within the time-scale that he has outlined and with the benefits that he has promised. It is to be hoped that the delicious irony of such a situation will appeal as much to the consultant as it often does to the client! It will certainly sort the consulting men from the consulting boys, the practitioners from the theoreticians!

Taking on a task such as this may however have significant consequential impact on other aspects of the consultant's activity, about which he may have to take careful stock. For example, the program of re-organisation and rectification may be lucrative but demanding in the time that it will take to complete, and what will happen to the other names on the consultant's client list? Of course, the CEO who wishes to engage the consultant in an executive capacity is looking only to meet the needs of his own business and will have understandably no particular concern about what this will do to other relationships that may have taken months to develop.

This can present some challenging alternatives. Does the consultant wish to back out of a relationship which is now clearly mature and which will repay many hours of developmental work? Can he afford to turn his back on other clients, and effectively return to a salaried existence? If the new salaried position on offer is of a fixed term duration, what cost will be re-invoked if there is an ultimate return consulting, with a need to revive contacts that were allowed to wither previously?

Unless a return to full blown salaried employment has been the aim all along, some form of compromise should be attempted whereby the consultant enters a part-time employment contract while trying to service his other clients concurrently. This may not be an easy exercise and some firmness may be needed to ensure that the prospective employer respects the pressures of the situation and is suitably flexible. Hopefully, the relationship will have become sufficiently strong for an amicable arrangement to be negotiated that will satisfy all parties.

This phenomenon of a mixture of consulting and quasi-executive functions is a relatively new but growing feature among independent consultants. In spite of the extraordinary rigours that consulting can exert from time to time, the prospect of a return to steady salaried employment conditions can look increasingly unattractive. Freedom and flexibility, and an evergreen variety of new challenges makes independence ever more preferable to the role of what the Japanese call a "salaryman" and what westerners more disparagingly refer to as a "wage-slave".

Of course, the opportunity to earn a steady and predictable fee in the form of a quasi-salary is tempting when compared with the inveterate uncertainty of an earn-as-you-contract fee income. However this must be balanced against the creative and inventive opportunities that arise from being one's own man in the pursuit of remunerative work.

The portfolio worker

This term, which has been coined by Charles Handy, admirably describes the mode in which many independent consultants now work. Having become aware of the uncertainties and lack of security that salaried employment under modern conditions can imply, often learned through personal experience, independent consultants prefer no longer to rely on a single income source for their livelihood.

Portfolio working calls for a different set of personal management skills from that needed in salaried employment, as indicated above where the successful consultant is called upon to combine a quasi-salaried position with his other responsibilities. Individually, each relationship may yield only moderate earnings but the aggregate result often renders an income level that is as satisfactory as it is stable. Additionally, the exposure to several different business situations concurrently enables the portfolio worker to cross-fertilise his experience so as to maximise his contribution to, and thus his value to, each relationship.

Apart from the need for skill in the management of a number of income sources, the portfolio worker must also exercise care with respect to confidentiality. Sometimes the workload can cause some confusion, and caution is needed to avoid conflicts of interest and the mistaken disclosure of information to the wrong party.

On the other hand, portfolio working is stimulating with the mixture of business contacts usually rendering a varied stream of opportunities that will make a working life vividly colourful in comparison with the routine of salaried employment.

A current drawback with this work and lifestyle is that it has yet to become common currency in social and business circles. On being asked what one does, it is often difficult to describe oneself accurately and succinctly. To claim to be a "consultant" covers a multitude of occupations, including no occupation at all. To try to list one's current activities in a few words may be impossible and may stimulate incredulity in the ears of the listener. Similarly, to describe oneself as a "portfolio worker" usually incurs blank stares but at least the term is an accurate summary of what many consultants actually do, so it is worth using the phrase as often as possible, and also explaining what it actually means.

Ageism and the skills mix

The composition of the work portfolio is likely to vary, and to change depending on age. In fact, the nature of consulting activity can be heavily influenced by ageist factors, as CEO's usually tend to equate age with a perceived level of expertise and ability – particularly in the case of smaller companies.

(Sexism may also play a part but this is often less relevant, not because it is less important, but simply as among the ranks of independent consultants, men still heavily out-rank women. This seems to be a statistical consequence of the continuing prevailing shortage of females in management and hence of those who are leaving salaried employment to pursue consulting activities. The authors strongly hold the view that women have much to offer the world of consulting, and for several reasons have the potential to be more effective than their male counterparts. In this context, a companion volume is now under preparation as a guide for women consultants.)

Many CEO's still adopt an ageist approach in determining whom they may employ to advise. This bias may be a reflection of their own self-esteem and the belief that someone younger is unlikely to be able to match their knowledge and ability, and unable to do a good job. In many instances, this view may be justified. After all, the search for assistance is a serious matter and may have far-reaching consequences for the future of the enterprise. The CEO may perceive placing responsibility for change in the hands of a younger person as an unacceptable risk.

From the viewpoint of the consultant, it is important to recognise that age may perhaps have greater impact on his marketability than his academic and business educational background. The authors have encountered younger would-be consultants who have expressed keenness to enter SME consultancy work on the back of a university degree, plus limited commercial experience at a junior management level, and a second degree at masters level in business studies. When asked what type of work would be their preference, they often state unequivocally "consulting on business strategy".

In reality many CEO's simply do not see this as a subject in its own right, despite the fact that they practise it well or indifferently every business day. Unsurprisingly, they exhibit little enthusiasm for assistance that adopts business studies type phraseology. Thus the younger consultant is likely to have to be content with mundane work in the early days where he can be more credible and so persuasive in his dealings with the client.

By way of guide concerning what a newcomer may expect to be the best means of starting a consulting business, we have chosen to segment on an ageist basis as set out below. The divisions and the opinions are generalised but they should give an indication of what to expect.

In the 20's: It is unlikely that anyone will have the experience or the credibility to perform effectively as an independent consultant unless a particular skill is to hand e.g. some special abilities in the area of computer programming. If consulting is a long-term ambition, it would be preferable to try to join an established consulting group in a junior capacity, or better still to seek work on the other side of the fence i.e. in an industrial or commercial company.

Practical hands-on experience is a an essential precursor to consulting and it is worthwhile spending a number of years either by gaining a variety of experience in one company or by moving between companies and industries. This is an excellent means of education and training; bear in mind that real life experience of badly run companies and of inept or unhappy or inefficient working colleagues is a base from which to study better methods. Watching things done incorrectly can be of enormous use when trying to convince others about the value of change and improvement.

In the 30's: Being thirty something is really the earliest one can seriously expect to make one's way in independent consulting, although a shortage of commercial experience might still mitigate against achieving success. Redundancy and de-manning is no longer an affliction only of managers in their 40's and 50's, and an unexpected change of circumstance may necessitate serious consideration of consulting as a career alternative rather earlier than might otherwise be desirable.

At this age, it can be difficult to build a consulting practise following generalist principles alone, and it may be advantageous to pursue business solicitation on a more specialised service format. For example, skills such as cost reduction, ISO 9000, regulatory compliance, IT and computer services may provide the way forward. The portfolio approach can be of considerable benefit in this regard because the proffering of specialist skills may bring the individual to the attention of the CEO more effectively. This may provide an avenue for return to the employed workforce either on normal salaried conditions or against a specific time contract.

We advocate this approach strongly at this age, as it provides the means of building knowledge and expanding experience to enable a smooth transition to full time independent consulting later.

In the 40's: Typically there is an age difference between the redundant from a large corporate organisation and the CEO of a more mature SME. The redundant who has become an independent consultant will have had experience of statistically similar management responsibilities (number of subordinate staff, authority for capital expenditure levels, responsibility for trading performance etc) to those held by the CEO. As previously discussed however, the large corporate ex-employee may not have had the same exposure to *command* as opposed to management but provided he adjusts his attitude, words and expectations, he should be well equipped to talk on equal terms with his client.

We believe that this is possibly the most lucrative decade of a consultant's career. He should carry the requisite weight of authority without necessarily feeling the weight of his years. Independent consulting is hard work and can be physically demanding, particularly if it involves a lot of solicitation calling and related travelling. Thus a high level of activity may be a concomitant of consulting at this age, but this should stimulate a broad and exciting range of opportunities. It has been noted that in this age group, CEO's are on occasions interested in recruiting consultants either for senior management positions in their companies, or occasionally as their potential successors.

A generalist attitude and approach is really a sine qua non at this age, and the consultant should be mindful of and fully receptive to the diversity of opportunities which could come his way. At the same time, the need for self-education remains pressing and a commitment to staying abreast of technology will be a useful aid. Familiarity with practical issues in new technology and their related strategic potential is still quite a scarce resource in this age group (and more so as we move up the age scales). The ability therefore to advise on the advantages and opportunities that technological cutting edges can offer, if only in a strategic sense, may be a valuable weapon in the armoury.

In the 50's: By this stage, one should feel a right to be more selective about the type and range of work contemplated. Generalism should remain the byword with respect to the nature of individual consulting assignments but concurrently, selectivity may be sensible regarding the type of projects taken on. Industry specialisation may begin to take precedence, reflecting a preponderance of experience and thus inside knowledge in certain quarters. For example, a consultant may have a preference for concentrating on leisure or property as over the years by fortune or design he has found himself undertaking a majority of assignments in those sectors, and has so become an acknowledged expert.

One of the authors has chosen to concentrate his own efforts in new business start-ups that require either the application of new technology, or the creative conjunction of existing technologies to create fresh business opportunities. This may sound an esoteric combination of qualifications but it is interesting to note the degree to which his workload increasingly conforms to this pattern, while still demanding that his approach to each assignment is generalist rather than specialist.

In the 60's: By now, the consultant is very likely looking to reap the fruits of his labours in a less rigorous and demanding fashion. He may well have noted that CEO-founders of companies, particularly SME's, have difficulty in relinquishing the reins and he should be alive to the perils that hanging on for too long can present both to the individual and to the company. On the other hand, the consultant should be well placed to continue to provide useful help and advice to his client base. He may by now be assuming board positions. (Hopefully his experience and memory will keep him alive to the warning implicit in the old joke about the difference between supermarket trolleys and non-executive directors i.e. the former have minds of their own while the latter have a greater capacity for food and drink).

There is no reason why active consulting should not continue at this age, and situations do occur where independent consultants will take a youngster under their wing. In return for a share of the income, the latter undertakes the legwork and the more physically demanding activities, while enjoying the advantage of learning at first hand from an experienced practitioner.

In the 70's: Perhaps there is by now a diminished interest in active consulting but assumption of the elder statesman's role can be an attractive means of "keeping one's hand in" and staying alert. The involvement is now likely to be far more to do with non-executive board membership of an SME but there is really no reason why someone of this age cannot actively contribute in guidance and quasi-management issues. There is no substitute for experience if balanced with sound judgement.

In the 80's: Well, why not? In the run-up years to the Millennium there has been an escalating recognition of the shortage of people versed in the older computer programming languages and it is not beyond the bounds of possibility that octogenarians have been re-called to the colours. If one believes in the cyclical nature of business evolvement, who knows what presently obsolete skills may be sought out again to tackle as yet unidentified future problems? Although the authors do not plan to reach this advanced age just yet, they do not see much attraction in conventional retirement, and they intend to be actively contributing to the business scene for many years to come. They are looking forward in *their* 80's to providing a counterbalance to the cult of youth which contributes so much good, and sometimes things not so good, to the modern business scene!

A broad range of opportunities

In summary we believe that consulting offers a superb range of opportunities for a diverse and interesting career. Undoubtedly motivation and ambition will vary widely with experience gained, and the latter quality will in large part be driven by age. The younger one starts, the more likely it is that personal evolution will embrace a pattern of consulting interlaced with corporate employment at differing levels of seniority.

Consulting yields the capacity to remain open minded about career alternatives while being well informed on the respective advantages and disadvantages. Combining its disciplines with employment experience should create a potent and valuable category of multi-talented business executives.

Finally, we consider it sensible that the individual sets up a disciplined methodology for monitoring his personal progress and development. It is normal to be aware that one has a lot of experience but it may not be easy to summarise quickly and succinctly the nature and extent of that experience. Failure to accomplish this could be costly as from to time, it may be necessary to describe in a readily absorbable fashion what has been one's experience, as an integral part of selling one's services.

In this context, the self-audit which we advocated in Chapter 4 is relevant but rather than repeat this discipline too often, a short cut is to refer to and update the self-evaluation of skills, rather as we have set out in **Appendix G**. If completed with thoroughness, this document can be employed as a useful tool of personal promotion not only in prospective collaboration arrangements with other consultants, but also in convincing the client of the value of the services on offer.

Summary points

- *Consultants must continually re-invent themselves as change is intrinsic*
- *Expect variety; prefer generalism over specialism*
- *Consulting is in forefront of change*

Client as employer?

- *Consulting can lead to fresh employment opportunities*
- *Client may require consultant to enact the advice given*
- *Consider impact of partial/ full employment on other consulting obligations*
- *Choice may be critical – safety of a salary or freedom and independence?*
- *Mixed employment situations are growing more common*

The portfolio worker

- *Results from desire to avoid risk of reliance on a single income source*
- *Requires a different set of personal management skills*
- *It can be a stimulating means of earning a living*
- *Not yet a widely recognised employment term*

Ageism and the skills mix

- *A consultant's typical work portfolio will change with his age*
- *Many clients view older age positively in consultant selection*
- *Youth is perceived as lacking experience and offering less value*
- *In the 20's: too young to consult, get more practical experience*
- *In the 30's: the earliest for independence, specialism more likely*
- *In the 40's: potentially the most active and successful age group*
- *In the 50's: more selectivity in work range and types of contracts*
- *In the 60's: a tendency towards the non-executive director role*
- *In the 70's: the role of the business elder statesmen*
- *In the 80's: there are still possibilities*

A broad range of opportunities

- *Motivation and ambition will vary with age*
- *An open mind can exploit consulting as a career development tool*
- *Disciplined self-monitoring of progress and development is recommended*

Chapter 15

Planning and managing an independent consultancy

The decision whether to start up one's own consultancy requires careful analysis. As we have tried to show, working for oneself in an activity where for much of the time one is working alone is quite a different way of life from the norm of salaried employment. However attractive consulting might appear, we strongly advise that a decision be deferred until all the factors have been taken into account and duly weighed.

Independent consulting is frequently directed at improving the affairs of small and medium sized enterprises that have encountered difficulties, often stemming from poorly thought out strategies and inadequate planning. The independent consultant is of course his own one-man SME and it therefore behoves him to apply to himself the same planning and organisational disciplines that he intends to promote to his clientele. In other words, he must practise on himself what he plans to preach to others.

On the assumption that the decision has been taken to commence a business from scratch, features of what to expect are described in the sections below relating to the first two years of operations.

Year 1: building the business

A new business start-up is a strenuous and time-consuming matter because there is so much to be done concurrently in different areas. This is an expensive time because funds have to be found for several expenditure categories, while income may not be received until much later.

Income gestation: The cash flow in consulting work is almost invariably strongly negative i.e. work is undertaken and expense is incurred now against the client paying up at some future, unfixed date. Unless a staged payment program has been agreed, the consultant can never be certain when the client will pay whereas expenses are a fixed and immediate commitment.

Even with a deal that faces no hitches, substantial delay may eventuate and the elapsed time could assume the following pattern:

	No of weeks
Search of database for suitable targets	1
Elapsed time in telesales before securing an expression of interest	2
Client solicitation program (meetings, phone calls)	3
Engagement letter now signed	-
Execution of consulting contract	2
Presentation of recommendations / report	-
Acceptance of recommendations / follow up discussions	1
Presentation of invoice	-
Delay before client pays invoice	3
Total	**12 weeks**

This shows that a three-month minimum period should be expected before income will be earned, and in many instances the elapsed period from start of client search to settlement of invoice could be closer to six months. Note also that time expended in servicing one client contract may reduce significantly the time available to pursue another. Thus in the early days, before a momentum and a critical mass has been built up, there may be significant intervals between the signing up of income producing clients.

For sake of caution, it is recommended that the first year sales should be targeted at no more than 10 – 20% of targeted turnover for the business once it has matured. From this it should be concluded that the business might incur a substantial hidden establishment cost through the need for the consultant to provide for his living expenses until his consulting income has consolidated. It is wise to be conservative and we recommend that the consultant should plan to support himself from other income sources or from his own capital for a 6 to 12 month period.

This scenario also emphasises the attraction of business derived from the "natural market" (as discussed in Chapter11) provided that it is at a realistic earnings rate and that it does not preclude the development of other income opportunities, once this source has dried up.

Fixed assets: This expenditure category should not be excessive but it is important that money is spent to good effect. The office and its furniture need not be stylish but must ensure a pleasant and comfortable working environment. The room should be devoted to the consultant's sole use and in a quiet part of the house; long hours will be spent here and any discomfort, noise or interruption will impede performance. The area should be well lit and ventilated, and large enough to allow for expansion; the smallest spare bedroom or box room of a typical house is unlikely to be adequate.

Apart from a desk, allow room for a subsidiary table, for the computer, fax and other communications, and for a decent sized filing cabinet. The latter will soon be necessary as files and paper will grow rapidly and efficient information retrieval will become critical quite soon.

The minimum office equipment required will be a personal computer (embracing word processor and spreadsheet functions, and with a substantial memory capacity), a printer, modem, fax facilities, data line and at least one separate telephone line. Approach different telecoms companies (including the local cable supplier) to identify the cheapest service provider.

Replication of reports and correspondence can be a significant factor so consider carefully the type of printer to be used. An ink jet system may appear preferable on basis of first cost but laser printers, while nominally more expensive to buy, usually provide superior print quality, operate faster and produce proportionately many more copies per cartridge refill. Photocopiers are very expensive compared with the total cost of this inventory; it is most cost efficient to look for a local shop facility and try to negotiate for a discount in respect of bulk usage.

Working disciplines: Establish with other family members the principle that the office is a formal place of work, and that it should be respected as such. It may also be wise to set down specific working hours when social/ family interruptions are as unacceptable as they would be in a conventional office environment. Likewise, the dedicated telephone line should be used only on business matters.

Transportation: A similar code of understanding may be needed regarding use of the car in a one-car household. Public transport in some cases can be more effective but in most instances, business meetings will require the flexibility and convenience of one's own vehicle. Note also that meetings are greedy for time because of the importance of allowing for travel so as never to be late at meetings. One of the authors has found a motorcycle to be a most efficient tool for travel related to consulting in both urban and rural areas.

Office consumables: Always hold buffer stocks. Otherwise, important items often have a habit of running out at the wrong moment. Major savings on stationery and related supplies can be obtained by using one of the major mail order discount wholesalers. Alternatively, many big centres have stationery stores that discount heavily; the quality can vary widely but it is usually adequate for most everyday needs. Always stock a small amount of high quality stationery for the odd prestige letter or similar communication where style of presentation and creation of a favourable impression are important factors

Personalised letterheads and stationery prepared by outside printers is expensive and usually unnecessary (except for business cards). The personal computer should be able to provide for virtually all personalised stationery needs.

Information sources: Review and re-organise your personal technical library so that you can recall easily what works it contains, and how to access them quickly. It is advisable to spend time studying the shelves of the local lending library and technical bookshop to be familiar with the type of books that are available in subjects with which you will be concerned. Technical books may appear expensive but far less so when compared with the time and cost of buying technical or professional advice from other people.

Ensure that you remain well informed about current business events as not only may these be directly relevant to your business, but also they are issues that your clientele may wish to discuss with you. Reading should include the business section of a daily national broadsheet paper and the local newspaper.

Review the availability of trades journals and magazines that relate to any areas of particular expertise or knowledge in which you intend to specialise.

Image promotion: It can be valuable to instigate a program of self-promotion through support of various business related and representative bodies e.g. chambers of commerce, trade associations, professional institutes and organisations. Participation in events which they organise can be enjoyable, informative and a good means of staying in touch with business people, other than clients. Restraint may be needed; the temptation can be strong to attend a multiplicity of amusing quasi-social events, at the expense of concentrated new client search.

Information storage: Develop your own marketing database on the companies that you plan to approach in your solicitation program. This database should include static data (e.g. address, activities etc), dynamic information (reported profits, turnover etc) and gossip, rumour and informed speculation. An example of database entries is provided in **Appendix F.**

It is valuable also to develop a secondary database for local accountants, lawyers, independent financial advisors etc. This may be used as the basis for a secondary promotional campaign (mailshot, telesales, physical meetings) to advertise your services, and so to encourage third party business introductions. These contacts may also be of use when seeking technical or professional collaborative assistance in more complex contracts.

Create an album of business cards received. Annotate on each the date and place of the meeting, and if space allows one line comments about anything significant discussed. It can be worthwhile amplifying the business card album with a contact directory. This is a personal record of people who have been met at business or social gatherings whose activities or services could be of use in the future.

If the business solicitation program is focussed on the local area, study the local newspapers carefully and take press cuttings, duly annotated and dated, about local companies and businessmen.

These cuttings should be filed in such a fashion for use later in conjunction with approaches to prospective clients.

Ensure that you are stocked with the latest copies of the trade telephone directories (*Yellow Pages*, *Thomson's* and so forth), and also that you are aware of what additional directories are available at the local reference library.

Trading status: Opinions seem to differ about whether to operate as a sole trader or as a limited company. If income is received from other sources, more efficient taxation management may be possible by continuing to receive income from that source personally while directing consulting income and all related expenses to a separate limited company. This is an area where we recommend that views be sought from a qualified taxation advisor.

Generally speaking, we prefer the concept of operating a limited company as it helps to isolate all the consulting activity in one place. From time to time, ancillary business or investment opportunities may arise as a spin-off to consulting and these may be more efficiently "warehoused" with this company.

An off-the-shelf vehicle can be purchased at modest cost from organisations that specialise in company formations. The obligation to maintain proper records is not too onerous, and preparation of the annual return and submission of annual accounts are not costly exercises. The annual trading turnover has to reach a substantial figure before auditors must be appointed.

Certain important legal obligations accompany the creation of a limited company related to the roles of directors and secretary, as well as to the company itself. Companies House issues detailed and informative brochures describing these obligations and these should be read carefully. The staff are helpful about queries, but if there are any doubts and concerns, legal advice should be sought.

It is sometimes believed that a personally controlled company is a good vehicle through which to borrow money on perhaps advantageous terms. However, a bank will not lend without a proven track record, and will most likely require the personal guarantee of the directors thereby yielding no net advantage in this respect. In any event we do not recommend borrowing money for the reasons set out below.

Use of contracts: As we have explained elsewhere, the independent consultant will enter a variety of contractual commitments with other parties (clients, other consultants, advisors etc.), some of whom may be physically remote under the aegis of a "virtual company". These types of organisation may have legal but no physical substance: they have been described as "little more than a bundle of contracts".

We provide samples of some of the more common types of contracts encountered in consulting in the Appendices, and also details on where more specific legal advice may be obtained on these and similar documents. Nevertheless, it is important to develop the habit of reading thoroughly all contracts to which it is proposed that you should become a party. Contract reading can be tedious and in a previous corporate life may have been left to a specialist department, or to corporate lawyers. The independent consultant does not have that luxury and it is not cost effective to refer every document to his personal lawyer. Practise will quickly refine the ability to read contracts effectively.

Contracts which you sign will make you or your consulting company legally liable and common sense dictates that you should be quite clear about all aspects of the obligations being entered. If doubts remain, it is recommended that a simple book about Law of Contract be obtained from your local technical bookshop. Despite this, if a contract contains clauses or phases that are unclear, refer to the other party for an explanation as to what is meant.

If the other party cannot or will not explain, do not sign. If he objects to your referring the contract to your own lawyer, do not sign. If your lawyer says that the legal aspects are satisfactory, then still think very carefully about the commercial implications and the consequences that you will be assuming. If these are unduly onerous, do not sign.

Insurance: The habit of careful study of contracts should also extend to insurance policies. As a precaution, existing third party cover should be checked regarding the installation of an office in the home which clients might occasionally visit, and also the use of the motor car on business.

Professional Indemnity Insurance (PII) may be worth consideration but this needs to be reviewed carefully in the light of the nature of the business. Key risks usually reside in whether the client will actually pay for work done (which is not a PII type risk), and in whether a client's business has suffered as a result of the advice proffered by the consultant. The latter circumstances will be adjudged in the light of the specific facts of each case and it must be for the individual to decide whether cover is needed. It should be noted that some organisations will not enter agreements with independent consultants unless PII cover is in place. However the policy terms and conditions need to be closely studied, particularly the exclusions, to determine exactly the nature and value of the protection that is being extended in return for the premium paid.

Capital and finance: The golden rule in starting your own consulting business is that if you need to borrow money (bank overdraft or loan, hire purchase or lease finance) to get going, then abandon the project. Consulting can be lucrative but the income flow will be irregular. This lack of predictability makes the assumption of any outside finance with its regular debt service obligations a dangerous course, regardless of how attractive and convincing the plans and forecasts appear.

If forming a limited company, this may be achieved with only token capital with the balance of funding provided in the form of loans from the directors. However if the directors themselves have to borrow from third parties to provide these loans, the net impact is the same and again the project should be abandoned.

For specific reasons of taxation management, borrowing from a third party may be desirable but this should only be entertained providing that it can be adequately serviced out of income received from sources quite separate from the consulting activity. Also this course should only be considered in the light of expert taxation advice.

Financial and legal matters: Another issue to be addressed is the appointment of bankers. If a limited company is to be formed, it is recommended that this should use a bank other than your personal bankers (why should one bank be privy to all one's financial affairs?). Some offer a year's free banking for new corporate accounts.

Also, consideration should be given to registration for VAT. This is discretionary for small businesses but obligatory once gross annual turnover exceeds a prescribed level that is adjusted for inflation periodically. (At the beginning of 1999, the level was £50,000).

Accounting assistance may be considered necessary for taxation issues and maintenance of records. The decision obviously lies with the individual, but there are bookkeeping software packages available at modest prices that are perfectly adequate for small one-man businesses.

The do-it-yourself mentality: The foregoing will have identified that there is a lot of organisational and administrative work to be undertaken in addition to the prime task of finding and taking care of clients. Some of this administrative work will be recurring but despite the additional burden, we recommend that as much of it as possible be undertaken personally by the consultant, rather than contracted out to third parties. This will give a taste of the complexity of matters with which the CEO of an SME client has to contend.

In addition, a D-I-Y attitude is cost effective in most matters (except those like taxation and legal issues where expert advice may prove cheaper in the long run). Closely monitored expenditure and the search for value for money will be critical in the first 12 months when adequate income may be hard to generate. Over time, D-I-Y as a business maxim tends to become an operational habit.

Year 2 and beyond: consolidating the business

After 12 months of operation, hopefully a distinctive pattern to the growth and makeup of the business should have developed. The first year will have inevitably included some failures and disappointments, and these experiences will have incurred some expenses and perhaps quite a lot of unproductive time. However much study and training has taken place beforehand, some of the initial client calls will in retrospect be seen as wasted opportunities.

Do not get downhearted. Everyone occasionally makes mistakes and misses chances of doing business. From time to time you will encounter consultants who claim very high success rates in client solicitation right from their first days – but then there is a class of consultant who is accomplished at embroidering the truth.

Success in consulting is commitment laced with attention to detail, an ability to learn from experience, and sheer determined, dogged persistence – and then lots more persistence. By the end of the first 12 months enough experience should have been gained for promotional and interview techniques to have become well refined. Solicitation success rates should have begun to improve, and it should be evident that the rule of 7 and the rule of 4 do actually work.

By now the nature of the work content should have begun to change. Less time should be needed, or available, to pursue new clients although the obligation to find new sources of work is continuous as a consultant's business is only as sound as the value of the portfolio of income producing clients.

Nonetheless, while the amount of promotional work with potential new clients should have reduced somewhat, pursuit of return business from existing or past clients should be gearing up. Although obviously it is in the interest of both client and consultant that each contract be completed as effectively as possible, business is highly dynamic. Fresh problems can arise and the consultant through the process of cross fertilisation will have collected new ideas and skills.

Hence in parallel with new client solicitation, the consultant should be renewing contact on a regular basis with past clients. An existing contact that is already warm is an excellent place either to cross-sell other products and services, or to promote ancillary business. It follows that the **Database** should be under regular review to identify opportunities for this purpose.

The business plan

The remainder of this chapter is devoted to sample documents that have been designed to help in the planning process, cost identification, income and cash flow projections etc. This structure should assist in reaching the key decision whether the projected consulting activity should proceed.

Full evaluation of the relevant factors and attention to all the details now may avoid time and cost later; it is always far cheaper to re-design and modify a business on paper than to attempt this after it has been created and expenditure committed. It is thus recommended that this planning format be completed in full as there is little point in risking money and time on what might be a significant new venture without a viability assessment. For clarity, the plans appear as a series of modules.

Module A Is consulting right for me?

Self questionnaire:

A.1 What other work commitments must I fulfil, and will they conflict with my scarce resources of time and money?

A.2 How many hours or days per week can I commit to consulting?

A.3 I will be working for much of the time at home and is this acceptable to my family?

A.4 The building up of a viable consulting business should be approached as a one to two year project. Am I prepared to commit to such a long period to establish my business?

A.5 For how many years do I wish to work as a consultant, and does this justify a one to two year establishment period?

A.6 Have I fully audited my skills and experience base, and have I identified all the areas of shortcomings that will require my attention?

A.7 What measures should I take to seek outside help to improve my skills and what will these cost?

Module A Is consulting right for me? (continued)

A.8 Working days plan

How many days per year do I plan to devote to consulting?

For example:

Number of working days (52 weeks x 5 week days)	260
Less allowance for leave (__ weeks x 5 days)	
Less number of days on prior business commitments	
Sub total	
Add back proportion of working Saturdays (for admin. etc)	
Total number of consulting days	
Number of working weeks per annum	
Average days per week to commit to consulting	

A.9

Based on A.8, I plan to devote ___ days (excluding working Saturdays) out of a total possible number of annual working days of ___ i.e. ___%.

What level of gross annual income do I ultimately require from this share of my time?

Module B Gross income target plan

B.1 When fully developed, I will require my business to generate fee income of £________ and I target an average of £______ in fees from each client in every 12-month period.

B.2 I plan to find my clients through the following means:

Telesales	__%
Existing contacts	__%
Other means	__% (specify)

B.3 Targeted annual sales for mature business £_________

Generated from:	Telesales	Existing contacts	Other
% share	___%	___%	___%
Sales by source	£_____	£_____	£_____
Number of contracted clients	_____	______	______
Number of offer letters (Rule of 4)	_____	______	______
Average number of contacts before offer letter extended	7	7	7

Module B Gross income target plan (continued)

Of which average number of:			
Meetings	_____	_____	_____
Telephone contacts	_____	_____	_____
Letters despatched	_____	_____	_____
Estimated aggregate time spent per offer letter days/ hours)	_____	_____	______
Estimated total time in client solicitation (time / offer letter x no. of contracted clients x 4)	_____	____	_______

Query: *Is the number of days calculated as available for consulting (A.8 and A.9) sufficient to cover the gross fee income target and time required (B.3)?*

Module C Expense budget

Full and accurate tabulation of all capital and operating expenses is necessary to identify how much financial support the business will require in the establishment and early consolidation phase (years 1 and 2).

The year 2 figures should provide a reasonably accurate forecast of how the continuing expense figures will look in the following years.

The entry "nil?" suggests that the expense may be first year only.

Category	Year 1	Year 2
Capital items		
- Computer and printer		nil?
- Modem & peripherals		nil?
- Fax machine		nil?
- System software		nil?
- Subsidiary software (e.g. accounting)		nil?
- Office furniture		nil?
Current items		
- **Communications**		
Telephone		
Data line		
Internet subscription		
Mobile telephone		
Mail services		
- **Utilities**		
Heat & light		
Water		
Council rates		
- **Travel**		
Petrol		
Hire charges		
Vehicle lease		
Repairs & service		

Module C Expense budget (continued)

- **General expenses**
  - Accountant
  - Advertising
  - Bank charges
  - Computer maintenance
  - Consulting fees paid
  - Insurance
  - Legal
  - Professional subscriptions
  - Repairs & maintenance
  - Seminar costs
  - Stationery
  - Technical books
- **Self-education**
  - Courses
  - Seminars
- **Support costs funded from other sources**
  - Daily living expenses
  - Personal capital items

NB This module is designed to identify costs for one's own management accounting needs and personal financial planning needs. It must not be assumed that all the items are eligible for tax deduction against the income of the business. Specialist tax advice should be sought in this respect.

Module D Cash flow

From the previous Modules, it should be relatively straightforward to prepare a spreadsheet showing a cash flow projection for the first two years.

This should indicate how much support will be required for and/or income derived from the business on a quarterly or monthly basis.

Thus:

	Month 1/ Quarter 1	Month 2/ Quarter 2	Month 3/ Quarter 3 etc
Number of consulting days			
Receipts:			
Gross consulting income			
Earned income from other sources			
Investment income			
Outgoings:			
Capital items			
Communications			
Utilities			
Travel			
General expenses			
Support costs			
Personal taxation			

Module E Payback

Key questions which in the final analysis only the individual can answer for himself:

E.1 On the assumption that virtually all the start-up and capital expense costs will be incurred in Year 1, and that Year 2 should set the projected income pattern for following periods, how many years will it take to recover the initial investment?

E.2 Will the income derived from year 2 onwards provide a satisfactory return for the amount of time that will be devoted to independent consulting?

E.3 Do I have the ability to succeed and in view of the risks and uncertainties, is this a wise step for my career?

Summary points

- *Be thorough over evaluation of whether to enter consulting*
- *Apply evaluation standards that would be used for affairs of a client*

Year 1: building the business

- *Establishment of new business will take time*
- *Calculate income gestation periods from selling to contract completion*
- *Note that first year income should be only a fraction of that for mature business*

Fixed assets:

- *Minimise expenditure but ensure comfortable working conditions*
- *Full suite of IT and communications facilities is essential*

Working disciplines and transportation:

- *Establish with family protocols for working hours and use of vehicles*

Office consumables:

- *Always keep buffer stocks*
- *Use computer to minimise outside printing*

Information sources and storage:

- *Review and improve business library*
- *Review subscriptions to press and trade journals*
- *Develop databases and suitable clients filing systems*
- *Ensure trade directories are current and up-to-date*

Image promotion:

- *Set up attendance program for business events*

Trading status:
- *Evaluate whether to operate as limited company or sole trader*
- *Consider taking professional and taxation advice*

Use of contracts:
- *Develop discipline of effective contract reading*
- *Study the Law of Contract*

Insurance:
- *Evaluate need for Professional Indemnity Insurance*
- *Review exposure to third party risks*

Capital and finance:
- *Never borrow money to start a consulting business*
- *Appoint bankers*
- *Register for VAT*

The do-it-yourself mentality:
- *Develop the habit of trying to do most things oneself*
- *This helps to minimise cash outlays and improves understanding of the challenges of starting a small business*

Year 2 and beyond: consolidating the business

- *Within 12 months a distinctive business pattern should be apparent*
- *Be prepared to make mistakes and to learn from them*
- *Need for self-promotion should fall away as business builds up*

The business plan

- *A full and complete business plan is important to starting properly*
- *Complete all planning modules:*
- *A – is consulting right for me?*
- *B – gross income target plan*
- *C – expense budget*
- *D – cash flow*
- *E – payback*

Chapter 16

All change! Where next with employment?

How long is a career?

Anyone aged around 50 in the late 1990's will have witnessed many remarkable changes in the nature of work, and in expectations of a working career since he or she first joined the labour force. Some of these changes, and the problems they present have been explored in this book. However, the most singular factor affecting the lives of those once known as "baby boomers" in the aftermath of the Second World War is the manner in which the length of formal employment under wage or salary earning conditions has been telescoped.

It is now hard to believe that as recently as the early 1970's, some occupational pension schemes still anticipated that 65 years would be the normal retirement age, with the expectation of a single employer throughout a working career. At that time it was still usual to contemplate forty plus years of employment, a view largely sustained by the labour shortages of the 1950's and 1960's. Invitations to pension scheme members to opt for retirement at age 60 was perhaps the first inkling of the changes that were to come.

New forces aided the phenomenon of a foreshortened working career also at the front end. Post-war employment practices had derived partly from the minimum school leaving age of 15 years, and from recruitment practises focussed on young people with 'O' level examinations only. Employment requirements, even in many white-collar trades and professions, often did not stipulate 'A' levels as a minimum; graduate level recruitment policies were rare.

Apart from the hiatus resulting from two years of national service, it was common for young employees to commence at around age 16 with the expectation of staying with the same employer right through to retirement. A near half-century of work in the same place under a paternalistic management structure must have been a daunting prospect that is now fortunately virtually impossible.

The later emphasis on a full program of secondary and tertiary education has typically removed 5 or 6 years from the employment profiles of many young people. Formal employment conditions may not commence until the early twenties, while there is general acceptance of the redundancy threat from the early forties onwards.

This change in expectations over the length of a working career has only come about in recent years. It is extraordinary that issues arising from the halving of the time one might hope to be in formal work have received so little attention. In the 1950's and 1960's, an average life expectancy of about seventy years would have consisted of average 16 years spent in education and growing up, followed by 45 years in work and then 5 to 10 years of retirement. Today, education is taking longer, followed by a 20/ 25 year period of salaried employment as the usual expectation. With UK life expectancy at 74 years for males and 76 years for females (and rising), many now face the prospect of around 30 years of what would once have been retirement, but which might now have to be something rather different.

Is this a matter for concern? Should we care if we are confronted with the prospect of 20 years more freedom and leisure than our parents could have hoped for? Why should we worry about the past and about how things have changed over the last fifty years? Are historic comparisons important, or in any way helpful in planning our futures? An apologist for what has happened might try to argue that the Post War baby boom is largely irrelevant for modern society. He might feel that individuals have adapted and responded through better lifestyles and rising affluence, and that comparisons of differing social conditions over the last 50 years are not germane to the future.

This is an unsound argument. Most of the adjustment needed to accommodate these profound changes has been born by individuals who have had to engage in new lifestyles. They have been forced to make fundamental changes to their lives, often on an ad hoc basis and with minimal support from the "system". Indeed, it is remarkable that the system of rules and regulations that govern modern society and commercial practises have changed so little in this context.

For example, consider the thresholds of entitlement for the aged to receive state pensions, the manner in which long-term public and private sector savings programs are administered, and the conditions under which mortgage finance is extended. These and many other elements of the modern economic and financial order presuppose an adherence to stability and longevity in career patterns that no longer exists. The system is still fashioned in response to a social model allied to the employment concept of thirty years ago, which is far removed from current reality.

The impact of this change has been largely cushioned by circumstances. Rising affluence has moderated the effect of income instability while inflation has eased the real cost of personal indebtedness. In part these factors have been incidental to the process but they have played an important role in relieving what could have been an untenable burden of hardship for many people.

The absence of central guidance or of governmental recognition has rendered some curious factors. The anecdotal evidence suggests that the scale of superfluous capacity in the potentially employable section of the population is under-recognised, or under-recorded. There are obvious political benefits in not probing this too deeply. Many of the affected individuals unwittingly collaborate in this cover-up for a multiplicity of reasons associated with pride, self-esteem and the frequently misguided belief that one day a reversal of fortune will allow them to recover lost careers.

The core issue does remain, however. Just what does one do in setting out on a career of "retirement" that may be years longer than the period of paid employment that preceded?

Some implications of redundancy or early retirement

Unless the severance terms are generous enough to permit a hedonistic lifestyle, an individual who has recently been made redundant confronts a fresh range of sensations and challenges. Release from conforming to a 9 to 5 working day gives a heady sense of freedom. The chance for extended recreational activities and self-indulgence may have been the stuff of dreams for years previously. Complete discretion over how time may be organised is an unusual and exciting experience for people who have been shackled by the constraints of a working career, and who previously have only been able to explore freedom for short, finite periods.

However, the chance to revel in these pleasurable sensations often does not last long, and reaction can set in rapidly. Loss of an acknowledged position of responsibility and authority, damaged self-esteem, and a feeling of many future empty, work-less days are important psychological elements. In terms of stress levels, the trauma arising from redundancy or early retirement can match that associated with divorce or the loss of a loved one. The career worker is inculcated with disciplines such as obligation, responsibility and ambition, and readjustment to some alternative mind-set not modelled around the workplace may be a difficult mental task. Social interaction is largely driven by colleagues who are work-mates, and by recognition of "position" as associated with a definable appointment within an organisational structure.

The severing of this nexus can be hard, and it is not unusual to encounter individuals who still refer to "us" and "we" in the corporate sense when talking about ex-employers, months or even years after that employment terminated. Nostalgia for a previous employer is an understandable sentiment but this should have little place in the mind of someone who for pressing financial and social reasons needs to re-invent himself to face the future.

The need to address the new reality following loss of permanent, salaried employment might be urgent. While it may be possible to find a new job, the experience of career severance means that the work attitude can never be the same again. Detachment and objectivity replaces the sense of vocation and "belonging" that typically accompanies a career that had been intended to last a working lifetime. Further, lost belief in the concept of job permanence brings about a subtle yet firm shift in mental attitudes, which replaces the conventional sense of loyalty in the job-seeker's mind.

Changes in attitudes to work

In response to his altered state, the middle aged redundant usually adopts a tougher approach to negotiating the terms on which he will offer his labour in future. He becomes more mercenary in his demands and expectations, exploiting all the opportunities and resources at his disposal. The move away from the comparative comfort which salaried environment provides is not easy to achieve, but may in part be helped by that management phenomenon of the 1990s – Performance Related Pay (PRP).

This attempt to create through PRP, an entrepreneurial spirit within corporate structures adopts as a template some of the conditions that habitually face the self-employed individual. However, PRP might only pay lip-service to some of the underlying principles as all too frequently it is little more than a manipulative sham, more reflective of skill in playing the system and exploiting management accounting deficiencies, than in genuine incremental contribution.

For the ex-employee, now on his own, PRP is for real in every sense. It is all-embracing, concerned with the way in which owned assets are marshalled, working skills are deployed, benefits of past experience and training are exploited, and the manner in which obligations and liabilities are controlled.

Previously some of these elements might have been the responsibility of working colleagues in the corporate entity. Co-ordination of effort was orchestrated by an often remote chief executive on behalf of an even more remote board, in the interests of distant shareholders. The corporate structure thus allows segmentation of interest and responsibility through different levels of hierarchy, and through division of executive responsibilities.

The self-employed quickly learns that he is his own manager, chief executive, board and shareholder. He can no longer rely on the luxury of the corporate umbrella any more than he can seek to lay blame for failure on a colleague. Being self-employed leaves no doubt precisely where the buck stops.

The challenges of a change in direction

The process of necessary re-invention takes many forms, but most immediate may be the need for a new income source, and this may be a challenging objective. Opportunities open to the middle-aged redundant for establishing a new career of stable salaried employment are diminishing through the demographic changes outlined above. It may be possible in certain circumstances to beat the trend but this is no guarantee that the cycle will not repeat itself.

Many individuals who have suffered the trauma of redundancy more than once often have fascinating stories to tell. They exhibit the features of being battle hardened, objective and self reliant to an extent that is rare in someone with a stable career background. They show many of the attributes that the ex-employee should study and copy in his necessary fashioning of new life and work ethics.

The move away from salaried employment is a step into the unknown, and can occur at an age when living habits have generally stabilised. The effects of this disturbance can be unsettling. The sense of loss and the enforcement of quite fundamental changes can wreak havoc. Affected individuals can lose confidence and may become reclusive while the spouse may be confused over the root causes of the redundancy. Children who had enjoyed the security and continuity of the family's income stream, may find unaccustomed austerity frightening.

Successful transformation from a lifestyle centred around corporate employment to an enjoyable alternative requires the assumption of skills that may be alien, as well as overtly entrepreneurial in nature. Alien because however seemingly tough, the corporate lifestyle has many advantages which are not necessarily fully acknowledged but which do cushion the effects of error and under-performance. In that world there are usually plenty of checks and balances in place to ensure conformity in behaviour and consistency in results.

For example, in corporate life a bout of over-indulgence the night before may be accepted with a blind eye turned to the resultant diminished effort on the following day. It is easy enough to "coast" through the after-effects and few executives can honestly claim that they have never exploited the system for this purpose. Indeed it is only after such practices have become unduly disruptive that punitive action may be initiated from above. On the other hand, the over-indulgent self-employed entrepreneur is automatically punishing himself. Temporary reduction in his wits or skills means an irreplaceable loss of earning time. Unlike the corporate employee who is confident of his monthly salary payment, there is no reward for a day of zero achievement. This is PRP with a vengeance.

Other sources of pressure

The newly born entrepreneur faces additional economic and social pressures. It has been noted more that the most immediately felt loss arising from departure from corporate employment is in the expense account rather than in the salary. Perhaps surprising but really rather obvious. Travel, meals, entertainment, accommodation and those discreet out-of-pocket expenses account for much of the corporate executive's visible spending, as well as bolstering his sense of importance. The expense account provides the baubles that are the badges of office to the outside world signifying status, importance, authority, seniority etc.

Removal of these badges of office has a public impact. The absence of the smart late model executive car is noticeable to a far wider audience than the new, less visible challenge of meeting the mortgage payments. The transition from four-star luxury accommodation paid by the company to bed and breakfast paid for by oneself sharply reminds what has been lost. Equally, this process heightens the distinction between price and value, and focuses the mind on where lies the optimal balance between the two. The trade-off is in the recognition of Quality. The search for quality in work, lifestyle and rewards should be high on the wish list of every new entrepreneur and in his search for a satisfying alternative lifestyle.

To this end, previous career experience may be of only limited value in adjusting to the changes now necessary, and in middle age any fundamental change in direction, whether optional or obligatory, can be difficult. However, despite these hurdles, it is possible to make the change a success, and to find a fulfilling life in an alternative career.

The enormity of the personal change process

The people surplus with which we are concerned is typically the result of various corporate re-organisational exercises, justified by the latest management gobble-de-gook. It is a predominantly sexist and ageist phenomenon. Sexist because the still lamentable shortage of women in management yields numerically fewer female managers to be discarded. Ageist because a criterion of modern management is to diminish the value of experience, and because relative seniority by age implies, often erroneously, a reduced ability to respond to change, plus a proportionately higher employment cost.

De-manning that is driven by a policy of age displacement often has minimal sensitivity for comparative ability. Accordingly the newborn entrepreneur's immediate response should be to demonstrate that those capacities that the corporate system has rejected are still potent, vigorous, and there to contribute.

However, such determination is not enough on its own. A thorough self-assessment is essential in an objective self-evaluation. If perceived lack of flexibility has been a contributory factor in the candidacy for redundancy, then accept this at face value regardless of whether or not the view is justified. Experiment with change through quite simple means by looking at an opposing or different case – be it found in politics, music or even just newspapers.

To consider a different point of view from that normally adopted can be challenging, refreshing and even exciting. One's traditional view may not fundamentally change through this process. However, in seeing the other side and appreciating the motivation of the opposing causes, one's own beliefs and attitudes may become more tenable and reasonable in the eyes of others. If a sense of exhilaration derives from mature consideration of a hitherto revolutionary thought pattern, then the process of re-invention may have begun.

This presents a scenario markedly different from that which would normally be anticipated in retirement after a lifetime's corporate employment. That social model predicts a large degree of relaxation, social contact with ex-colleagues through reunions and the pensioners club, exercise gained through long walks in the country and golf several times a week. The middle-aged entrepreneur has to defer that cosy dream in the self-belief that he is still young enough and mentally sufficiently agile to make a contribution that will matter.

It would be nice if a neat and complete list could be produced of all the tasks needed for a comprehensive and effective exercise in re-invention. In fact the range of needs are as complex as human nature itself and it would be purposeless to try to bludgeon this complexity into a simplistic list of do's and don'ts. This subject and those people to whom it refers deserve better treatment. It is by applying a themed approach to the relevant issues and some of their environmental causes that we hope to help in the rejuvenation of a still valuable component of the workforce.

Steps into the unknown

The changes that we are witnessing in the demographics of employed labour are unprecedented. They promise to contribute to change in the nature of UK society in ways that we can only begin to understand. Components of the economic process that we have assumed to be immutable no longer enjoy sound foundations.

In years to come the notion of middle class employment that we presently consider to be standard may come to be considered quaint and out-of-date. Already the concept of the medium term employment contract embracing a salary supported by occupational pension rights and a package of fringe benefits is denied to significant numbers of otherwise capable middle aged people.

This is accompanied by growing cynicism in the minds of first time job seekers and younger executives that they will ever have the luxury of steady secure employment of the type that their parents had come to expect almost as a right. It is possible that future generations might view the model that has formed the backbone of white-collar employment in the 20th century as a short-term aberration in the developing panoply of modern economic and social activity.

Already it is clear that the lifetime expectations of the post war years categorised as 20 years of pre-employment, 40 years of employment, 10 years of retirement are obsolete. Life patterns are now well evolved into standards of disruption during the working phase. Developing this theme of career fragmentation, it is apparent that the typical 25 years working career will be broken up into as many as 5 or 10 contracts with different employers. Job mobility on this scale promises more departure from the traditional concept of employment stability.

What remains especially unclear and what is of specific concern to present generations are the implications of a standard 30 years plus of living after formal employment has ended. We anticipate that future career satisfaction will be much more a matter of individual initiative calling for greater measures of self-reliance and self-determination than would hitherto have ever been considered tenable in an employer-career stratified business world.

This places the middle aged, newly born entrepreneur of today very much at the sharp end of this step into the unknown. It was noted earlier how little the system had been modified to accommodate far reaching demographic changes, and therefore how much change has to be borne individually. The lag in systemic change will have major consequences for the response capacity of the centrally delivered services that earlier, more fortunate, generations took for granted.

Constraints on the system resulting from limitations on physical resources, population ageing and an increasing rate of exits from formal salaried employment conditions raises all sorts of interesting challenges for national planners and governments. At the micro or personal level, the questions are no less pressing. Just what is the individual going to do to fill all that time?

Governments may ponder the broad issues of care and social security for an expanding non-economically productive share of the population and they may well find their contingency planning for this uncertain future to be wanting. Equally many individuals, if they are honest, will find their personal planning processes to be deficient. On a material plane they may fear a shortage in supply of golf courses, bowls clubs and Spanish retirement villas (the Spanish are growing old also). Mentally, they may have a horror of the atrophy, moral decay and premature ageing that can accompany a life of hedonism and self-satisfaction stretching away into the future.

Conclusion

"I used to work for XYZ Ltd but for the past couple of years I have been working on my own as a self employed consultant". How often in a business forum or at a social gathering does one hear a comment like that, or something very similar? With growing frequency middle aged people whom in previous years would have been assumed to be safe in some salaried profession or activity are claiming now to have chosen to become self employed.

There are many derivations on the theme and different terms are used to describe what has been a profound and possibly traumatic change in someone's life. Phrases abound such as "I had always wanted to do something on my own" or "I could no longer tolerate the commute to the office and wanted to work from home" or "by working freelance, I could avoid company politics and really do something worthwhile".

Equally specific terms can actually mean something quite different. "Self employed" may in reality mean unemployed. "House husband" might indicate that the wife has far greater earnings power than her spouse. The term "consultant" itself covers a wide range of alternatives including near full time work, part-time or casual occupation, or a lot of unremunerated effort.

The speaker might try to portray the impression that transition from salaried employment was a matter of personal choice, and exercised at a time that was best suited to him. In part or in whole this may be a fabrication but may go unchallenged, out of courtesy or out of reluctance to probe into what might have been an unhappy period in a working career. Sometimes such kindness is misplaced because a frank sharing of experiences and the proffering of advice might make all the difference between success and failure in pursuit of a new career.

For a variety of reasons, the adoption of a role in consultancy may be viewed as a reasonable and easily assimilated development in a career path and superficially there would appear to be many advantages. Relief from the need to conform to corporate work schedules; absence of tedious business meetings; a world without company politics – these and other factors make self employed consulting seem attractive from the viewpoint of the stressed corporate executive.

These are undeniably cogent reasons for pursuing a move but there is a flip side. What is commonly overlooked is that accommodation of the change requires an alteration in attitudes, understanding and objectives that are as basic and as important as that needed to make a success of the move from school to university, or from university into employment.

No one need undertake such significant milestones early in life without help and guidance, from parents, teachers, career advisors, or prospective employers. A whole support network is available to ensure that the transition process is smooth, and that the investment of time and money in training and development is not wasted.

By comparison, the middle aged consultant starts with none of these aids and with little advice and guidance. The human resources department of his erstwhile employers is unlikely to have any residual interest in his case after the process of career severance is complete. Their interest is focused on closing the matter, and in moving on to tackle the next candidate. More enlightened employers may arrange the services of out-placement agencies. Their mandate though may be little more than an extension of the HR "tidying up" exercise, rather than an in-depth assessment of the future needs of the individual.

The individual himself is often misguided in his aspirations and over what he must undertake to fulfil them, and he may harbour quite unrealistic expectations. And who can blame him?

His life may have reached a crisis point, and he may still be recovering from the shock. He is entitled to feel resentful, confused, angry, lonely, or rejected. His family is facing fresh problems, anxieties and uncertainties. Contact with friends, acquaintances and ex-colleagues may be difficult and embarrassing. These are hardly circumstances under which it will be easy to form a balanced view of what to do next, and he may find that there is little or no objective help available to him.

A frequent response is to choose to set up in a role where previously acquired skills and experience can be packaged so that they can be sold for commercial gain. The motivation may be to sustain income levels or it may be simply that a life of doing nothing from middle age onwards after an active and demanding career in employment cannot be contemplated. Thus are many new aspiring consultants created.

Whatever influences are at work, the fact remains that most individuals who come into consulting under circumstances of this nature run a very high risk of failure. Lack of preparedness, inaccurate recognition of acquired skills and abilities, and failure to acknowledge the vital need for re-training are some of the causes.

The failure rate is a tragedy because many of these fledgling consultants are in this position through no fault of their own. They are victims of the rapidly changing nature of work and of the employment market but nevertheless, with the right guidance and stimulus they do still represent a vibrant, vital and needed element of the workforce. We hope that this book will contribute in that aim.

The end

but preferably,

the beginning!

Glossary of terms

Active client: A party who is paying for a consultant's services, or has entered into a binding contract to pay.

Affinity marketing: The practise of promotion through groups of potential clients who have a form of affinity, one to another. For example, they may be members of the same trade organisation or chamber of commerce, or they may share a similar type of technical or business problem. The affinity approach attempts to find clients who will refer or introduce other clients because of the shared nature of the issue. This can help to introduce scale economies into consulting promotion – which is hard to achieve by other means.

Ageism: Often the reason for the corporate redundancy which is the precursor to entry into independent consulting, it can be a positive marketing tool for the consultant. By stressing his age, the consultant is underlining his maturity and above all, the depth of his experience, and is thus providing comfort to the client.

Bandwidth: The concept that many clients have restricted ability to comprehend or digest a broad range of subject matter concurrently. Failure to respect the limitation of bandwidth may result in information overload, or in rejection of the consulting message. Measurement of bandwidth capacity is important in deciding the manner in which information is imparted to the client.

Body language: In face-to-face meetings, body language can be more indicative of the client's acceptance or rejection levels regarding points and proposals than any words that he may actually speak. However, so much has been written about this subject that body language is often exploited as a negotiating tool and may be used to mislead, and to signal precisely the opposite message.

Break even: The point at which income matches the amount of cost incurred in securing a contract, or an active client.

CEO: The chief executive officer of the client company, and the person through whom dealings should be promoted and directed in smaller organisations. With many small companies the CEO occupies one or more of the following roles: founder, chairman, managing director, technical director, majority shareholder.

Client cost: The aggregate average cost incurred to secure one consulting client. This costing methodology is individual to each consultant, computed on whichever costs he chooses to recognise, and may be a composite of actual and notional costs. It is an important figure to recognise because it is an indicator of what price will be paid in giving up on a existing client opportunity, or in looking for a new prospect (see also **Lead**).

Client contract: The written document specifying what work the consultant will undertake, and what fee the client will pay. No client may be considered "active" until he has signed this contract (see also **Engagement Letter**).

Code of practise: Sometimes drawn up by consultants as indicative of the terms on which they will do business in protection of the client's interests. May be used to assist promotional efforts, and may appended to the letter of engagement.

Cold call: The very first point of physical or telephonic contact between the consultant and a prospective client.

Collaboration agreement: A written agreement between two consultants to share work and fees in respect of an active client, or in jointly marketing their services.

Controllable client: A client who listens to the consultant, and is responsive to proposals and suggestions. The opposite is a client who signs a contract without due consideration of the obligations entered and who then fails to co-operate, or who through various actions makes it impossible for the consultant to undertake his contracted duties.

Corporate actions: The program of work that the consultant recommends should be undertaken as a result of his studies.

Corporate memory: An intangible but valuable facet of an organisation, it is the joint accumulated knowledge and experience vested in longer term employees in a stable working environment. The corporate memory is often an early casualty of redundancy programs, and its destruction can often negate the intended benefits of such programs

Corporate parasite: A potential client who welcomes the consultant with open arms, gives the impression of being interested in a contract, milks the consultant for his Intellectual Property (see **IPR**), and never pays a fee.

Cost reduction: A method of consulting whereby the fee is paid out of validated savings that the consultant has made in a client's operational expenses. Essentially a product rather than a relationship activity, it can be a useful adjunct to a general consultant's range of services. Cost reduction has the disadvantage that companies are increasingly aware of the savings that can be made without outside assistance; also special techniques are required to ensure that the **IPR** is not passed over before the client has contracted to pay for the service.

Cross sale: The sale of an additional product or service to an active client. An attractive technique because incremental income is earned at zero or minimal additional client cost (see also **Multiple sale**).

Deed of confidentiality: A deed entered between a consultant and his client whereby the former must treat all the information provided by the client as strictly confidential between the two (usually in perpetuity), and whereby information may only be released to third parties against specific written permission. (See also **Mutual non-disclosure agreement**).

Engagement letter: The contract by which the client engages the consultant's services (see Appendix for example)

Executive summary: A succinct and easily assimilated summary of the contents of a report that provides a thorough overview of the subject in hand. It should always precede the report, but is usually the final part to be actually written. If it exceeds two A4 pages in length, it is not an executive summary but something else.

Follow up: The process by which an initial contact is pursued, or by which further contact is maintained with a client or prospective client.

Front end: **fee** Also known as up-front fee. The payment of a fee, or part of an agreed fee, at the commencement of a consultant/ client contractual relationship. A useful mechanism to test the substance of a client's intentions if these are in doubt, or where the client appears to have unrealistic plans.

General consultant: A consultant who seeks to offer a broad range of services, and is thus more likely to relate, initially at least, to the CEO.

Gestation: The elapsed period between initiation of a contact and the signing of a letter of engagement. Frequently underestimated in planning new work opportunities and targeting income flow.

Hooks: The points given away by the target client in a solicitation or follow up interview which indicate that he has special problems or issues which could benefit from the assistance of a consultant. Usually the target client is unaware that he has said something that is of commercial potential in the consulting process. Hooks can therefore be used in the meeting summing up as a means of persuading him to enter a contract.

Independence maturity: The state of mind and demeanour by which an individual is able to work confidently and competently on his own in a freelance fashion.

Independent consultant: A consultant who is self-employed and who works entirely on his own i.e. without being employed by, or licensed to, or affiliated with, any formal or incorporated consulting group. Any co-operation with other consultants is likely to be restricted to limited period or task specific ad hoc collaboration agreements.

Internal focus: The state of mind or general attitude that concentrates on internal issues to the exclusion of recognition of the dictates of the customer base, or of the outside world at large. This is a common malaise among the employees of large organisations who are conditioned to submit to the corporate mores rather than to recognise that broader considerations and perhaps wiser counsels exist outside this closed arena.

IPR: Also know as Intellectual Property Rights, this is the consultant's core stock-in-trade and it is critical that this is sold through an enforceable client contract rather than given away without earnings being accrued. IPR is difficult and expensive to protect legally. Patents, copyrights, licenses and **mutual non-disclosure agreements** are the types of protection available but piracy is a fact of life and very common.

Laying pipe: A promotional effort with a possible future client which has no specific immediate sale in mind and is undertaken in the interests of building a warm relationship which may bear fruit at some indeterminate future time.

Lead: A business prospect.

Milestones: A summary of key actions and relative deadlines included in a consultant's report and recommendations.

Multiple sale: A situation where a number of different products or services can be sold to a single client (see also **Cross sale**).

Mutual non-disclosure agreement: Also known as a bi-lateral non-disclosure agreement, this is a legally binding agreement which may take many different forms but has the basic effect of binding two parties to share specific **IPR** between them, and not to disclose that material to third parties without mutual written consent. A stronger and more embracing contract than a **Deed of confidentiality**.

Natural market: The market which every individual enjoys when he leaves the corporate world, consisting of the contacts and goodwill garnered through his previous environment e.g. ex-employers, ex-customers, ex-colleagues, business and social friends and acquaintances. The natural market is always finite in time and exploitable value, and is a fragile and insecure base from which to build a sustainable, long term consulting business.

Nine dots: A simple figurative concept to describe the limitations and parameters of a client's business, economic and social environment. A consultant is not earning his keep if he is not taking his client beyond the constraints of the nine dots.

One more thing: The notion that regardless of how complete is a piece of work, there always at least one more thing that should have been included but has been overlooked.

Portfolio worker: A term coined by Charles Handy to describe the individual who is no longer prepared to risk his economic well-being in the hands of a single employer, and who therefore maintains a portfolio of viable activities which produce income from different sources.

Rebate: A down payment or deposit paid by a client as an act of good faith at the commencement of a task, to be off-set against payment of the fee on completion.

Rule of 4: The rule that for every four tenders issued to undertake consulting work, one should be accepted. If more than one in four is successful, the conclusion is that the tender price is too low (see also **Strike rate**).

Rule of 7: The rule that *on average*, it takes seven individual points of contact in the solicitation process before a client contract is signed.

Salaryman: Japanese term for **wage slave**.

Specialist consultant: A consultant who offers a single or small number of services, and whose specific disciplines are usually described in his title e.g. compliance, marketing, IT, ISO 9000. He may offer his services direct to clients or he may work as sub-contractor to a general consultant under a collaboration agreement.

Strike rate: The frequency with which approaches to prospective clients wins a positive response (see also **Rule of 4**)

Success fee: The concept of a fee paid on the basis of successful conclusion of a specific piece of work. Success fees should only be contemplated against carefully worded and binding client contracts, and the fee rate should be very generous compared with the consultant's standard **daily rate** – to take account of the risk factor and the opportunity cost. Usually success fee deals do not work out and should be avoided because they reflect a basic lack of commitment and confidence by the client. It is this minimal commitment to the "partnership" that militates against the consultant's efforts to complete a transaction successfully.

Time waster: Potential clients who are so vague, unprincipled, badly organised, uncommitted, lacking in self-determination or direction, that they refer to consultants for help more for self-serving psychological reasons than with any serious commercial intent (see also **Corporate parasite**).

Traps: Various points in a client contact where the consultant may be cornered. Examples: he may have been tricked into giving away rather than selling IPR; he may be stymied by presenting only closed questions; he may be on the defensive and having to justify his role; he may have lost control of the dialogue, and thus wasted the opportunity. Traps are invariably costly but can almost always be avoided by proper contact planning and control.

Virtual organisation: A new and increasingly effective form of company where there is little or no bricks and mortar investment in relation to the human resources engaged through various forms of telecommunications, and operating on a geographically remote basis. Virtual companies are expected to expand and become a significant economic force in step with the technological developments that aid commercial transactions in cyberspace and electronic commerce. Features of successful virtual organisations include major investment in state-of-the-art technology, high levels of direct income in relation to central overheads, and most activity devolved to remote operators. The National Lottery has many features of a virtual organisation.

Wage slave: Very common in conventional companies, he has consciously or unconsciously chosen to risk his income deriving from a single source and to deny himself opportunities for freedom and independence. Usually found wearing a suit (dark)

Walk-away: The point at which the consultant is determined to close a relationship as being no longer viable to pursue. Any further initiative will be left to be taken by the client; any response by the consultant will only be on the latter's terms.

Wavelength: The effective level of communication between the consultant and his client. Achievement of the right wavelength is essential for a financially beneficial and creative relationship.

Wired: The consultant who is fully equipped to exploit modern communications (telephone, email, the Internet and fax). A consultant who is not wired is not considered a professional.

Index

Index

Appendix A

Sample engagement contracts

The means by which a client may legally contract with a consultant to employ the services of the latter can take many different forms. We provide here two sample documents comprising a formalised consultancy agreement and a rather more informal letter of engagement.

These samples are provided for guidance and information purposes only. No warranty or guarantee is extended to the effect that either of the samples contained in this appendix constitutes the basis for a legally binding contract between the parties. It is recommended that qualified legal advice be sought as deemed suitable by the consultant prior to the entering of an engagement contract with his client.

Appendix A-1: Consultancy agreement

THIS AGREEMENT is made on the........th day of...........................199
between...............................of...............................(the "Client")
and...............................of...........................(the "Consultant")

1. Services

The Consultant as an independent contractor agrees to perform, during the term of this agreement, the following services on an exclusive/ non-exclusive basis:

....

2. Products

The term "Products" shall mean the Client's line of activities and services describe generally as...

3. Compensation

3.1 The Client shall pay the Consultant at the rate of £............. (pounds) per hour/ day for each hour/ day that the Consultant shall perform services during the term of this Agreement, provided that the number of hours/ days does not exceed ....hours/ days without the written consent of the Client.

3.2 In addition to the hourly/ daily compensation provided herein, the
Client agrees to pay the Consultant under the following conditions

....

3.3 All payments shall be subject to Value Added Tax.

4. Term

The initial term of this Agreement shall commence on the......day of ....199.. and shall terminate on the ....day of ....199... provided however that either party may terminate this agreement at any time during the initial term or any extension term by giving the other party not less than ..... days' notice in writing. This Agreement may be extended beyond the initial term or any extension term only by the written agreement of both parties prior to the extension of the initial term or any extension.

5. Designation of duties

The Consultant shall receive his requests for services to be performed from (name of officer) (title) (company name and address).

6. Restrictive covenant *(NB dependent on whether the services are exclusive or non-exclusive - see Clause 1.)*

During the term of this Agreement, the Consultant shall not make his services available to any competitor of the Client in the specific field in which he is performing services for the Client.

7. Patent rights

The Consultant agrees during the term of this Agreement and for a period of (12) months after the termination of this Agreement, to assign to the Client, its successors, assignees, or nominees, all right, title and interest in and to all inventions, improvements, copyrights, techniques and designs, and all other intellectual property made or conceived by him solely or jointly with others, relating to the Products, in the performance of this Agreement, together with all United Kingdom, European Union and foreign patents and copyrights if any which may have been obtained thereon by the Consultant, and at the

Client's request and expense, will execute and deliver all proper assignments thereof.

8. Confidentiality

The Consultant shall not disclose, publish, or authorise others to publish, design data, drawings, specifications, reports or other information pertaining to the work assigned to him by the Client, without the prior written approval of the Client unless required by Law until such matters come into the public domain. Upon the expiration or sooner termination of this Agreement, the Consultant agrees to return to the Client all drawings, specifications, data and other material obtained by the Consultant from the Client, or developed by the Consultant, in connection with the performance of this Agreement.

9. Reimbursable expenses

The following expenses plus Value Added Tax where appropriate will be invoiced in addition to compensation:

9.1 Travel expenses necessary in order to perform services required by the Agreement. Use of personal vehicles will be invoiced at ..per mile.

9.2 Hotel Accommodation and subsistence allowance at ...... per day.

9.3 Out-of-pocket personal expenses.

9.4 Telephone, telefax and telex charges.

9.5 Computer charges, printing and reproduction expenses.

9.6 Other expenses resulting from the performance of this Agreement.

10. Warranty *(NB More detailed warranties may be required)*

The Consultant's services will be performed in accordance with generally and currently accepted consulting principles and practises. This warranty is in lieu of all other warranties either expressed or implied.

11. Limitation of the consultant's liability

The Client agrees to limit any and all liability, costs, claims and demands of whatsoever nature including but not limited to........................ or the total amount of compensation, whichever is the less, on account of any error or omission on the part of the Consultant.

12. Payment terms

Terms of payment are as follows:

due on signing this Agreement
due monthly on the ....th day of each month
due at completion of the assignment

All invoices shall be regarded as delinquent if remaining unpaid for more than 30 days and a charge equivalent to ...% per month will be added in respect of all delinquent funds due to the Consultant. In the event that the Consultant shall be successful in any legal action for non-payment of sums due to it under this Agreement, the Consultant also shall be entitled to recover reasonable legal costs and expenses for bringing and maintaining any suit as a part of damages.

13. Variation of agreement

Any variation of this Agreement shall not be valid unless it shall be in writing and signed by both parties hereto.

14. Legal jurisdiction

This Agreement shall be subject to English Law and the English Court shall have exclusive jurisdiction.

IN WITNESS WHEREOF, the parties have signed this Agreement.

For and on behalf of (the
Client)..................of..

For and on behalf of (the
Consultant)…………………of………………………

Witness to the signatures above ....

Appendix A-2: Informal letter of engagement

(Consultant's address and date)

(Client's name and address)

Dear........

I write to confirm the basis on which I (as Consultant) will provide advisory and consultancy services to (name of CEO) of (name & address of Client) (the Client) in connection with ..../ for review of general business activities/ ....for the purpose of conducting a health check of the Client's business activities/...................for a special survey of...................

1. The nature of the engagement

Under the Engagement, the Consultant will perform investigation, review and advisory services as required by the Client including, as appropriate, the following:

1.1 ....etc

1.2 ....etc

The structures, solutions and strategies expressed by the Consultant and the advice given by the Consultant to the Client as a result of this work will remain confidential between the Client and the Consultant, and will not be disclosed or referred to in negotiations or otherwise with third parties without mutual consent unless required by Law until such matters come into the public domain.

2. Fees and commission

In consideration of the Consultant accepting the Engagement, the Client agrees to pay to The Consultant or his nominee the following amounts:

2.1 A fee for a minimum of £ / which will be paid in four instalments of minimum £ . The first instalment will be payable immediately upon acceptance of this letter, and the remaining at quarterly intervals thereafter/ the total fee shall be paid at the conclusion of the assignment described in Paragraph 1. above.

2.2 Reimbursement of reasonable travel, accommodation and out-of-pocket expenses, refunded concurrent with payment of the fee/ fee instalments specified under Paragraph 2.1.

2.3 Any external advisors, such as accountants, technical or specialist consultants, lawyers, engineers, quantity surveyors, interior design consultants or sub-contractors will be commissioned only following the written approval of the Client. All costs associated with such services will be borne by the Client.

2.4 All fees and expenses will be subject to Value Added Tax where appropriate, and all invoices issued by the Consultant shall be due for settlement within 30 days.

3. General

3.1 This agreement shall be effective from (date) until (date) or completion of the assignment, which shall be not later than (date).

3.2 During the term of this Agreement, the Consultant shall not make his services available to any competitor of the Client in the specific field in which he is performing services for the Client.

3.3 This agreement will be governed and construed in accordance with English Law and the English Court shall have exclusive jurisdiction.

Yours sincerely,

(The Consultant)

The terms and conditions set out above in this letter are agreed.

....

(The Client) (Date)

Appendix B
Sample collaboration agreement

This sample is provided for guidance and information purposes only. No warranty or guarantee is extended that it constitutes the basis for a legally binding contract between the parties. It is recommended that qualified legal advice be sought as deemed suitable by the consultant prior to the entering of an engagement contract with his client.

(Consultant's address, Date)

(Name & address of sub-contractor)

Dear

I refer to recent discussions about our proposed collaboration in a project to advise (name of client) of (address) (the "client") on (general description of the project or of consulting mandate). As discussed, it has been agreed with the client that part of this work will include (general description of sub-contractor's work and duties) into those areas covered by the consulting contract.

1. Nature of the collaboration:

1.1 I will engage your services in the capacity of sub-contractor for the express purpose of covering (more specific description of duties) for the client, in accordance with the terms and conditions of the contract with the client, a copy of relevant clauses of which are annexed hereto.

1.2 Upon successful publication of the work program specified in paragraph 1.1, the collaboration shall be terminated.

1.3 All contact direct with the client, be it written or verbal shall be through myself, unless I agree otherwise in writing.

2. Split of workload:

You shall be directly responsible for the timely and efficient completion of all work relating to (description), and you will provide all recommendations, reports and proposed work programs direct to myself for onward transmission to the client. In addition you will be required to make yourself available at least weekly for joint review meetings with the client and until your contracted work has been successfully completed, and your obligations under this agreement have been completely discharged. At least three business days' notice will be given of such review meetings.

3. Intellectual property:

The copyright relating to all work which you produce of a written nature shall pass to the client upon payment of your fees.

4. Reimbursement of costs:

4.1 Normal office expenses incurred in the project such as communications, stationery and sundry costs shall be reimbursed by ourselves within fifteen days of presentation of claims and supporting receipts or other documentation provided always that we shall at the time have received payment of such expenses from the Client.

4.2 Additional expenses such as travel and accommodation incurred in connection with the project shall be subject to prior agreement by us.

4.3 All fees and expenses will be subject to Value Added Tax where appropriate, and your invoices shall be due for settlement within 30 days.

5. Fees:

You will be reimbursed at the rate of £ (pounds) per day plus VAT for a period not exceeding (number) days, being your estimate of the time that it will take to undertake the sub-contracted work.

6. Time-scale:

The project shall be subject to submission of interim/ final reports by:

7. Non-competition:

You agree not to solicit business or other work from the client beyond that described in this agreement prior to the expiry of our contract with the client which is scheduled for (date) and for a period of ( ) months thereafter.

8. Indemnity

You shall hereby indemnify and hold me harmless against all losses, claims, liabilities, damages and expenses of any nature, directly or indirectly arising out of or as a result of any act or omission by you, or your agents or subcontractors in the performance of this Agreement.

9. Early termination

I shall have at my sole discretion the right to early termination of this agreement without compensation of fees and expenses due in the event of your failure to complete any part of your sub-contracted duties within ( ) days of any deadline mutually pre-agreed in writing.

10. Additional work

I agree to allow you the right to first refusal in respect of any additional work prospects related to (general description of sub-contractor's work and duties) that I may identify with the client during the duration of our contract.

11. Governing law

This agreement shall be subject to the laws of England and the English Court shall have exclusive jurisdiction.

Yours sincerely,

(Name of consultant)

I accept the above-mentioned terms and conditions......... (Name of sub-contractor))

Appendix C
Code of practise, confidentiality and mutual non-disclosure

The examples of engagement contracts set out in **Appendix A** *include clauses regarding the confidentiality with which information provided by the client is to be treated. However, some clients are sensitive about the treatment and disposal of commercially valuable material, and they may require the consultant to be specifically bonded through a separate document. The offer to enter into such a binding declaration may prove an assistance to the promotional effort should the client be in some doubt whether it is wise to be as full and frank as the consultant may require in order to do an effective job.*

We have provided three types of document that may help to allay the client's fears. Firstly there is an example of a Code of Practise that sets out the standards upon which the Consultant has decided to conduct his business; this might be appended to an engagement letter. We recommend that every consultant should prepare his own Code of Practise.

Secondly, we provide a standard deed of confidentiality in three versions. Version C-2a adopts a very simplistic format whereas C-2b is a deed for use where the consultant is trading in his own name and C-2c is applicable to business undertaken in the name of a limited company.

Finally, we provide a mutual non-disclosure agreement. This document provides equal protection to the consultant as well as to the client. The competent consultant has much of value to offer in the intellectual property rights that he controls or owns. Thus confidentiality is a two way street and the client should be equally bound not to abuse the commercially sensitive information that might be an integral part of the consultant's stock-in-trade.

These samples are provided for guidance and information purposes only. No warranty or guarantee is extended to the effect that any of the samples contained in this appendix constitutes the basis for a legally binding contract between the parties. It is recommended that qualified legal advice be sought as deemed suitable by the consultant prior to the entering of an engagement contract with his client.

Appendix C-1: Code of practise

I, (name of consultant) or we, (name of consultant's company) ("the consultant") hereby undertake at all times to adhere to the following standards and principles in the conduct of my/ our business on behalf of clients who have engaged my/ our services in the areas of general or specific business consulting, advice and guidance:

The consultant will:

1. only undertake assignments which it is competent to fulfil and where the client's requirements have been fully documented and agreed through a signed Contract of Engagement ;

2. advise clients of potential conflicts of interest before accepting any assignment;

3. provide full explanation of the relevant services and their costs, including ancillary expenses, terms of business, and schedules for completion of assignments;

4. never approach any third party in connection with an assignment without first obtaining clearance from the client

5. ensure strict confidentiality at all times concerning the information provided by the client or its nominees;

6. only engage in a collaborative manner the services of other consultants, advisors or technical experts who are of proven competence and who are similarly bound to confidentiality, and always subject to the prior consent of the client;

7. respond promptly and expeditiously to all requests by the client within the parameters of the agreed assignment;

8. provide full and complete reports and recommendations to the client at the completion of the assignment in the form and structure agreed at the outset;

9. maintain prompt and regular communication with the client throughout the assignment;

10. refrain from undertaking any consulting or advisory work on behalf of any known competitor of the client for a period of 12 months from the completion of an assignment.

Signed ....(consultant)

Appendix C-2a: Confidentiality agreement

I, (consultant's name) of (address) do hereby agree and affirm that all technical and administrative data concerning the activities of (client's name) provided to me by (name of officer of client) and his colleagues shall remain strictly confidential to me indefinitely unless required by Law until such matters come into the public domain.

In accepting the information concerning (client's name) and other related data provided by (officer of client), I recognise without reservation (name of client's officer) as my sole intermediary and future correspondent in respect of all matters concerning (client's name), and I do hereby agree to conduct all and every subsequent business concerning the (client's name) through (officer of client) or any other officer of the company whom he may expressly choose to nominate to act for him.

Signed: (consultant)

Acknowledged: (officer of client)

Appendix C-2b: Personal deed of confidentiality

THIS DEED OF UNDERTAKING is made the day of 199 by ....of...................................(the "Consultant") in favour of ………………………of ………………………...(the “Client”)

WHEREAS:-

(A) The Client has contracted to provide intellectual property to the Consultant

(B) The Consultant has at the request of the Client agreed to enter this Deed in favour of the Client

WITNESSES as follows:

1. The Consultant hereby covenants and undertakes to the Client:-

1.1 To treat and retain as secret and confidential all information relating to the Client or any systems or operations of the Client or any customer of the Client and any information derived therefrom as disclosed, communicated or supplied to the Consultant by the Client (whether orally in writing or by any other method) or otherwise acquired or obtained or held or arrived at by the Consultant including, without prejudice to the generality of the foregoing, all tapes, discs, diskettes, handbooks, manuals, drawings, designs, specifications, charts, diagrams and any such documents or materials containing any such information. The said information and all documents, media and materials recording or containing any part or parts of the same and any copies thereof are herein collectively referred to as "the Information";

1.2 Not to have in his possession any of the Information or to take copies of any of the Information except in the course of and only to the extent necessary for the proper performance of the designated duties as a consultant to the client;

1.3 To return to the Client forthwith on termination of his contract with the Client for whatever reason any originals or copies of the Information howsoever recorded in his possession or under his control.

2. The obligations to the Client hereunder shall continue in full force and effect during and after termination of this contract with the Client for whatever reason unless required by Law until such matters come into the public domain.

IN WITNESS whereof the Consultant has executed this deed the day and year first before written.

Signed as a deed by..

In the presence of:..(Witness)

Appendix C-2c: Company deed of confidentiality

THIS DEED is made the day of 199
between
.................................of..........................(the “Consultant”)
and ....of.............................(the “Client”)

WHEREAS by an exchange of letters between the Consultant and the Client dated .... and ....respectively (together "The Engagement Contract") it is agreed that:

(A) to enable the Consultant to carry out its duties under the Engagement Contract the Client will supply to the Consultant certain information relating to the Client and/or its customers; and

(B) the Consultant is entering into the Deed to record the terms upon which it will receive and hold such information which may be provided by the Client or any of its associated or affiliated companies and/or its customers.

WITNESSES as follows:-

1. The Consultant hereby covenants and undertakes:-

1.1 To treat and retain as secret and confidential all information relating to the Client (and all its associated/ affiliated companies) or any systems or operations of the Client or any customer of the Client as disclosed communicated or supplied to the Consultant by the Client (whether orally in writing or by any other method) or otherwise created or acquired by the Consultant under or in connection with the Engagement Contract including, without prejudice to the generality of the forgoing, all handbooks, manuals, drawings, designs, specifications, charts, diagrams, tapes, discs, diskettes and any other documents or materials containing any such information unless required by Law until such matters come into the public domain. The said information and all documents, media and materials recording or containing any part or parts of the same or any copies thereof are hereinafter collectively referred to as "Information";

1.2 To use Information solely for the purpose of performing its duties under the Engagement Contract;

1.3 To use all reasonable endeavours to protect Information from and against theft or damage or unauthorised copying or disclosure;

1.4 To use all reasonable endeavours to restrict access to Information to those of its employees and directors directly engaged in providing services under the Engagement Contract;

1.5 Not to allow any persons who are not employees of the Consultant (other than employees or authorised representatives of the Client) to have access to Information or any copies thereof;

1.6 The Consultant warrants that each of its employees has or will sign a confidentiality agreement on being employed by the Consultant. The Consultant will use all reasonable endeavours that the Consultant's employees and directors who will have access to Information are aware of and comply with the Consultant's obligations under this Deed;

1.7 In the event that any of the Information shall be copied, disclosed or used otherwise than as permitted under this Deed then without prejudice to any rights or remedies of the Client in respect of such copying, disclosure or use the Consultant shall forthwith notify the Client of such an event and if requested take such steps (including the institution of legal proceedings) as shall be necessary to remedy (if capable of remedy) the default and/or to prevent further unauthorised copying disclosure or use;

1.8 To return to the Client the originals and copies of the Information in the Consultant's possession or under its control if so requested by the Client unless any due payment by the Client to the Consultant remains outstanding.

1.9 The Consultant hereby undertakes to comply with all relevant provisions of the Data Protection Act 1984 and any statutory modification or re-enactment thereof or regulations and statutory instruments made pursuant thereto from time to time ("the Act"). In particular the Consultant will agree in advance with the Client its procedures for holding and processing personal data (as defined in the Act) and its security measures for storing Information and will not alter any such agreed procedure without the prior written consent of the Client. The Consultant confirms that it will effect and maintain all necessary registrations under the Act.

1.10 The Consultant's duty of confidence hereunder shall continue in full force and effect notwithstanding termination of the Engagement Contract and compliance with the provisions of clause 1.8 above.

2. The Consultant undertakes that if it shall be supplied with any headed notepaper or other documents bearing the Client's name and / or any devices which reproduce symbols of the Client or facsimile signatures of any employee, manager, or director of the Client, the Consultant shall ensure that such notepaper, documents and devices are only used as permitted by the Client and are kept in a secure place and access thereto and supervision of the use thereof restricted to senior and responsible members of the staff of the Consultant the identity and positions within the Consultant's organisation of whom have been previously notified to the Client in writing. The Client shall have the right to require the Consultant not to allow access to the

materials in question to any such employees as the Client shall designate. The Consultant further undertakes to return such notepaper, documents and devices to the Client forthwith upon request.

3. The Consultant hereby acknowledges that the Information and all copies thereof shall be and remain the property of the Client.

IN WITNESS whereof the Consultant has executed this Deed the day and year first before written.

Signed as a Deed by Consultant

In the presence of:

Witness

Appendix C-3: Mutual non-disclosure agreement

This bilateral non-disclosure agreement (hereinafter called "Agreement") entered into and effective as of the date entered below:

Between:	of	(hereinafter called “the Client”)
And:	of	(hereinafter called "the Consultant")

As the Client is engaged in the (general description of business activities or specific project) under (description) conditions at (location) and in connection with this activity/ program has in its possession certain valuable Confidential Information relating thereto;

As the Consultant is engaged in the business of (general description) and has in its possession certain valuable Confidential Information relating thereto, including without limitation (such Confidential Information hereinafter called in certain provisions Consultant's Confidential Information): and

As the parties are willing to exchange their respective Confidential Information subject to certain terms and conditions outlined below in order to permit each other only to evaluate the other party's Confidential Information for the purpose of developing the.....................................

In consideration of the covenants hereinafter contained and other good and valuable consideration, the parties agree as follows:

1. The Client agrees to disclose to the Contractor such portion of the Client's Confidential Information as the Client considers necessary and appropriate in the circumstances for the purposes indicated

above in the recitals. The Consultant agrees to disclose to the Client such portion of the Consultant's Confidential Information as considered necessary for the purposes set out in the recitals above. All Confidential Information disclosed hereunder in written, printed or some other tangible form shall be clearly and conspicuously marked by the disclosing party with the word "Confidential" or "Restricted" or otherwise identified by an appropriate stamp or legend indicating its confidential nature. All Confidential Information disclosed hereunder verbally or visually and identified by the disclosing party as confidential when disclosed to the receiving party shall be confirmed in a written resume within 30 days following such disclosure. Any such resume shall be marked by the disclosing party in the same manner as described above.

The parties agree to hold all Confidential Information disclosed hereunder by the other party in confidence for a period of two years from the date of receipt hereunder and to use the same degree of care, but no less than a reasonable degree of care, to prevent any unauthorised disclosure or publication thereof as they use to protect their own Confidential Information of a like nature. The parties agree not to disclose or divulge any of such Confidential Information to anyone except their employees who have a need to know same and are directly involved in the above-mentioned exercise(s) provided such employees have executed a secrecy agreement with their employer in advance of any disclosure of such Confidential Information that provides for at least the confidentiality and restricted use obligations that apply to the parties pursuant to this Agreement.

2. The parties further agree not to use any Confidential Information disclosed hereunder by the other party for any purpose other than the purposes(s) described above for the same period of time identified in Paragraph 1. above from the date of its receipt hereunder without the prior written consent of the disclosing party.

Nothing in the Agreement will be construed as a representation or inference that either party will not independently pursue similar opportunities, provided that its obligations set out in this Agreement are not breached.

3. All Confidential Information disclosed pursuant to this Agreement and all documents relating thereto disclosed hereunder shall remain the property of the disclosing party and shall be returned promptly by the receiving party to the disclosing party together with any copies thereof upon receipt by the receiving party of a written request from the disclosing party therefore which the disclosing party may make at any time and from time to time except for one copy of each which the receiving party may retain for dispute resolution purposes only in connection with this Agreement. Each party shall have the right to make a reasonable number of copies of confidential documents as required in order to carry out the above mentioned purposes of this Agreement.

4. The foregoing obligations imposed upon each of the parties to keep all Confidential Information disclosed hereunder by the disclosing party in confidence and not use any thereof for any purpose other than the purposes described above shall not apply to any such information which the receiving party can show:

a) is already in the possession of the receiving party at the time of receiving the same from the disclosing party without the obligation of confidentiality as shown by the prior records of the receiving party;

b) is published or becomes available within the public domain otherwise than as a consequence of a breach by the receiving party of its obligation not to disclose any of the disclosing party's Confidential Information;

c) is lawfully received by the receiving party from any third party without restriction on disclosure or use;

d) is independently developed without any breach of this Agreement by the receiving party's personnel who have not had access to any of the disclosing party's Confidential Information; or

e) is approved in writing by the disclosing party for release or other use by the receiving party according to terms stipulated in such approval.

5. Except as otherwise expressly permitted hereunder, no license under any trade secret, patent, patent application, industrial design, trademark, copyright, mask work, confidential process, formula, plan, computer program, data or other valuable Confidential Information or know-how is granted to the receiving party or can be implied by disclosure to the receiving party by the disclosing party of any of the disclosing party's Confidential Information hereunder. The parties shall use reasonable effort to attempt to provide information hereunder to the other party that is accurate; neither party, however, shall assume any responsibility whatsoever with respect to the accuracy of such information.

6. This Agreement shall continue for a period of two years from its effective date subject, however, to the proviso that either party may terminate this Agreement at any time during the period upon at least thirty days prior written notice to the other party. Unless previously returned pursuant to Paragraph 3. above or otherwise agreed, upon the expiration or termination of this Agreement, the parties shall promptly return all Confidential Information and all documents relating thereto disclosed to them hereunder together with any copies thereof except for one copy of each which the receiving party may retain for dispute resolution purposes only in connection with this Agreement. The obligations concerning disclosure and use of Confidential Information imposed hereunder shall survive the expiration or

termination of the Agreement and shall continue to bind the parties, their successors, permitted assignees and their representatives for the balance of the period of time identified in paragraph 1 above then outstanding from the date of first receipt of such Confidential Information hereunder or with respect to any applicable portion thereof, until the effective date of any of the events recited in paragraphs 4 (b) to 4 (e) above, whichever occurs first.

7. This Agreement contains the entire agreement of the parties relating to the subject matter hereof and supersedes all proposals, negotiations, representations, warranties, conditions and agreements, collateral or otherwise, oral or written, relating thereto made prior to the execution hereof. Any modification or amendment to this Agreement must be in writing, having direct reference to this Agreement and must be signed by both parties. The invalidity of any provision hereof shall not affect any remaining provisions.

8. This Agreement and the rights and obligations granted to and undertaken by the parties shall not be assignable or transferable, in whole or in part, by either party without the prior written consent of the other party.

9. This Agreement shall be governed and interpreted in accordance with the applicable laws of England. The parties shall comply with applicable law relating to the import, export and re-export of Confidential Information disclosed pursuant to this Agreement.

10. Each party appoints its employee listed below as its respective Data Control Co-ordinator to provide and receive on its behalf all Confidential Information in a tangible form exchanged under this Agreement. Each party may change its Data Control Co-ordinator by giving written notice of the new Data Control Co-ordinator's name and address.

All notices, requests and other communications pursuant to this Agreement shall be in writing and shall be given by sending same by fax and confirmed by prepaid recorded or by registered post or by courier or by hand delivery and signed for on receipt or by prepaid registered or certified post with return receipt request to the other party addressed in the case of the Client:

(Names and address) Attention:...........................

and in the case of the Contractor:

(Name and address) Attention:............................

Any notice, request or other communication forwarded hereunder shall be deemed to have been received if delivered by fax, on the date of issuance at the sending party's terminal of a notice of confirmation of receipt at the receiving party's terminal, if delivered by courier or by hand, on the date of delivery, and if mailed, on the fifteenth business day (days other than Saturdays, Sundays, statutory holidays and locally observed company holidays) of addressee after it has been mailed except, however, in the event of an interruption of mail service in the country where either party resides as indicated above in which case receipt shall be deemed to occur when such notice is actually received.

Each party may change its address for service hereunder by written notice to the other party of its new address.

11. Each party agrees not to use the other party's name in any way for advertising or promotional purposes or to make any disclosure to any third party or any public announcement regarding the existence or content of the Agreement without obtaining the prior written consent of the other party.

12. The parties understand and agree that discussions hereunder are exploratory only and that no commitment or representation has been or is made by the Client to Consultant or vice versa that will result in the development, manufacture, marketing, sale or supply of any product or service by either party for or to the other party whatsoever. The Client and the Consultant are under no obligation to incorporate any suggestion, idea, feature or specification exchanged between them under this Agreement in any products or services developed, manufactured, marketed, sold or supplied by either party.

Neither party shall make under this Agreement any commitment or incur any charge or expense for or in the name of the other party. Neither party has any obligation by virtue of this Agreement to procure any products or services from the other party. Neither execution nor performance of this Agreement shall be construed or deemed to have established any joint venture or partnership or have created the relationship of principal and agent between the Client and the Consultant.

13. The parties agree that the reproduction of signatures by way of tele-copying device will be treated as though such reproduction were executed originals, and each party undertakes to provide each other with a copy of this Agreement bearing original signatures as soon as possible after acceptance.

IN WITNESS WHEREOF the parties hereto have caused this Mutual Non-disclosure Agreement to be signed by their respective duly authorised representative as of the date written below.

.....................for the Client ....for the Consultant

(Date)

Appendix D
Pro forma interview questions

The more the consultant knows about the affairs of his client, the better equipped he will be to work competently. Information gathering is a continuing task, even for the smaller business undertaking, and can never be considered complete. Nonetheless, the consultant has to take a decision at some stage to commit to views and recommendations, while being aware that he still needs to know more. At that point, he should at least be certain that he has covered all the appropriate topics, even if the information on some areas is scant.

As explained in Chapters 8 and 9, the collection of data is a complex matter calling for the application of interrogative and observational abilities that will become more refined and effective with practise. To ensure that complete coverage is achieved, a structured approach is to be preferred, but always allowing flexibility for the discussion to follow its own or natural course, and to be responsive to the manner in which the client wishes to impart his information. The adoption of a series of questions in the manner of a questionnaire is too rigid, will give the impression that the consultant is an amateur at work, and will swiftly alienate the client.

The questions set out below are in an order that could be considered appropriate for a potential investor carrying out a due diligence exercise on a target company. In many ways this is a suitable analogy because consulting is a highly judgmental process. The consultant's views and recommendations should always be researched and presented in the expectation that they will form the basis for decisions involving the commitment or expenditure of real money. Good consulting is not a theoretical exercise; it is fashioned on the premise that someone is going to place hard cash where the consultant's mouth has been.

Sample questions:

1. Principal activities

1.1 What are the precise activities/ products/ services ("activities")?

- Relationship to each other
- Rationale for the mix
- Major/ minor activities
- Relative contribution of each to turnover/gross margin/ net profit
- History, background and logic for each

1.2 What are the particular features of each activity?

- Reputation
- Price
- Useful operating life
- Attractive aspects
- Fashion or necessity
- Quality
- Product lifecycle
- Packaging and presentation
- Service support
- Guarantees and warranties

1.3 What other information is relevant to understanding the significance of each activity?

- Uniqueness
- Customer loyalty
- Branding
- Premium appeal

2. Customers

2.1 What is the profile of the customer base?

- Number
- Aggregate value
- Average value
- 20% largest customers
- Exposure to large customers
- Number of small customers

2.2 What is the profile of the typical customer?

- Age, gender
- Personal or corporate
- Typical needs and expectations
- Reason for being a customer

2.3 How are sales made?

- Contract or open trade
- Lead times
- Programmed or spontaneous purchasing
- Repeat sales factor
- After sales support
- Average transaction size
- Seasonal factors
- Pattern of and reason for demand fluctuations
- Predictability of fluctuations

2.4 What is the contribution to gross margin of each activity?

- Historic pattern of growth over last 3/ 5/ 7 years
- Declining or growing sales per activity
- Degree of help needed for weaker activities
- Comparison of gross margin with net contribution per activity

2.5 What is the position with the order book?

- Historical comparisons
- Underlying trends
- Ability to satisfy on schedule

3. Markets

3.1 How is the market measured?

- Global, International, European, national, regional or local
- Value
- Number of customers
- Number of suppliers
- Based on own activities or inclusive of additional possible substitute activities
- Inclusive or not of foreign customers and suppliers

3.2 What is the position with the defined market?

- Size of market share
- Methodology used for measuring market share
- Share growing or contracting
- Individual activity shares growing or contracting
- Pace of change accelerating or decelerating
- Technology and product substitution threat

3.3 Are there any plans to change significantly the market position?

- New or replacement activities
- Activities to be withdrawn
- Promotional programs for new geographic sectors or customer types, or different positions within existing market sectors

3.4 What logistical issues arise from proposed changes in market position?

- Market research
- Advertising
- Packaging
- Distribution methods

4. Competition

4.1 Who are the main competitors?

- Size and representation
- Number
- Their competitive advantages
- Growing or diminishing threat

4.2 Has foreign competition been fully evaluated?

- Impact of changes intra-EU regulations
- Tariff changes
- Far eastern/ third world/ eastern European competitive forces

4.3 What future patterns are expected in the development of competition?

- New technology
- Product substitution
- Low cost suppliers
- Pricing wars

5. Marketing

5.1 What commitment is made to marketing?

- Existence of marketing department
- Recognition of difference between marketing and sales
- Importance attached at senior management levels

5.2 What reliance is placed on expert assistance?

- Strength of internal marketing department
- Use of external sources of help
- Ability to identify and respond swiftly to market changes

6. Suppliers

6.1 What is the nature of procurement?

- Number and identity of suppliers
- Reliability and quality consistency
- Undue exposure to and reliance on particular names
- Nature of contracts
- Price stability

6.2 Have alternative supply sources been investigated?

- Availability of better quality/ reliability/ price
- Alleviation of risk
- Contingency factors

7. Physical Resources

7.1 What is the nature of the property assets?

- Age, condition
- Suitability
- Room for expansion
- Health & safety factors
- Access
- Proximity to main markets/ suppliers/ raw materials
- Asset utilisation
- Yield on assets

7.2 What is the nature of the plant and equipment?

- Age, condition
- Maintenance standards
- Depreciation
- Replacement policy
- Utilisation factors
- Technology substitution

7.3 Is the Information Technology infrastructure adequate?

- Book-keeping and control systems
- Stocks & debtors control
- Management information
- Extent of IT use among managers and staff
- Compliance issues (Y2K, sector regulation etc)
-

7.4 What manufacturing systems are in use?

- Labour productivity
- Efficiency factors
- Quality control
- Production flexibility
- Waste rates
- Environmental issues

7.5 How is production scheduling controlled?

- Nature of systems
- Predictive capacity
- Co-ordination with marketing/ sales/ finance

7.6 How adequate is warehousing and distribution?

- Control systems
- Stock levels
- Information retrieval
- Security of storage

- Loss and pilferage factors
- Proximity to suppliers and customers
- Efficiency of layout and co-ordination with manufacturing

7.7 Is inventory properly controlled?

- Adequacy of computer system
- Age and condition of stock
- Value (forced sale or market)
- Buffer stock policy
- Supplier relationships and co-ordination

8. Management and employees

8.1 What is the organisational structure?

- Organogram
- Departmental/ divisional structure
- Staff numbers/ gender/ age range
- Training and development
- Recruitment policies
- Terms of employment
- Unionisation
- Staff turnover and loyalty

8.2 How well balanced is the management team?

- Mixture of expertise and skills
- Training and background
- Individual authority levels
- Inter-departmental co-operation and communication
- Team skills or individual players
- CV's of principal managers

8.3 What is the remuneration policy?

- Salary structure
- Performance recognition

- Bonus schemes
- Employee participation in equity
- Comparison with competition/ industry/ local standards

8.4 How relevant are labour regulations?

- European works councils
- Health & safety
- Working hours
- Minimum wage legislation

8.5 What fringe benefits are provided?

- Employee facilities
- Health insurance
- Overtime policy
- Holiday policy
- Pension scheme

9. Financial Issues

9.1 What is the historic financial record?

- Profit record for previous five years or longer
- Contribution per activity
- Balance sheets
- Capacity to generate cash flow
- Growth of shareholder equity
- Ratio analysis
- Isolation of non-recurring or exceptional items
- Debt policy
- Off balance sheet finance

9.2 What are the forecasts for the business and how realistic are they?

- Business plan
- Current management accounts
- Sales forecasts and projections

- Budgetary planing process
- Projected profits – aggregate and divisional
- Contribution per activity
- Cash flow and capital appetite
- Capital expenditure needs
- Assumptions supporting projections

10. Proprietorial issues

- Age and health of owner
- Remuneration package
- Retirement and pension planning
- Family succession
- Remaining ambitions and aspirations

11. Other matters

The following are additional issues to be investigated:

- Trademarks and licences
- Insurance
- Contingent liabilities
- Litigation
- Major contracts
- Research & development
- Independent asset valuations
- Product literature

Appendix E
Sample company health check report

BUSINESS ANALYSIS: **UVW Ltd**

PRINCIPAL CONTACTS:

Tony Smith	Managing Director
John Smith	Foreman (son of MD)
Ms Annie Long	Bookkeeping clerk

1. BACKGROUND & TRENDS:

Company started nine years ago. Operates a vehicle maintenance and repair workshop. Good service standards and fine pricing have resulted in rapid growth in last three years. Year-on-year turnover growth was 13%, 18%, 21%. Profitability in same period has grown 4%, 3% and 7%. Staff numbers are now 10. Company owns its premises.

Although sales growth has been good, local competition is getting stronger, helped by more modern workshop equipment.

Mr Smith plans to retire within next 2 years and will hand business to his son.

2. CONSULTANT'S MANDATE

2.1 General health check of business.
2.2 Review ways to improve profits.
2.3 Review debt funding and recommend improvements.

3. COMPANY'S RESOURCES REVIEW

3.1 Premises
- presently adequate
- need for more room in 12 months
- lease on next door premises expires in 5 months
- expansion by taking adjacent space?

3.2 Workshop equipment
- mainly OK for present needs
- some new tooling required
- possibility of lease finance.

3.3 Office & stores
- stores records still manually maintained
- space adequate for future needs
- stores could be more efficient if closer to office

3.4 Computer system
- suitable for this size business
- not properly utilised for stores controls
- debtors records incomplete

3.5 Staff
- appear technically competent
- training in IT skills for stores staff needed

4. DAILY OPERATIONS

4.1	Workshops	-	no comments
4.2	Stores	-	could be better located
		-	require computerisation
		-	stock control appears acceptable
4.3	Office	-	need for better management information
4.4	Accounts	-	new debtors management system needed
		-	regular review of exposure per account name required
4.5	Finance	-	bank overdraft level inadequate
		-	lease finance should be investigated
		-	factoring appears too expensive

4. SPECIFIC RECOMMENDATIONS & ACTION RESPONSIBILITIES

IMMEDIATE	introduce new debtors system (bookkeeper)
	approach bank for increased overdraft – security? (MD & consultant)
IN ONE MONTH	renegotiate factoring terms (MD)
	negotiate lease for new tooling (MD)
IN TWO MONTHS	relocate stores (Foreman)
	computerise stores records (Consultant)
	basic IT training for storeman (Consultant)
IN FOUR MONTHS	approach next door's landlord regarding lease of those premises (MD)

Appendix F
Sample of a potential client database

Information gathered for potential future use grows rapidly in active consulting. The creation of viable methods for logical storage is integral to operational effectiveness. There will always be more potential than active clients and most will not justify their own files until real business is in prospect. However, collecting and recording data from a number of different sources is a valuable means of improving client solicitation. Set out below is a sample of a database:

Name Address/ Tel No	CEO/ Senior Managers	Activities	Comments
ABC Plumbing Ltd 10 High St	A. Jones MD	Implied	Mailshot 2/3/99 deferred call Next contact 1/7/99
DEF Ltd 5 Low St	B. Brown Finance Director	Wholesale Distribution	T/O £3.5M Rumoured to be in financial difficulty Have lost major customers recently Existing client XYZ owed £30K overdue by DEF

Appendix F Sample of a potential client database

GHI Metals Ltd 6 New St	R. Green MD	Steel traders	Contacted 3/2/99 Refused any approach at all. Very aggressive. No priority
JKL Printers Ltd 8 Old Street	G. White Chairman	Printers	T/O £14M Feature article 1/12/98 in *Chronicle* (see Newspaper clippings file). Expanding rapidly. Known to be in crowded premises. Met White briefly at Chamber of Commerce lunch 4/2/99. Appear to be short of adequate skilled management. Priority target. Diarised for April mailshot & telesales program
MNO Caterers Ltd 9 Fore Street		Contract catering	Started business Dec 1998
PQR Signs Ltd	Letter of engagement d 1/10/98 - See active client file		
STU Sales Ltd 12 Bridge Road	A. Rowe MD	Pharmacy chain	Several tries for meeting 1998 - always postpones. Possible time waster. Last try diarised May 99.

Appendix G
Skills self-evaluation

Part 1: Industry sector experience: categorise each sector/ industry

(1 = expert skills, 2 = technical skills, 3 = operational skills, 4 = some practical exposure, 5 = minimal working understanding)

Primary	**Experience level**
Agriculture – advisory and service support	
Agriculture – crops	
Agriculture – livestock	
Coal mining	
Fishing	
Forestry	
Market gardening	
Metal mining	
Mining & quarrying	
Oil & gas extraction	
Plant products & extracts	
Timber products	
Water resources	

Secondary

Experience level

Building construction
Chemicals & allied products
Clay, glass & stone products
Clothing & apparel
Computer hardware
Computer software
Control & analysis equipment
Electrical equipment & components
Fabricated metal products
Food products
Furniture & office fittings
General manufacturing activities
Heavy construction
Industrial & commercial machinery
Leather products
Motor manufacturing
Paper & allied products
Petroleum refining & allied
Pharmaceuticals
Pipelines
Primary metal products
Printing, publishing & allied industries
Railway equipment
Rubber & misc. plastic products
Specialised construction
Textile products
Tobacco products
Transportation equipment
Vehicle components

Tertiary (services)

Experience level

Air transportation

Automotive dealers

Bank & finance

Building materials & allied

Business services

Cinemas & theatres

Clothing & apparel sales

Communications

Couriers

Food & drink establishments

Food sales & distribution

Gas

General merchandising

General retail

General utilities

Health services

Home furnishings & equipment sales

Hotels & general accommodation

Insurance

Insurance broking and agency

Investment companies

Leisure

Legal services

Local transportation

Motor freight

Museums & exhibitions

Nursing care

Personal services

Petroleum distribution & sales

Postal

Real estate

Social services

Wholesaling

Part 2 Primary skills

(1 = expert skills, 2 = technical skills, 3 = operational skills, 4 = some practical exposure, 5 = minimal working understanding)

Experience level

Accounting & bookkeeping
Advertising
Branding
Budgeting & costing
Business modelling & planning
Business strategy
Change management
Compliance control
Configuration management
Contract negotiation & drafting
Disaster & contingency planning
Documentation control
Feasibility assessments
Financial administration & control
Fixed asset planning & management
Industrial relations
Internal audit
Manpower development
Market analysis
Market research & development
Marketing
Operations management
Organisation & methods
Organisational development
Outsourcing management
Personnel
Procurement
Product planning & launch
Program management

Project leadership
Property management
Risk management
Quality assurance & control
Sales & distribution
Stock management
Systems testing & development
Technical authoring
Training
Warehouse management
Workflow planning & control

Part 3 Information Technology Skills

(1 = expert skills, 2 = technical skills, 3 = operational skills, 4 = some practical exposure, 5 = minimal working understanding)

Experience level

Business analysis
Change management
Compliance
Development management
Electronic commerce
Operations management
Process analysis
Program direction/ management
Project direction/ management
Security
Software design & development

In the dynamic complexity of business life, these lists can be considered little more than a starting point for the creation of an "inventory" of skills. The individual should review his own profile frequently, and augment and up-date as necessary to give a current picture of his true worth.